ROUTLEDGE LIBRARY EDITIONS:
ACCOUNTING HISTORY

Volume 34

PIONEERS OF A PROFESSION

PIONEERS OF A PROFESSION

Chartered Accountants to 1879

JAS. C. STEWART

Routledge
Taylor & Francis Group
LONDON AND NEW YORK

First published in 1986 by Garland Publishing, Inc.

This edition first published in 2021
by Routledge
2 Park Square, Milton Park, Abingdon, Oxon OX14 4RN

and by Routledge
52 Vanderbilt Avenue, New York, NY 10017

Routledge is an imprint of the Taylor & Francis Group, an informa business

British Library Cataloguing in Publication Data
A catalogue record for this book is available from the British Library

ISBN: 978 0 367 33561 9 (Set)
ISBN: 978-1-00-304636-3 (Set) (ebk)
ISBN: 978-0-367-53255-0 (Volume 34) (hbk)
ISBN: 978-1-00-308114-2 (Volume 34) (ebk)

Publisher's Note
The publisher has gone to great lengths to ensure the quality of this reprint but points out that some imperfections in the original copies may be apparent.

Disclaimer
The publisher has made every effort to trace copyright holders and would welcome correspondence from those they have been unable to trace.

PIONEERS OF A PROFESSION: CHARTERED ACCOUNTANTS TO 1879

Jas. C. Stewart
(with a new introductory note by T. A. Lee)

Garland Publishing, Inc.
New York and London
1986

For a complete list of Garland's publications in accounting
please see the final pages of this volume.

This facsimile has been made from a copy in the Library of Congress.

Library of Congress Cataloging-in-Publication Data

Stewart, James C. (James Cathcart)
Pioneers of a profession.

(Accounting thought and practice through the years)
Reprint. Originally published: Edinburgh :
Scottish Committee on Accounting History, Institute of
Chartered Accountants of Scotland, 1977.
Includes index.
1. Accountants—Scotland—Biography. 2. Accounting—
Scotland—History. I. Title. II. Series.
HF5604.S73 1986 657'.092'2 [B] 86-25636
ISBN 0-8240-7888-8

Design by Bonnie Goldsmith

The volumes in this series are printed on acid-free, 250-year-life paper.

Printed in the United States of America

This book has been published on behalf of
the Scottish Committee on Accounting History
of the Institute of Chartered Accountants of Scotland.

Introductory Note

It is generally accepted that contemporary professional accountancy owed its formal beginnings to the Scottish accountants who, in the mid-nineteenth century, created the various bodies which now are part of the Institute of Chartered Accountants of Scotland. James Stewart is a Past President of the Institute, and in this book offers unique insights into the lives and careers of its founding members. He provides valuable information for the accounting historian on the backgrounds, education, places in the community, work styles and the integrity and credibility of nineteenth-century accountants in Scotland.

T.A. Lee

PIONEERS

OF A

PROFESSION

QUAERE VERUM

18 54

Endpaper map:—

From Forbes & Wilson's Plan of the City of Edinburgh and its Vicinity . . . (c 1853)

Scale: 9 inches = 1 mile

Both Old and New Towns are shown, much as they are today, the Old leading up the Royal Mile to the Castle, and the New north of Princes Street. Differences include a *round* garden in Charlotte Square, King's Bridge for Johnston Terrace, only *one* art gallery at the Mound (the National Gallery projected), and the streets off Leith Walk at the planning stage only.

The city ended on the west at Melville Street, part of which appears here.

At the eastern boundary of the map is the Royal High School. Edinburgh Academy is near the northern boundary. These two schools provided many pioneer C.A.s.

(The endpapers were printed by John Bartholomew & Son Ltd. The maps were kindly lent by Mr Peter Bartholomew, M.C., C.A., Chairman, whose great-great-great-grandfather, George Bartholomew, engraved the original of the Edinburgh map.)

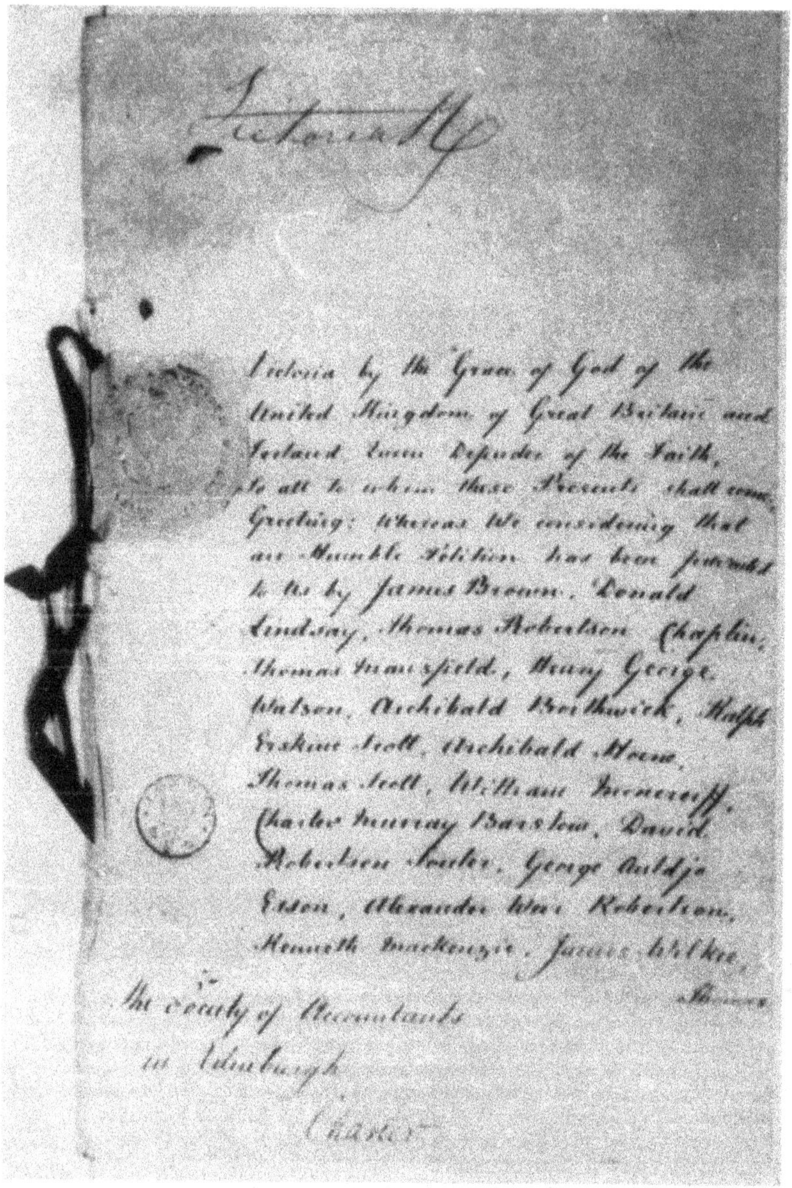
Victoria R

Victoria by the Grace of God of the United Kingdom of Great Britain and Ireland Queen Defender of the Faith, To all to whom these Presents shall come, Greeting: Whereas We considering that an Humble Petition has been presented to Us by James Brown, Donald Lindsay, Thomas Robertson Chaplin, Thomas Mansfield, Henry George Watson, Archibald Borthwick, Ralph Erskine Scott, Archibald Horne, Thomas Scott, William Moncreiff, Charles Murray Barstow, David Robertson Souter, George Auldjo Esson, Alexander Weir Robertson, Kenneth Mackenzie, James Wilkie,

The Society of Accountants in Edinburgh

Charter

First page of the Royal Warrant (dated 4th November, 1854) for the original Charter of The Society of Accountants in Edinburgh, renamed The Institute of Chartered Accountants of Scotland, in 1951, on the granting of a supplementary charter, following the amalgamation of The Institute of Accountants and Actuaries in Glasgow (Charter dated 1855) and The Society of Accountants in Aberdeen (Charter dated 1867) with the Edinburgh Society.

(Reproduced with the approval of the Keeper of the Records of Scotland)

PIONEERS OF A PROFESSION

CHARTERED ACCOUNTANTS TO 1879

being BIOGRAPHICAL NOTES on the
members of the Scottish Chartered societies
1854 to 1879
compiled with a
PREFATORY ESSAY
by

JAS. C. STEWART, C.A.
a Past President of
The Institute of Chartered Accountants of Scotland
and Membre d'Honneur of the
Union Européenne des Experts Comptables, Economiques et Financiers

SCOTTISH COMMITTEE ON ACCOUNTING HISTORY
THE INSTITUTE OF CHARTERED ACCOUNTANTS OF SCOTLAND
27 Queen Street
Edinburgh
1977

ISBN 85099 026 2

Printed by William Blackwood & Sons Ltd., Edinburgh

Acknowledgments

The support of the members of the Scottish Committee on Accounting History is gratefully acknowledged by the author. The membership of the Committee is as follows:—

Dr Robert Donaldson	†Professor R. H. Parker, F.C.A.
Miss Anna B. G. Dunlop	Dr N. T. Phillipson
*A. Scott Finnie, C.A.	§T. Robertson, F.C.A.
Professor T. A. Lee, C.A.	Robert C. Smith, C.A.

James C. Stewart, C.A.

* *Convener from 1976* † *Convener 1971-76* § *Secretary*

This book could not have been published without the financial sponsorship of the following, to whom the Scottish Committee on Accounting History is grateful:—

The Institute of Chartered Accountants of Scotland
Arthur Young McClelland Moores & Co.
Coopers & Lybrand
Davidson Smith, Wighton & Crawford
Deloitte & Co.
Mann Judd Gordon & Co.
Thomson McLintock & Co.
Thornton Baker & Co.
Touche Ross & Co.
Whinney Murray & Co.

Notes for the Reader

I Because Scotland has its own independent legal system certain terms used in this book may not be familiar to non-Scottish readers. Of these the most frequently recurring are:—

(*a*) **W.S.** These are the designatory letters used by members of the Society of Writers to Her Majesty's Signet—the senior Scottish society of solicitors.

(*b*) **S.S.C.** These designatory letters are used by members of the Society of Solicitors in the Supreme Courts of Scotland—another important society of solicitors.

(*c*) **Advocate.** Where it appears in this book the term normally denotes not, as in general Scottish usage, a barrister, but a member of the Society of Advocates in Aberdeen—the local society of solicitors.

(*d*) **Cautioner.** As used in relation to Indentures of Apprenticeship (Articles of Clerkship) this refers to the third party, normally the apprentice's parent or guardian, who because the apprentice was not of full legal age accepted responsibility for the due performance by him of his part of the contract, in fact acted as guarantor.

II In order to avoid frequent repetition of the full titles of the three Chartered bodies these are normally referred to as the "Society" or "Institute" as the case may be. The context will make clear which body is intended.

III The main sources used in the compilation of the book were:—

Minute books of the Scottish Chartered bodies.

Register containing copies of Indentures—Edinburgh Society.

Register containing copies of Applications for Membership—Glasgow Institute.

Official Directories of Scottish Chartered Accountants (1897 onwards).

Relevant local Directories.

A History of Accounting and Accountants. Ed. Richard Brown. (1905; and London: *Frank Cass & Co.*, 1968.)

A History of the Chartered Accountants of Scotland to 1954. (Edinburgh: *The Institute of Chartered Accountants of Scotland*, 1954.)

A History of Accountants in Ireland. H. W. Robinson. (*The Institute of Chartered Accountants in Ireland*, 1964.)

The History of the Institute of Chartered Accountants in England and Wales and its founder bodies 1870-1965. (London: *Heinemann*, 1966.)

The Accountant's Magazine. (Edinburgh, 1897 onwards.)

The Accountant. (London, 1874 onwards.)

Contents

Illustrations

Acknowledgment is made, for some of the illustrations, to:—

Aberdeen Public Library.
Peter H. Bartholomew, M.C., C.A.
Edinburgh City Libraries.
Mitchell Library, Glasgow.
The Scottish Record Office.
The Society of Advocates, Aberdeen.

The remaining illustrations were taken from the archives of The Institute of Chartered Accountants of Scotland.

Foreword

This book is timely in that it records the beginnings of the profession of chartered accountancy over a century ago, while it is still possible to trace back to these early days.

"Pioneers of a Profession" not only gives valuable information about these great men who laid the foundations of the profession as we know it today, but it records for the first time, in the appendix, the links with firms founded by some of the pioneer C.A.s. Many of the original firm names are, of course, now out of use, as a result of these firms having become part of national or international firms.

The section on "Origins and Background of a New Profession" makes most interesting reading and follows the changes in political, social and industrial conditions through which the accountancy profession grew in stature and built up for itself a reputation for integrity and professional competence, which led to the acceptance of accountancy as a respected and honourable profession. That is a heritage which those of us who are chartered accountants today must guard with all the force we can command.

The enterprising author of the book, James C. Stewart, a Past President of the Scottish Institute, has been more than generous in the time he has devoted over a long period of years to affairs of the Institute. He has obviously undertaken very careful and time-consuming research to produce such full biographical notes on those far-sighted early accountants. He has lifted his pen, not for the first time, and I congratulate him on this latest work, which I am sure will deservedly command an important place in accounting history.

President (1976-77),

March 1977 — *The Institute of Chartered Accountants of Scotland*

Author's Preface

This book had its origin in a proposal made by the then Convener of the Scottish Committee on Accounting History of The Institute of Chartered Accountants of Scotland—Professor R. H. Parker, F.C.A.—that the Committee should undertake or sponsor an enquiry into the social backgrounds of the early Scottish Chartered Accountants. As a starting point for such an enquiry it was obviously necessary to establish a list of the persons concerned and I undertook to attempt to do this.

To keep the project within reasonable limits it was agreed that the enquiry should cover only those who within twenty-five years after the granting of a Royal Charter to the Society of Accountants in Edinburgh in 1854 were entitled to use the professional designation "Chartered Accountant". That designation was adopted by the members of the Edinburgh Society almost immediately following the grant of their charter. This example was followed by the members of the Glasgow Institute and later, from its formation in 1867, by the members of the Society of Accountants in Aberdeen. It emerged that, up to 1879, there were in all 346 men who were entitled so to describe themselves and a list of these was drawn up. The list contains the names of 180 members of the Edinburgh Society, 144 members of the Glasgow Institute and 22 members of the Aberdeen Society.

In the process of compiling this list, my interest was sufficiently aroused to impel me to go further, though in a slightly different way from that originally proposed by Professor Parker, who is now developing and expanding his own original project. Having been encouraged to continue, I have tried to bring together such biographical notes about the first chartered accountants as could fairly easily be assembled without undertaking research on a scale for which I have neither the skill nor the temperament. It then seemed appropriate to provide an introduction setting the scene in which the new profession came into existence and in which the first chartered accountants carried on their work. This introduction again is based on no special research but is intended merely as a reminder of the great and continuing changes in the social and economic conditions within which the profession has developed, and not as a significant contribution to accounting or social history. It is so difficult to recall what things were like even during my own apprenticeship that I felt that some such outline might be welcomed by readers.

As the product of an amateur author working outside his normal field the book suffers from obvious defects, and there are substantial gaps in the biographical information. I apologise for all the faults, despite which I hope that the book may provide a starting point and perhaps even a guide and an incentive to some more skilled and dedicated researcher. The faults would have been even more obvious and the gaps greater but for the interest taken and assistance given me by other members of the Scottish Committee on Accounting History, by the Institute's librarians and by a number of members of the Institute who have provided me with information about ancestors or predecessors in the profession. To all of these I wish to express my thanks but I wish particularly to thank Miss Anna B. G. Dunlop, the keeper of the Institute's Antiquarian Book Collection and former editor of *The Accountant's Magazine*, without whose continued interest and encouragement I should never have persisted in the work, and Mrs Morag Stirling, my former secretary, without whose continuing ability to decipher my handwriting it would have got no further than a collection of untidy and almost illegible notes.

Today's members of The Institute of Chartered Accountants of Scotland who are the professional successors of these "Pioneers of a Profession" will, I hope, find the book of some interest and perhaps even find in it some inspiration to maintain the great tradition established by the founding fathers.

Origins and Background of a New Profession

About the middle of the 19th century accounting, which had existed for centuries or even millenia, as a rather dull and obscure occupation, began its rapid transition to its present position as one of the most influential professions of modern civilisation. The first steps in this transition were taken, almost unwittingly, by the men of whom some account is given in the latter part of this book, in a small, not very affluent country on the fringes of Europe. The question why this should have happened then and there is one which must surely be of interest to all their professional successors, and especially to those of them who are members of The Institute of Chartered Accountants of Scotland, the institute which grew from the small provincial societies which these men founded and which they fostered through their early days.

There had, of course, been earlier associations of accountants than those founded in Scotland in the 1850's, but all had faded away leaving scarcely a trace of their existence. Notably in Italy, the country in which the art, or science, of account-keeping in the form which remains basic to modern practice originated, several bodies were founded from the 16th century onwards, up to a short time before the formation of the Scottish societies; but of these none still exists.

Was there then something in the economic circumstances of the mid-19th century and in particular something which was peculiar to Scotland, which provided the stimulus for the formation of a great new profession? Even the designation "Chartered Accountant" used in many parts of the world today to distinguish members of that profession (a usage frequently based more on imitation than on the existence of a relevant legal charter) was the invention of a committee of the Scottish pioneers.

In search of an answer to that question, it may be helpful to take a short look at the circumstances of time and place in which the first chartered accountants emerged. Circumstances in which these pioneers of a profession lived their lives and carried on their professional vocation, but which were so soon, so radically and so rapidly, to change.

* * * *

A long era of relatively slow change, throughout which agriculture and the processing, mainly for local consumption, of natural products had provided men with their main occupations and were the sources of whatever degree of wealth and prosperity they enjoyed, came to an end around the 18th century. There then began, and still continues, a period of great and rapid changes both in the nature of the commodities of commerce and in the scale of their production and distribution. These changes, made possible by man's increasing control over nature, gave rise to our present so-called technological civilisation in which change and growth have themselves become dominant motives.

About the same time revolutionary changes in political and social conditions were also taking place. By the middle of the 19th century it was possible to assess at least some of the effects of the changes which had taken place in the economy, and, by analogy with the parallel political movements, the process of economic change acquired the label "the industrial revolution".

Looking back from a later age it can now be seen as an evolutionary rather than as a revolutionary movement and as involving more elements of economic activity than purely those of industrial production. The interaction of changes in transport and communications and in the framework within which industry and commerce operated and were legally controlled and financed can now be seen to have been as important as the actual changes in the technology of industrial production. Furthermore, the problems which have arisen in these fields have proved more troublesome in their effects and more difficult of solution than the purely technological problems.

The need to deal with the problems to which the industrial revolution as it gathered momentum gave rise in the ancillary fields of record-keeping and finance is the basic reason why an independent accountancy profession began to emerge at that particular time.

There had throughout the middle ages, to look no further back, been a steady development of international trade matched by certain developments in financial practices and the records kept of commercial and financial transactions. The extent and speed of the expansion of trade was, at that time, seriously restricted not only by the limited means of production available, but by the limitations imposed by existing methods of transport. The size and speed of ships was governed by the only known means of propulsion—wind power or man power. On land again, apart from the absence of any roads which reached even the standard of the Roman roads, by then largely fallen into decay, the size of the load and the speed with which it could be moved was limited by the tractive power of the horse.

In consequence the volume of trade was necessarily restricted and commercial operations were on a scale which could in general be personally supervised and controlled by the merchants concerned. Furthermore there was no incentive to increase production beyond the point at which it could be readily distributed. Nevertheless, credit transactions had developed and bills of exchange were in regular use. Merchants also regularly took steps to reduce their risks by entering into marine insurance contracts; though the premiums, like the risks, were high. Bills of exchange themselves, however, like the specie in which settlement of them was eventually made, were treated as a kind of commodity the physical possession of which was more important than the record of them in a merchant's or banker's books. The banker's function was, as to a degree it still is, to act as a clearing house and, by lending the use of his name, to provide the assurance that settlement, in specie or by substitution of other acceptable paper, of bills bearing that name could be relied on. The actual settlement was a matter rather of physical exchange than, as in our time, of book entry. The bill fairs held at various centres in Europe during the 16th century and later exemplify this. At these fairs trade in bills of exchange between bankers or their agents took place alongside or in some instances in complete substitution for trade in commodities between merchants.

But though the scope of trade slowly developed and with it banking and insurance, and some joint stock companies in a somewhat primitive form existed, industry and commerce remained predominantly in the hands of individuals who, if they felt that records were required, kept their own private records and did not recognise any need to employ accountants other than such of their confidential clerks as might be dignified by that title.

* * * *

The first significant improvement in inland transport, in capacity if not in speed, resulted from the widespread construction of canals. The construction of canals also called for mobilisation of capital on a scale not previously required, and while a considerable part of the capital required was found by the landowners through whose lands the canal routes passed, not all could be raised in this way. Without the improvements in the speed of transport, however, which resulted from the application of steam power to the propulsion of vehicles and ships it would have remained uneconomic to exploit the productive potential of the newly discovered source of power and the mechanical inventions which had been made about the same time. To produce goods on a scale greater than the distribution system could handle has, it seems, never been a major economic problem.

In the 19th century it was the conjunction of the two applications of power—to production and to transport—which gave rise to a virtual explosion in the volume of production in such established industries as textiles. In turn, the needs of the new transport systems themselves for iron and steel for rails and ships and engines and for coal to drive them multiplied demand and created the need for new forms of organisation requiring finance on a scale beyond the capacity of the individual merchant or manufacturer.

This changing pattern of production and trade led to changes in and to the expansion of the banking system. It also led, through the development of the joint stock company operating in all sections of the economy—production, transport, finance—, to that divorce of management from ownership with which we are now so familiar. This in turn led the non-active shareholders, or partners as they really were, to require from those to whom management was delegated, at first usually themselves also partners, an account of their stewardship and so to the emergence of the independent accountant to verify the account so given. The need to provide this attest function, now one of the main functions of the public accountant, was not, however, the immediate stimulus to the development of a separate accounting profession. That came rather from the failures of the new system than from its successes; from the need to determine the rights and obligations of creditors and of partners, as stockholders were before the introduction of limited liability, in concerns which could not meet their external liabilities. These partners might number hundreds, many of whom, especially in banking companies, might also be debtors or creditors, and the cross claims which could arise created sometimes enormous complexities. Difficulties of this kind could not arise so readily in England, where banking companies were restricted to six members, and where the rules for the ranking of partnership claims against the estates of the individual partners were different from those in Scotland.

From about the middle of the 18th century, a few men found that they were able to make the adjustment of business accounts which had fallen into a state of confusion, or the supervision and realisation of bankrupt estates and the settlement of the competing claims on the proceeds their sole business and began to designate themselves "accountants". Very often these individuals had acquired their accounting skills while acting as book-keepers or cashiers in mercantile offices and, with a reputation for skill and knowledge, had also gained the good opinion of those with whom they did business as being men of character and integrity. It was natural, therefore, that resort should be made to their services when complicated or disputed transactions required to be unravelled and acceptably adjusted.

Already when local directories began to be published in Britain towards the end of the century, a number of those whose names appeared in them were described as "accountants". The first London directory in 1799, a date which curiously enough is later than that given for the first publication of a number of provincial directories, included eleven accountants. Six years earlier than that it has been said that no more than three accountants were known in England; one in Liverpool and the other two in Bristol. It does seem unlikely, even though both these cities were thriving ports and commercial centres, that they should have had accountants before the capital, but such is the report. The Incorporated Society of Liverpool Accountants was certainly formed in January 1870, ten months before the Institute of Accountants in London, and in 1966 a Bristol firm was described as being "the oldest established firm in the Institute (of Chartered Accountants in England and Wales) having been founded in 1780".

Dublin also, on the evidence of its directory, must have had accountants before London, and perhaps before any city in Great Britain. That city's directory was first published in 1752, but it was in 1761 that the designation "accountant" first appeared in it. The demand there for accountancy services cannot have been great because not until 1767 did that designation again appear. This can probably be taken as indicative of the fact that in these early days, when accountancy was emerging as a distinct occupation, it was frequently a part-time occupation, carried on in conjunction with some other activity which might well be given precedence in describing a man's business in a directory entry.

In Scotland, not surprisingly in view of the lead which that country later took in the establishment of the profession, the designation seems to have been adopted rather more quickly. The first Edinburgh directory, when it appeared in 1773, included the names of seven accountants. Ten years later the first Glasgow directory had six. Thereafter, these numbers steadily grew.

It may, perhaps, be not too fanciful to suggest that the very poverty, comparatively speaking, of Scotland, and of Ireland, had something to do with the early appearance in them of the specialist accountant. The Scots predilection for litigation may well also have contributed to the demand for persons of skill to elucidate accounts and assist in establishing claims. Certainly, the Scottish Courts were more willing to recognise the standing of the independent accountant than were Courts in England. The organisation of the latter, too, where matters of accounting were dealt with by Masters in Chancery, which in Scotland were commonly remitted for investigation and report to a person of skill, not a functionary of the Court, may have had a part in this.

Certainly there is a marked contrast between the view of their status in the eyes of the Courts which members of the Edinburgh Society felt they were entitled to claim when, in their petition for incorporation by Royal Charter, they stated "That in the extrication of these numerous suits before the Court of Session which involve directly and indirectly matters of accounting, an Accountant is almost invariably employed by the Court to aid in eliciting the trust . . . such investigations cannot be prosecuted by the Court itself without professional assistance on which it may rely, and the Accountant . . . performs in substance all the more material functions which the Petitioners understand to be performed in England by the Masters in Chancery" and the view of accountants expressed by a Queen's Bench Judge at the trial of a fraudulent bankrupt at Bristol many years later. At that trial Mr Justice Quain complained of the conduct of the trustee, who was a professional accountant, and after referring to solicitors as "gentlemen" went on to speak of "an ignorant set of men called accountants" whose encroachment into bankruptcy cases was "one of the grossest abuses ever introduced into law".

The Glasgow petition for a charter also made reference to the accountants' work for the Courts. In the western city, of course, accountants were not so directly involved with the superior Courts as were their Edinburgh contemporaries, so their reference was suitably modified to include reference to involvement also with the Sheriff Courts. The Glasgow petitioners repeat the reference to the functions of the Masters in Chancery.

The conjunction, then, of a rapid growth in the scale and complexity of industry and commerce, with financial difficulties arising partly as an aftermath of the Napoleonic wars and partly from the speculative boom occasioned by the railway mania, brought about conditions in which to quote again from the Glasgow petition ... "to the due performance of a profession such as this a liberal education is essential and that the object in view ... to maintain the efficiency as well as the respectability of the profession in Glasgow ... will be ... greatly assisted by the formation of the Petitioners into a body corporate ..." which, to quote this time from the Aberdeen petition, "... would tend to secure in the members of their profession the qualifications which are essential to the proper performance of its duties".

These then were the conditions which explain why the slow emergence of public accountancy as a distinct calling should culminate on 23rd October, 1854, the date on which the Royal Charter incorporating the Society of Accountants in Edinburgh was signed, in the birth of a new profession, and to some extent explain why then and why there.

* * * *

The attributes which distinguish a profession are more readily recognised than defined and listed. There have been many claims by the followers of various vocations to be added to the ranks of those commonly acknowledged to be professionals, not all of whom have been able to demonstrate their right to the description. Yet, if there are no rigidly definable standards, there are a number of accepted characteristics of a profession in the absence of which no body could justifiably claim to be professional. These include the possession of special knowledge and skills, acquired from those already initiated, by means of a regular system of training and demonstrated to the satisfaction of the prior initiates; the submission to discipline at the hands of fellow professionals; and the acceptance of certain obligations to society, offset by the recognition by society at large of a special professional status. All of these marked and still mark, both in primitive and advanced societies, those who claim to be professionals, be they priests or wizards, physicians or witch-doctors, lawyers or ju-ju men. They also predicate the existence of a closed association of initiates to guard and develop the skills of practitioners and to exercise disciplinary control over them.

Man's competitive instincts are highly developed, but he is also by instinct a gregarious animal. Wherever and whenever a numerous body of men have, even though engaged in a measure of internecine competition, a clear common interest in the matters involved, the latter instinct will in general take precedence. The result will be the formation of some kind of association to regulate the competitive element and to promote the common interest so that it may not be frustrated by too high a degree of contention. Apart from other conditions conducive to the growth of a new occupation, the position had been reached in the middle of the 19th century when a sufficient number of people had come to be engaged in public accountancy to bring these centripetal forces into play and to encourage the formation of a professional association or associations. In the conditions of the time the associations which were formed tended to be local, but pressures to seek a wider unity were early felt and from the first there was consultation and a measure of collaboration between the newly formed Society and Institute, in which the Aberdeen Society later shared. These pressures eventually led after nearly a century to the unification of the three bodies, and the movement towards co-operation on a still wider scale, indeed to world-wide international co-operation in the formulation and maintenance of professional standards of conduct and practice, continues.

So it was that in 1853 groups of accountants in both Edinburgh and Glasgow decided that the time had come when they should seek recognition of their occupation as a separate and distinct profession and that to this end formal organisation was necessary. The movement was entirely spontaneous. There was no legislative pressure nor even any official encouragement. The new bodies gained no special legal protection. Many practising accountants remained outside the chartered bodies, as some still do, but those who helped to promote them had as one of their goals from the first the achievement of recognised professional status. Their policies were directed always to that end and in a relatively short time they achieved the recognition which they sought.

* * * *

The first move in Edinburgh was made by a very small group. A letter was addressed by A. Weir Robertson to 14 accountants in the city inviting them to attend a meeting in his office. The letter presumably followed discussion with at least some of those invited and possibly with others. In response to this invitation eight men met in Robertson's office on 20th January 1853. Two days later there was a second, somewhat larger meeting and a draft constitution was considered. On the last day of the same month, 47 men attended yet another meeting, at which the Institute of Accountants in Edinburgh was formally constituted. It was under that name that the petition for incorporation by Royal Charter was later presented, but the Charter itself entitled the new corporation The Society of Accountants in Edinburgh. Presentation of the Petition for a Charter was approved at the first annual general meeting, which was held on 1st February, 1854, and the Petition was signed by 54 members, the full number of ordinary members at that time. The Charter was signed on 23rd October, 1854. Supplemented by an additional Charter granted in 1951, it is still the constitutional foundation of The Institute of Chartered Accountants of Scotland.

In Glasgow a somewhat larger number of accountants were originally involved, and the initial proceedings took a rather different form. Twenty-seven men who had begun to practise in the city at various dates from 1841 to 1853 signed a requisition addressed to 15 of their fellow practitioners who had all been practising since before 1841, requesting them to consider the formation of an association. The request was favourably received by the seniors, and a joint meeting of all those interested was held on 14th November, 1853 at which a constitution for the Institute of Accountants and Actuaries in Glasgow was adopted. In July, 1854 it was decided to follow the example of the Edinburgh Society and to apply for the grant of a Royal Charter incorporating the Institute. The petition was signed by 49 members (five fewer than the number of signatories to the Edinburgh petition), but two of those originally concerned do not appear to have become members. One, James Watson, was among those to whom the letter of requisition was addressed, the other, J. McGeorge, who had been in practice since 1849, was a signatory to the letter. Both of these men were primarily stockbrokers, but for a number of years they described themselves as "accountants and stockbrokers". Watson was a prominent man in the city, chairman of the Stock Exchange Association in 1852-53, and as his role as a recipient of the requisition letter was in any case passive his decision can be readily understood. He later become Lord Provost of the city and was knighted. Why McGeorge should have signed the letter and then done nothing further is not so readily understood. A number of those who did become members, however, seem to have regarded membership as unimportant, and several in the early years were expelled from membership for non-payment of the trifling subscription, though from what can be learned, they were men of good standing and reputation. At least McGeorge avoided this. The charter of the Glasgow Institute was dated 15th March, 1855. It was surrendered, with that of the Aberdeen Society, when the three Scottish bodies united in 1951.

Twelve years after the incorporation of the Glasgow Institute, accountants in Aberdeen decided that they also should form a society. The number of men involved in Aberdeen was, naturally, smaller than in the other two cities and they proceeded directly to petition for a charter of incorporation without the preliminary procedure of forming a society and adopting a constitution, as the Edinburgh and Glasgow accountants had done. The number of signatories to the petition presented in 1867 was only twelve and, in the light of the experience of English accountants just three years later, it is a little surprising that they do not seem to have had any difficulty in securing their objective. In 1870 when the newly formed London Society of Accountants, a much larger body than the three Scottish societies together, proposed to petition for a charter, they were advised by Mr Goschen, then Chancellor of the Exchequer, to acquire corporate status by registration under the Companies Act of 1862. The London Society having declined to follow this advice, it was not until 1880 that the efforts to obtain a charter were successful and The Institute of Chartered Accountants in England and Wales was incorporated.

Shortly after the granting of their charter the members of the Edinburgh Society decided to adopt the use of the professional description "Chartered Accountant" and of the designatory letters "C.A.". Their example was almost immediately followed by the members of the Glasgow Institute and by those of the Aberdeen Society from its incorporation. The words "Chartered Accountants" were included in the title adopted by the English Institute on its incorporation, although they did not appear in the original titles of any of the three Scottish bodies; they were introduced in the name of the Scottish Institute in the supplementary Charter of 1951. Members of the English and Irish Institutes have, since the granting of their respective charters in 1880 and 1888 used the style "Chartered Accountant", but, having two grades of membership have prefixed F or A to the plain C.A. of the Scots, who alone, in Britain and Ireland, may use these letters unqualified by some additional indication of category or geographical location.

It is clear that not all those who considered themselves to be practising as accountants were invited to join the new associations. Nor, after the associations had been formed, did all the active accountants in their areas seek to become members. In Glasgow in particular, for some years after the founding of the Institute, the number of accountants listed in the local directory who were not members grew somewhat more rapidly than did the roll of members. One can only guess how far this may have been because many, especially of the older men, failed to see any advantage in joining the new body when they had already established themselves or how far it was due to knowledge of the discrimination exercised in the admission of members and the fear of a possible rebuff to which this knowledge might give rise in the minds of perfectly respectable practitioners to whom even the possibility of it would, because of their age and established connections, have been an affront. It is true, certainly, that from the beginning, even before the institution of anything more than purely formal examinations, all applications for membership were very carefully considered and enquiries made as to the applicants' suitability for membership.

* * * *

The ages of those becoming members in the early days covered a fairly wide range. A few, including James Brown, the first President of the Edinburgh Society were in their sixties, while in Glasgow, Donald Cuthbertson was already past seventy. Not many were under forty. For a few years the new members continued to include men in their thirties and forties but within a relatively short time a pattern of entry after serving a regular apprenticeship and submitting to examination established itself, and the average age at entry fell to well below thirty.

Among the original members of the Edinburgh Society were a number of men connected with insurance companies, who could more properly have described themselves, as indeed some did, as actuaries. The Institute in Glasgow had adopted as its full title "The Institute of Accountants and Actuaries in Glasgow", but in fact very few of its early members had any claim to the alternative description. The highly specialised role of the professional actuary had not at that time clearly been distinguished, though the Institute of Actuaries, based in London, of which some of the Edinburgh men were members, had been established in 1848. In 1856 the Scottish members of that Institute withdrew from it and set up a Scottish counterpart, "The Faculty of Actuaries", of which during subsequent years a number of Edinburgh Chartered Accountants became members. In fact five of the first fourteen Presidents of the Edinburgh Society were Fellows of the Faculty of Actuaries, but no Glasgow office-bearer was.

In Glasgow there was on the other hand a very close link with the Glasgow Stock Exchange Association, involving not only personnel but for a number of years premises also. The Glasgow Stock Exchange Association had been formed in 1844 with an initial membership of 28. Most of these combined stockbroking with accounting and no doubt it was the nature of the former activity, which virtually required the existence of an association to enable it to be carried on in an orderly way, which led these men to combine in an association of stockbrokers before the idea of forming an accountancy society was raised. Nineteen of the original members of the Institute were also members of the Stock Exchange Association, and twelve of the first sixteen chairmen of that association were or became chartered accountants. The Institute also, until it acquired its own premises in 1873, made use of the Stock Exchange premises for council meetings and other formal business.

The Edinburgh Stock Exchange was founded in 1845 but the links between it and the Society were never so close as those between the two Glasgow bodies.

* * * *

Since the middle of the 19th century immense changes affecting not only man's environment but his very mode of thought have taken place. These affect every sphere of life, science, art, music, transport. To appreciate the differences one need only couple a few names from the past whose theories in 1854 seemed solidly established with those of some of their successors—Newton and Einstein; Dalton and Rutherford; Rembrandt and Picasso; Mozart and Schoenberg; Stephenson through the Wright Brothers to Neil Armstrong. Accountancy still awaits a name which might be similarly linked with that of Pacioli, whose ideas have perhaps held the field too long, but to whom Sandilands does not seem quite the right successor. With these changes, but affecting our lives as accountants more directly, we have seen so many technological innovations and achievements, which continue at an ever accelerating pace, that we tend, even while admitting our own inability to cope with the changes, to regard our forebears of the last century as completely unenterprising and unprogressive and to forget how much of our vaunted progress was in fact initiated by them.

Great social and political changes—the growth of trade unions; the extension of the franchise; amelioration in many ways of social conditions—as well as new psychological insights and virtually new methods of thought originated with or owe much of their development to the men of the dark ages of Victorianism. It was into that very different climate in which the winds of change were rising, though not yet blowing with such force as to disrupt social stability and orderly progress, that the new accounting profession emerged.

The way in which the new associations were incorporated reflected the existing commercial and social order. The only ways in which they could readily acquire a corporate identity were through the grant of a Royal Charter or under a Private Act of Parliament, and the latter method was so expensive and time consuming as to be quite inappropriate for such a purpose, though it had to be used by canal, railway and other public utility companies. Within a short period the introduction of legislation controlling the incorporation of companies had changed this, and, as has been noted, it was only with some difficulty that in 1880 The Institute of Chartered Accountants in England and Wales was able similarly to adopt that, to them preferable, method of incorporation by Royal Charter, rather than accept the alternative and more commonplace course of registration under the new Companies Acts.

In more recent times several accountancy bodies, first registered as companies, have after long and honourable histories successfully petitioned for the granting of Royal Charters, largely for the purpose of securing in this way recognition of the high standing which they had already earned. Others have failed in their attempts to do so.

In the mid-19th century, company legislation, which provides and regulates so much of present day public accountancy work, was at a primitive stage. A small number of chartered incorporations were engaged in commercial enterprises—in Scotland notably some of the banks and the Carron Company. The growing number of public utility enterprises, canals, railways, gas and water supply companies, were in general incorporated and their operations governed by the provisions of Private Acts of Parliament. The promotion of such Private Acts was a long-drawn-out process, and many a venture was submerged by the flood of promotional expenses before even a start could be made on the creation of the works which were its object. The so-called joint stock companies were little more than unwieldy partnerships in which the advantages gained from the use of an apparently convenient organisational framework and from the transferability of shares were offset by many legal inconveniences, especially if the company proved unsuccessful and had to be wound up.

* * * *

In the absence of company legislation, the accountant's chief concern with the law was the Bankruptcy Statutes. These governed the winding up of insolvent "companies" as well as the estates of individual bankrupts. It is not surprising, therefore, that in the petitions for the granting of the Royal Charters, as well as in the announcements, as then permitted, by individual accountants of their willingness to place their skills and knowledge at the service of the community, knowledge and experience of bankruptcy matters figure prominently. Understandably enough, too, the first committees appointed by the newly incorporated societies were to consider the pending changes in the bankruptcy laws and to offer advice on these. It is a little surprising, however, to find how little corporate notice seems to have been taken of the Act of 1855 which introduced in Britain the principle of limited liability for stockholders or of the wider implications of the Companies Act of 1862.

In these early days of the profession little auditing work was done, and recurrent annual fees were exceptional. Such fees mainly accrued to those practitioners whose business included the factorage of continuing trusts or the management of landed estates, both of which tended to be in the hands of lawyers, rather than of accountants. Reckoned by number, a high proportion of the fees earned were at first very small—commissions on the collection of debts, on insurance premiums and similar items. On the other hand the fees in the more important bankruptcy cases, though few in number, could be very substantial in amount, and all in all the accountant, especially if he had connections in the legal profession, as many in Edinburgh had, was in no danger of being regarded as a poor relation by members of other professions.

This pattern of work changed fairly quickly and, within the lifetime of many of the original chartered accountants, was already more akin to that with which we are still familiar. The changes were mainly linked to the new company legislation. Although not at first a statutory requirement, auditing increased in importance, appointments as secretaries or managers of the growing number of financial and investment companies were available to practising accountants on a part-time basis, and those with the right connections and reputation found ready employment in connection with the promotion of the new undertakings which rapidly sprang up in the financial, commercial and industrial fields. Not infrequently this latter type of work led to appointments as directors of companies of various kinds.

Audit procedures remained somewhat primitive, and the importance of the auditor's role was only slowly recognised. It was not till two years after the spectacular and scandalous failure of the City of Glasgow Bank in 1878 that the banks as a whole adopted a system of voluntary audit by two professional accountants of independent status. Only in 1865, indeed, had the Clydesdale Bank given a lead by publishing an abbreviated form of Balance Sheet; a lead slowly and apparently reluctantly followed by others.

Work under remits from the Courts was at this time of greater relative importance than it is now, as was other work in connection with the Courts, such as acting as expert witnesses. The Scots have always been a litigious people and, as the terms of the petitions for the Charters make clear, the Courts regularly remitted accounting questions to independent accountants for investigation and report. Many practitioners also acquired reputations as expert witnesses and, at a time when accounting records were neither so complete nor reliable as they later became, their services in that capacity were frequently in demand.

The promotion of public utility undertakings, either by companies or by the re-invigorated municipal authorities, and later the acquisition of company undertakings by local authorities frequently gave rise to enquiries somewhat analogous to those relating to planning permissions, with which we have become familiar, and evidence by accountants figured largely in these proceedings. These, as well as enquiries into the conduct of concerns which had collapsed, sometimes followed by criminal proceedings, and also ordinary litigation involving accounting matters all provided remunerative employment for those who could establish a reputation as skilful and reliable expert witnesses.

One important section of present day professional work which contributed little to the early accountant's work load was taxation. This reflects the relatively light burden which tax at the then current rates imposed.

We have, of course, no access to the accounts of the old accounting firms and so must attempt to assess the relative penury or affluence of the early chartered accountants from such evidence as we have about their mode of life, where they lived and what leisure pursuits they followed. From this it can be safely assumed that few found themselves in financial straits though, then as now, the occasional chartered accountant would, like other professional men, meet with financial hardship. Where this did happen, their professional colleagues were, from the earliest days, willing to help, as is illustrated by a grant made in 1892 to one of its members by the Glasgow Institute. The possibility of setting up a widows' fund was one of the earliest projects discussed in each of the bodies, and benevolent associations were set up in Glasgow and Edinburgh after some years.

The cities in which the first chartered accountants carried on their profession, while differing in many ways from the Edinburgh and Glasgow of today, would, especially the former, have been readily recognisable to us, their successors. The greater part of the New Town had been built and many of the principal bank and insurance offices had already been erected. Some of these still imposing buildings must have impressed contemporaries as symbols of the strength and stability of the financial system which they were erected to serve, as well as witnesses to faith in its future. In trying to view the civic scene with contemporary eyes it must be remembered that in 1861 the population of Edinburgh was only about 168,000 and that in 1865 the total amount of Scottish bank deposits was under £60 million. Against that can be set the rather staggering fact that the new Head Post Office in Edinburgh, which was opened in 1866, cost a total of only £120,000, while the British Linen Bank building in St Andrew Square, built in 1852, cost only one-fourth of that figure.

In the same year of 1861 Glasgow's population was under 400,000 in spite of having nearly doubled during the preceding 30 years. It continued to grow rapidly until well into the next century. The rate of population growth in Edinburgh was not quite so fast, and for the country as a whole it was, between 1831 and 1881, appreciably slower than in the two main cities. This was, indeed, the period in which the movement of population from the country to the towns was reaching its flood. In 1851 the census showed for the first time that one-half of the population of Britain could be classified as urban, a situation which according to the economic historian J. H. Clapham "had probably not existed before in a great country at any time in the world's history".

Yet the towns had not yet any great amenities to offer to the ordinary citizen, and the impressive palaces of finance contrasted sharply with the poor dwellings of the average citizens. Movement within the cities was still mostly on foot—not until 1870 in Glasgow and 1871 in Edinburgh were tramways authorised, and for many years thereafter they were horse-drawn. The change from company to municipal water supplies took place just a little earlier, and neither the quantity nor the quality of the companies' supplies could be considered at all adequate, though they strongly resisted the loss of their rights of supply.

Gas companies had been operating since before 1820, and some of the earliest chartered accountants had professional connections with these. Electricity, however, as a public utility, was still some way in the future.

Such has been the rate of change during the last hundred years that it is hard to realise that the pioneer chartered accountants were nearer in time to the institution of mail coaches between Glasgow and Edinburgh (in 1758) and between Glasgow and London (in 1790) than we are to the founding of the accounting societies. To these pioneers also the coming of railways was more recent than the beginning of commercial aviation is to us.

Rail transport, indeed, if not so spectacular in its technical manifestations, grew at a rate that was comparable to the rate of development of air transport. The first public railway from Stockton to Darlington, a mineral line 25 miles long, was opened in 1825. By 1848 there was a direct rail link between Glasgow and London, and the through connection between Edinburgh and London previously broken by the absence of bridges over the Tweed and Tyne was completed in the same year. By that same year, 1848, less than twenty-five years after the first line opened, 5,000 miles of railways were operating, the mileage having grown from 2,000 miles to that figure in five years. Between these years, in 1845 the number of new railway projects before the public was 620, involving capital of £563,203,000, and during that one year 225 railway Bills were introduced in Parliament, of which 120 passed. Had it not been for the delays and expense caused by the necessary parliamentary proceedings, the rate of expansion might have been even more rapid. The losses to investors might also have been greater, as there seemed to be no difficulty in finding subscribers, notwithstanding that in some cases the promotional costs were so great that the sums subscribed were wholly swallowed up before construction work ever got under way. The total capital raised for railways between 1830 and 1884 was equal to the whole National Debt, and so great an impact did the railway finance mania have on the economy that in his presidential address to the Insurance and Actuarial Society of Glasgow in 1884 James Wyllie Guild, C.A., one of the leaders of the young accountancy profession, said, "It is a financial problem of no small importance to solve what is to take the place of railway investment for the future savings of the nation". Technological developments unforeseen by Wyllie Guild and his contemporaries have since provided ample outlets for the national savings. Like the railways, these, unfortunately, have by no means always proved to be to the financial benefit of the savers.

Prior to the railways canals had provided the only large scale medium for widespread mobilisation of capital, but canal finance never attained the volume or the frenzied level of speculation reached by the railway boom.

Another activity in which the early accountants were greatly involved was insurance business. The middle years of the 19th century saw a great expansion in insurance business of all kinds. In the local directories of the period a great many accountants not only describe themselves as insurance agents, but specify the companies for which they act. The companies, too, appeared to be eager to publicise the names and addresses of their agents and frequently included lists of these in their advertisements. These advertisements constituted by far the greater part of all the advertising which appeared in the directories.

About the same time a number of investment and deposit companies of various kinds were formed. Few of these were investment companies as we now understand them: there were not in fact available investments for purchase of which the funds of such companies could have been employed. Property Investment Companies, resembling in some ways building societies, began about 1867. All of these took deposits and invested their funds either in the purchase of or in mortgages secured on heritable properties. By 1879 there were fifteen of these companies in Scotland and also twelve similar companies which invested their funds in foreign or colonial properties. The management and direction of this type of financial concern provided a fair amount of work for accountants, especially in Edinburgh. If the number of companies seems small it is to be remembered that so too was the number of chartered accountants. Several of the pioneer chartered accountants owed their first professional trips abroad to their connection with colonial or American land companies; as, at a somewhat later date, a number of what are now leading international accounting firms originated from the despatch overseas of a British, frequently a Scottish, chartered accountant to investigate or supervise the interests of British investors.

In view of the role which the accounting profession now plays in relation to the admission of securities to quotation on the Stock Exchange, and the reliance placed on the profession by the Exchange and by investors generally, it is of interest to note that the foundation of organised Stock Exchanges considerably pre-dated the emergence of a recognised accountancy profession. Of the securities first dealt in, a high proportion were government or other fixed interest stocks, in relation to which accountants' reports do not have comparable significance even now, but this is no complete explanation. The most active dealings then, as often still, were in highly speculative stocks about which comparatively little factual information was available, or even sought. In spite of today's different official attitudes and of increasingly stringent rules and regulations intended to provide for the investor's security, it might perhaps be said of the attitudes and methods of many stock exchange operators "Plus ça change, plus c'est la même chose".

The London Stock Exchange dates from before the end of the 18th century. About fifty years after, in 1844, a group of men who had been carrying on business in Glasgow as accountants and share brokers decided that the time had come to organise a regular stock market in that city and formed the Glasgow Stock Exchange Association. In the following year the Edinburgh Stock Exchange was established.

The number of stocks quoted in Glasgow's first official list was 59 and the number of transactions in these stocks was very small. On occasion a day would pass without a single transaction being recorded, and one wonders how some forty men came to think that here was a source of income of such importance as to demand the creation of an association to protect and regulate it. Certainly, the majority of those involved were described as being also accountants; yet not for nearly a further ten years did they think that the formation of a society for the regulation and protection of that part of the business was necessary.

At first the number of quoted stocks increased slowly, and ten years later the stocks of only 89 companies were included in the list. The promotion of numerous railway and other public utility companies brought a number of new stocks to the market and by 1879 there were 319 stocks listed in Glasgow. The years following the passing of the 1862 Companies Act had seen a great increase in the number of companies. The shares in by no means all of these, however, were dealt in on any of the Stock Exchanges. Between 1862 and 1865 over 2,500 companies were registered, the nominal capital of which amounted to more than £567 million. Of the 319 items in the 1879 list, nearly one-third were railway stocks, and general industrial companies were still virtually unrepresented.

There are in the records references to days "of hectic and excited dealings", and there was undoubtedly a great deal of speculation. It is difficult now to imagine how this could be conducted without the "advantage" of the telephone and at a time when even a fair proportion of country mail was still carried by mail gig.

* * * *

The absence of any public transport in the cities meant that those professional men not sufficiently affluent to have their own horses or carriages on or in which to ride to their offices had perforce to live within easy distance of their work. In some cases, home and office still remained in the same premises, and of one of the early Edinburgh Presidents it was later recalled by a former apprentice that his dining room was used for breakfast and for dinner but between these meals it served as a cash room.

It has already been noted that, by the middle years of the century, the city centres included a number of still existing office buildings, but the total urban and suburban areas were very much smaller, so that it was easily possible to reach the business sections on foot from the then comparatively new and fashionable residential terraces. Many of these, as in the case of the Institute's premises in both Edinburgh and Glasgow, were later to be converted to office use and later still many have been demolished to make way for the human filing cabinets which have too often been substituted for civilised civic architecture.

But if many of the exterior features of the mid-century buildings remain, the office interiors have undergone complete transformation. Even since the author began his apprenticeship, the changes have been very great, so great that it is difficult to recall the old conditions, so Dickensian do they seem in retrospect. Gone are the high sloping desks and tall stools, the open coal fires, clumsy copying presses and messy duplicators and the pillar telephones. That period of change covers only a little over fifty years, less than half the total span of the Institute's history, and the first half must have seen changes just as great, if not greater. The earliest chartered accountants had even more primitive copiers and duplicators—only the most advanced offices had either. Telephones and typewriters had not even been invented. Only in 1852 had the Clydesdale Bank introduced a copying press, and a successor of James Meston, the founder of the Aberdeen Society, recalled that Meston did not see the need for such an appliance, since, being a heavy man, he could produce better copies by sitting on the letter book. Yet Meston was not a complete reactionary, for his office had one of the first telephones in the North.

It could be a mistake, however, to assume that the absence of all mechanical aids to speedy communication meant an absence of pressure and a wholly leisurely professional life. Time was taken up in writing and copying; in moving from place to place within the cities; and in dealing with routine matters now wholly or partially mechanised. Then as now, all the professional man had to sell was time and skill, and the former at least is strictly limited, so that if spent in one way, however unimportant or unproductive, it is not available for use in another. Ways may be discovered for recycling all sorts of waste, but it is not possible to recycle lost or wasted time. While our forebears may have had to find what seem to us easier solutions to easier problems, the pressures under which they had to seek these solutions were probably little, if any, less than those of today, and even if time was available for deliberate constructive thought it does not seem to have been given to consideration of accounting theory, for little in that field was published in Scotland in the second half of the 19th century; and it was not until the profession was nearing its jubilee that an accounting journal was published there. The first Scottish accounting journal was *The Scottish Accountant*, a short lived periodical produced by the Scottish Institute of Accountants in 1891. That Institute had been formed in 1881 in an attempt to provide provincial accountants in Scotland with an alternative to membership of one of the three city bodies, but met with no real success.

From time to time the societies arranged series of lectures, or sometimes just single lectures, on professional subjects. A number of these and also papers delivered to other professional bodies and learned societies by chartered accountants were subsequently published in pamphlet form. Most of these dealt with matters of mainly topical interest and did not contribute anything radically new to accounting thought. Not until well into the present century and certainly not until the profession was nearer to celebrating its centenary than its jubilee could accountancy realistically claim a place as an academic discipline in its own right, the existence of an ancient chair at Alexandria notwithstanding.

* * * *

While accountancy was establishing itself as a distinct profession, changes in the scale, organisation and techniques of industry were also taking place, and at an unprecedented speed. Some of the ways in which these changes affected the new profession were connected with the legislation which was found to be necessary, not only to regulate directly the growing industrial and commercial concerns, but also to deal with the social framework within which these concerns operated.

New forms of local government were introduced, a virtually new educational system came into being, and it was found that increasing urbanisation called for new measures for the protection of the health of the population through better water supplies and improvements in public hygiene.

Until 1833 town councils had been virtually self-perpetuating bodies with no real basis of popular election. The Edinburgh Town Council, as it existed in the 1820's, was described by Lord Cockburn as ". . . omnipotent, corrupt, impenetrable. Nothing was beyond its grasp; no variety of opinion disturbed its unanimity for the pleasure of Dundas was the sole rule for every one of them. . . . Silent, powerful, submissive, mysterious and irresponsible, they might have been sitting in Venice". So inefficient and corrupt indeed was the system and was even seen to be so that, from 1772, it had been found necessary to remove certain functions from the Town Council and to vest them in special bodies of Commissioners. Yet notwithstanding this the city had in 1833 to declare itself bankrupt. Robert Christie, who was in practice as an accountant in Edinburgh at that time and whose son was later an original member of the Society of Accountants in Edinburgh, was appointed accountant to the trustees for the city's creditors and was responsible for preparing a scheme for settlement with the creditors by the issue of a 3% permanent stock.

Yet the town council's activities were not uniformly discreditable. These same men who incurred Cockburn's strictures, or some of them, had the vision and drive to promote the planning and construction of the New Town, which improved living conditions for many of the city's inhabitants beyond recognition; though an incidental result was a separation of the classes which had not previously existed but which followed the removal to the New Town of most of the professional and other more affluent sections of the population. By 1830 the number of houses in the new quarter had reached about 5,000, and the people who moved to them, many of them professional families, at first mainly lawyers. but soon to include chartered accountants, were the real leaders in the city's life.

At about the same time as Edinburgh, other towns including Aberdeen, Dundee, Paisley and Dunfermline all became bankrupt, so that the need for a new system of local government and of local government accounting and finance was obvious.

Glasgow escaped bankruptcy, though there was a good deal of mismanagement, if perhaps rather less corruption. Generally, however, the position was much the same, and from around 1800 many functions were taken out of the control of the Council and transferred to Commissioners. In Glasgow, too, with a much smaller proportion of professional people, civic leadership was more in the hands of the merchants. This may or may not have been beneficial financially.

The passing of the Scottish Burgh Reform Act of 1833, following on the national electoral reforms of 1832, saw a complete change in the electoral system, though the size of the electorate still remained very small in relation to the total population. The whole basis of local government was also reformed, and in 1872 the educational system underwent major changes.

All these changes directly or indirectly affected the accountancy profession. The accounts of the numerous new authorities and public utilities required to be audited. The developments all had to be paid for and, in so far as paid for or supported by the national exchequer, taxation began to assume a growing importance which meant, of course, that greater importance attached to the proper determination of the taxpayer's liability. In retrospect it would seem that the founding fathers had chosen a very appropriate time to launch a new profession.

In spite of the need to increase the national revenue, however, it was not till many years later that Income Tax could be said to constitute a noticeable burden. In 1873 what would now be called the basic rate was 4d. in the £ (1·66%) and in the 1880's it varied from 2d. (under 1%) to 6½d. (2·7%). Not until 1911 was a surtax applying to incomes over £5,000 per annum introduced, and even in 1914, before the outbreak of the first world war, the basic rate had risen only to 1/4d. in the £ (6·66%).

* * * *

The extent of the industrial expansion and of the opportunities which this opened up for accountants may be judged from consideration of just a few statistics illustrating the changes which took place during the first 25 years of chartered accountancy.

The first ironworks on any scale in Scotland was established at Carron in 1760. Production of iron increased very slowly for over half a century, and even in 1836 when railway construction had already begun and after the hot blast process had been invented the total annual production amounted only to 75,000 tons. Thereafter there was an amazingly rapid increase. By 1845 the annual production was 475,000 tons and by 1855 825,000 tons. It was the same in shipbuilding. The construction of iron ships began in Scotland in 1818 and up till 1830 not more than 5,000 tons of steam ships had been built on the Clyde. In 1861 the output on the Clyde had grown to 81 steamers of a tonnage of fully 60,000 and by 1868 these figures had nearly trebled at 227 ships of a tonnage of 175,000.

In textile manufacturing the story was the same. The quantity of cotton goods manufactured in Scotland more than doubled between 1830 and 1850 and in the next decade it nearly doubled again.

New products also contributed to the country's industrial growth. The manufacture of linoleum started in Kirkcaldy in 1847 and that town had the only factory for this material till 1866. It is interesting, incidentally, to note that Kirkcaldy was one of the first places apart from the four main cities where there is a record of the existence of a practising accountant in Scotland. The North British Rubber Company was established in 1855, by which time rubber was already beginning to have some importance as an industrial material for the manufacture of such things as boots and shoes, coats, leggings, hoses, tyres for traction engines and vulcanite products. Between 1852 and 1857 the quantity of rubber imported into Britain increased fourfold from 2,195,984 lbs. to 8,932,672 lbs.

Another index of the increasing opportunities for accountants may be found in the Stock Exchange lists. It has already been noted that the number of stocks quoted in the Glasgow list had grown from 59 in the first official list to 319 in 1879. More relevant than the mere growth in the number of stocks quoted is the composition of the lists. The 1854 list comprised stocks of 43 railway companies, 8 gas companies, 13 insurance companies, 13 Scottish banks and 12 miscellaneous companies (water, canal, cemetery and iron companies). Railways, banks and insurance companies still figured largely in the later list, but the total number of these, although approximately double the earlier total, represented a smaller proportion of the whole list. Indian, Colonial and Foreign Government Stocks now provided about one-fifth of the list, but from the accountant's point of view the most interesting and important feature was the diversification shown by the appearance of significant numbers of companies under the classifications Tramways; Shipping, Telegraphs; Mines, Minerals and Metals; Bond, Loan and Trust Companies; and Miscellaneous—mainly land, property and financial concerns. The number of commercial companies rapidly increased following the company legislation of the fifties and sixties, but their advancement to public quotation moved more slowly.

• • • •

Occupational patterns were changing also. In the 1851 census the ten largest occupational groups in Britain still included important hand trades like tailors, shoemakers etc., whose products were soon to be replaced by factory made goods. During the sixties, the number of clerks doubled and in the following decade doubled again, yet in 1881 only 19 females were classified as clerks. A high proportion of all those employed around this period were employed in domestic service of one kind or another, and their number continued to increase until 1911 when it reached a maximum of a million and a half or 1 in 7 of all those in employment. This reflects the quite different social conditions in which the first chartered accountants lived, in what was still an age of privilege. But, though it was an age of privilege, opportunities to break into the privileged circles existed for those with energy, ability and integrity. It was for some easier to find these opportunities in the new profession than, for instance, in the legal profession where privilege was more firmly entrenched and family connections and influence of more importance. These differences can be traced in the careers of some of the pioneer accountants, where in Edinburgh family background played a larger part, while in Glasgow and Aberdeen most had to make their own careers from the bottom.

In Edinburgh the earliest directories show about one in three of the entrants as following a profession, while only one in eight could be classified as a business man. In Glasgow, these proportions were almost exactly reversed. The influence of the hereditary element in the legal profession, from which in Edinburgh a large proportion of the early accountants sprang, can be seen from the fact that throughout the long period from 1690 to 1829, 60% of those who became Writers to the Signet were sons of lawyers, landowners, crown servants, or ministers, and only 15% the sons of merchants or tradesmen, the last being an insignificant number.

In terms of what a hundred years ago would unashamedly have been described as "class" or social status the chartered accountant today, like other professionals, has certainly fallen back or, to use the current jargon, the differential in his earnings and living standards has narrowed quite dramatically. As late as the turn of the century an income of between £500 and £1,000 per annum, an income well within the reach of an accountant becoming established in practice, even had he started with no advantages of inherited means or connections, was adequate to provide a good standard of living with an appropriate domestic staff. Conditions have so changed since that any attempt at direct comparison is really futile. In monetary terms, after making allowance for inflationary changes, professional incomes on average have probably increased, but the whole pattern of domestic expenditure has changed, and even for those who might be able and willing to afford it domestic staff is unobtainable. In fact, domestic equipment has changed just as much as office equipment, and the wife of a pioneer accountant would feel as little at home in a modern kitchen as her husband would in a modern office.

* * * *

Are all these changes, however, only external? Are the men the same, or, if not, how have they changed? The biographical notes contained in the main part of this book may suggest answers—perhaps different answers to different readers. Here it may be attempted to reach some general conclusions as to the type of men who were the "Pioneers of a Profession". Perhaps the first thing that will strike the reader are the differences, particularly the differences between the Edinburgh and Glasgow men—differences in social origins, in education, in the routes by which they, especially the earliest of them, entered the profession, and even to some extent in the kind of practices which they built up and in their modes of life. Many similarities will also be noted; and both differences and similarities will be seen to have their counterparts still. This would lead to the general conclusion that, in fact, the pioneers of the accounting profession were a fair cross section of the men of their class and time. If, in these comments, the early Aberdeen members appear to be given less prominence this is only because relative to those in the other cities they were few in number, and they were also a little later in time.

The element of family succession within the legal profession in Edinburgh has already been noted and in that profession there may well have been a similar element in Glasgow. There was, at an early stage of the evolution of accountancy in Edinburgh, because the seat of the superior Courts was there, a strong link between the law and the new profession. Many of the early Edinburgh accountants had received at least part of their training in legal offices and a number had family connections in the legal profession. In Aberdeen, too, the two professions in the early days would seem to have been almost interchangeable. Of the 22 members of the Aberdeen Society whose admission to membership pre-dates 1879, six had either practised as advocates or trained in the offices of advocates. Few of the early Glasgow members, however, and these mainly migrants from Edinburgh, had served in legal offices or were the sons of lawyers.

As might be expected, since so many of the early Edinburgh members were the sons of professional men, a large number of them had been educated at what were then the city's leading schools—the old High School and the newer Academy. Fully one-half of the 180 men who became members of the Edinburgh Society before 1879 were the sons of men of the professional or landed classes: 45 are known to have been educated at Edinburgh Academy and 16 at the (Royal) High School. In Glasgow, the proportion of fathers in the professional classes was much lower, probably no more than one-quarter, but the occupations of sufficient of the remainder are known to suggest that it is probable that at least an equal proportion were merchants or followed some commercial occupation. Only four are known to have attended the city's ancient Grammar School, by then known as the High School, and even fewer to have been pupils at the relatively new Glasgow Academy for, as the prospectus described it, "the sons of gentlemen".

* * * *

In those early days professional education, other than learning on the job, was virtually unknown, Of a fair number of early members it is recorded that part of their education had been obtained at a university; in the majority of instances, Edinburgh University. Not many seem to have graduated, so these references may have been to attendance at one or other of the law classes, before such attendance became compulsory, as it did within about ten years of the founding of the Society and Institute. At that time, too, it was not unusual for a young man to attend some classes at a university without any intention of proceeding to a degree.

The legal aspect of the accountant's work, mainly bankruptcy, was the only part in which any formal instruction could be obtained or which was dealt with in existing text books, and many of the earliest letters of application for membership of the Glasgow Institute include references to the applicant's past attendance at or intention of attending the Scots Law Class at the University in order to acquire the knowledge of the law of bankruptcy, possession of which was obviously expected to be accepted as evidence of his fitness for admission to membership.

The "accountancy" books which did exist were almost all elementary explanations of the Italian method of book-keeping or books of the "merchant's companion" type. There had not then appeared, nor for a considerable time afterwards did there appear, any books treating of the theoretical or academic aspects of accountancy, and, unlike the older disciplines of mathematics, law, medicine, philosophy or theology, there are no such surviving treatises from classical times, however out of date their theories may be.

During the period from 1853 to 1879, which covers the admission as chartered accountants of all those dealt with in the biographical section of this book, there were published in Scotland only 19 books or pamphlets on accounting subjects considered worthy of note in "Accounting in Scotland", the 2nd edition (1976) of the bibliography published by the Scottish Accounting History Committee of The Institute of Chartered Accountants of Scotland. Several of these were designed for school use and only one, "Practical bookkeeping adapted to commercial and judicial accounting" by Frederick Hayne Carter, C.A., could by any stretch of the imagination be described as an accountancy text. This book, incidentally, was the first book by a chartered accountant to be published. The first edition appeared in 1861 and five other editions followed. the last of which, published in 1890, was revised and edited by the author's son, F. W. Carter, C.A.

It was to be many years before accountancy could claim, and some believe it cannot yet do so, to have progressed from being a superior kind of trade, mental rather than manual, to being a serious academic discipline.

If in these early years few books competed for inclusion in the accountant's professional library, it would seem that even fewer readers competed for the use of those which were in the societies' libraries. Both the Edinburgh Society and the Glasgow Institute set up libraries for the use of their members within a few years of their incorporation; but in 1867 the council of the Institute was compelled to take note of the fact that, during the seven preceding years, an average of only three members each year had made use of their library.

In England publication of the journal, *The Accountant*, began in 1874 before the amalgamation of the early local bodies resulted in 1880 in the incorporation by Royal Charter of The Institute of Chartered Accountants in England and Wales—of which amalgamation *The Accountant* was from its first publication a vigorous advocate. In Scotland, the founding of a professional journal followed the formation of the professional societies only after many years. The first was *The Scottish Accountant*, to which reference has already been made. Then in 1897 *The Accountant's Magazine*, now the official journal of The Institute of Chartered Accountants of Scotland, began publication. It was originally, like *The Accountant*, an independent venture, but from the first it received official encouragement and, when required, financial support from the three societies.

* * * *

It should not be assumed from what has been said, however, that the early chartered accountants were not interested in the theoretical side of their profession, nor that they were by any means illiterate or even non-literary men. Several are known to have built up substantial private libraries, and a number were themselves authors of books on a wide range of professional and non-professional subjects. A number, also, contributed papers to bodies such as the British Association, the Royal Society of Edinburgh and the Royal Glasgow Philosophical Society, many of which were later published in pamphlet form. Several, too, took an active interest in music, either as performers or administrators, while others collected pictures or were otherwise interested in art. A few were numbered among the very early motorists, and others became prominent in connection with their hobbies as naturalists or photographers.

A different sphere in which not only individual members but the Edinburgh Society and the Glasgow Institute in their corporate capacities played an active part was the Volunteer movement. Accountants' companies of the local volunteer corps in each city were formed with financial support from the societies, and a large number of the early members held Volunteer commissions. Some gave many years of service in various corps and reached the rank of lieutenant-colonel or colonel before retiring. The Edinburgh Society also gave a substantial donation to the new Edinburgh Infirmary, and the Glasgow Institute subscribed towards the cost of the great hall (the Bute Hall) at the newly built University. The last mentioned donation did not pass without opposition; a petition against it was organised by a member who, oddly enough, was himself a graduate of the University.

The organisation of local government in those years did not present quite the same chances for service as elected representatives as later opened up; but in all three cities chartered accountants were prominent in the work of the town councils during the last quarter of the century. The county councils and other local councils which were constituted about that time also drew into their membership members of the developing profession.

A very high proportion of all the "pioneers" were active in church work and in the work of many and varied charitable organisations. Not a few were, in fact, sons of the manse, so it was to be expected that a number of these would hold office in the churches, established or free, with which their fathers were connected. At that time, too, the churches held a more central position in the nation's life than now, though any church court today may still be expected to include a number of chartered accountants which is disproportionately high in relation to their total numbers as compared with the whole population. In the field of public service, then, the early chartered accountants played a full part, as their successors have continued to do.

In other ways also they were a fair sample of their age. Their sporting activities covered a wide range. As well as pursuits of the country gentleman—a role which many doubled with their professional activities, as did many members of the legal profession—pursuits such as hunting, shooting and fishing, the peculiarly Scottish pastimes of golf and curling had their share, or more than their share, of enthusiasts. There were a few who, in their younger days, were notable as athletes or cricketers, and among the Edinburgh Academicals were several who had learned at school the new style of football, including one who was a member of the Scottish side in the first international rugby football match against England in 1871.

The period covered by the lives of those here designed as pioneers is long, extending to about eighty years in all, because while the line was drawn to include only those admitted to membership in or before 1879, a number of these survived to celebrate their jubilee as members and to see the roll of Scottish Chartered Accountants vastly increased, with members spread throughout the world and the whole role and status of the profession completely changed. The last of the original members died in 1918, only ten years before I myself became entitled to design myself "Chartered Accountant".

Scottish chartered accountants began to move about the world almost from the beginning. At least ten of the 346 pre-1879 members spent all or substantial parts of their careers in various parts of the world—in India, Australia, Ceylon, Japan and New Zealand. Others, although remaining home based, made numerous journeys abroad on their clients' business at a time when the transatlantic crossing took more days than it now does hours. To the impression created by those early emigrants can be traced the beginnings of the high reputation which, almost since his invention, it may be claimed that the Scottish Chartered Accountant has enjoyed and deserved.

Drawn by Thos. Shepherd: engraved by W. H. Lizars *(By courtesy of Edinburgh City Libraries)*

The Bank of Scotland, at the top of the Mound, Edinburgh, as it was in 1830. It was built in 1806 and was not encased in its present enlarged and more ornate stone shell until 1870. This is the building as many of the pioneer CAs would see and use it.

From James Pagan's Sketches of the History of Glasgow *(By courtesy of the Mitchell Library, Glasgow)*

British Linen Bank, Ingram Street, Glasgow, 1847. The engraving at left shows the Gorbals Church, and that on the right St Enoch's Church (now demolished).

George Washington Wilson Collection, (By permission of Aberdeen City Libraries) Aberdeen Public Library

Princes Street, Edinburgh, 1856. "The world's first instantaneous snap-shot street photograph." The photographer was George Washington Wilson, an Aberdeen man. The Scott Monument had been completed ten years earlier. The General Post Office and North British Hotel (both now behind it) had not yet been built. The side street is Hanover Street.

George Washington Wilson Collection, (By permission of Aberdeen City Libraries) Aberdeen Public Library

Holburn Junction, at the west end of Union Street, Aberdeen, 1868. Most of the buildings facing the street have been substantially altered, several have been replaced, and the street itself has been materially widened. This part of the street was then called Union Place and had originally been a narrow lane giving access to the back of a row of houses on the south side.

George Washington Wilson Collection, (By permission of Aberdeen City Libraries) Aberdeen Public Library

The east end of Union Street, Aberdeen, 1870. The construction of the Town House was one of a number of major developments within the city which reflected the fundamental economic and social changes which were taking place at the time.

Buchanan Street, Glasgow, c. 1870. *(By courtesy of the Mitchell Library, Glasgow)*

Buchanan Street first opened in 1778 as a residential street, laid off in lots "with sufficient room backwards for garden plots. The situation . . . pleasant and convenient and affords a prospect rural and agreeable''. It developed and changed rapidly. Now, and for long, noted mainly as a shopping street, it would, as it was in the 60s and 70s, be well-known to pioneer C.A.s, several of whom had their offices there.

From Grant's Old and New Edinburgh *(By courtesy of Edinburgh City Libraries)*

Queen Street, Edinburgh, c. 1870. The Society of Accountants in Edinburgh later (1891) bought No. 27, which is today the central part of the headquarters of The Institute of Chartered Accountants of Scotland.

Actual size; from the Antiquarian Collection of The Institute of Chartered Accountants of Scotland

£100 note, dated 12th November, 1877, of the City of Glasgow Bank, which went bankrupt in 1878. The church on the left is Glasgow Cathedral, still showing its two west towers, although they had been demolished in 1846. On the right is the Royal Exchange, now Stirling's [illegible]

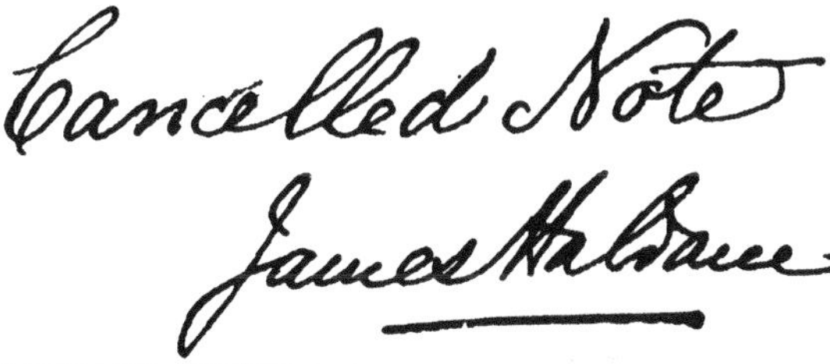

The back of the City of Glasgow Bank £100 note shows the signature of James Haldane, C.A., who was one of the pioneer C.A.s and a liquidator of the Bank.

From Building News, 13th June, 1879. *(By courtesy of the Mitchell Library, Glasgow)*

City of Glasgow Bank: architect's drawing (Campbell, Douglas & Sellars), 1879. Although the Bank had already failed, plans for the building were carried out (but for the top storey), and the building then sold as part of the assets of the Bank. It was demolished in 1959

Biographical Notes

The entries are arranged alphabetically. Names beginning with Mac or Mc follow those beginning with M.

In the headings to each of the biographical notes the dates, if known, of the birth and death of the subject are given. Between these dates appears the initial letter of the body to which he belonged, followed by the year in which he became a member. It was possible to distinguish those Glasgow members admitted in 1853, before the Charter, but the first definitive list of Edinburgh members is that of those who, in 1854, signed the petition for a Charter.

JAMES AFFLECK

b. G 1877 d.

James Affleck had served an apprenticeship of four years with McClelland, Mackinnon & Blyth, the last of the firm names under which the first President of the Institute carried on practice. His apprenticeship expired on 5th August, 1876 so that at the date of his admission Affleck was probably in his early twenties. Shortly after his admission he became a partner in the firm of Bird & Affleck which had an office at 92 St Vincent Street, Glasgow. Affleck may have been the son of a Mr John Affleck who in 1879 was assistant manager of the Union Bank of Scotland. It is an unusual name and in that year both had the same residential address. As a young man he held a commission in the 3rd Lanark Volunteers. He was apparently dead before the end of the century as his name does not appear in any of the official directories which were first issued in 1896/7.

He is one of the few early members whose names do not appear in the lists appended to Richard Brown's *History of Accounting and Accountants* although probably dead before 1905. It may be, however, that he ceased to be a member for some other reason.

P. H. AIKMAN

b. G 1877 d. 1921

At the time of his admission P. H. Aikman was working in London with William Edwards & Co., Accountants, 18 King Street, Cheapside and his was the first application for membership bearing a London address. His admission number was 125.

Prior to going to London he had served for five years in the offices of McFarlane & Hutton.

Shortly after admission he returned to Glasgow and formed a partnership with Ninian Glen who had also been with McFarlane & Hutton and was admitted to membership in the same year as Aikman.

Aikman does not seem to have taken any very active interest in Institute or public affairs but was interested in the affairs of the United Free Church of Scotland. He was an elder in and congregational treasurer of Wellington Church, Glasgow and was also joint convener of the Central Fund Committee of the United Free Church.

He was married, and had a family of 3 daughters and 1 son. In March 1921 he retired from business and died later that year.

RICHARD S. AITCHISON

b. 1850 E 1878 d. 19-ii-1936

Richard S. Aitchison was born at Haddington. His early education was received in East Lothian, presumably at the local parish school. He was then sent to Edinburgh to the Royal High School, and at the age of 17 was indentured to Murray &

Romanes. On completion of his apprenticeship in 1872 he did not seek to become a member of the Society as he did not at that time intend to practise. Later, however, he decided to make professional accountancy his career and was admitted to membership of the Society. Three years later, in 1881, he became a partner in the firm with whom he had trained, and the whole of his professional career, covering a period of 66 years, from his apprenticeship till his retiral after being senior partner of the firm for 19 years, was spent in the one office.

When Murray died the firm name was changed to Romanes & Aitchison. It remained the same when Romanes died in 1914 and later when Aitchison's son in turn became a partner.

The busy professional life which he led throughout his long career left little time for outside interests, and Aitchison took no part in public affairs. He was highly regarded by his fellow chartered accountants and, having served a term on the Council of the Society, was invited to accept the Presidency, an honour which he did not see his way to accept.

His principal recreation was gardening for which he had a great enthusiasm. He also played golf with no great distinction and was a member of the Mortonhall Club.

Although not active in public life he took a full part in Church affairs and was an active member of Morningside High Church where he was an elder for 47 years and acted as congregational treasurer for 26 years.

Aitchison was married and had a family of 2 sons and 1 daughter. His younger son was a chartered accountant and became a partner in Romanes & Aitchison. He and the daughter survived their father, but the elder son was killed in Gallipoli in 1915.

Aitchison lived to the advanced age of 86.

ROBERT AITKEN

b. 22-viii-1806 G 1855 d. 19-vii-1890

Robert Aitken was the eldest son of another Robert Aitken, a banker.

He was one of the group of accountants in practice in Glasgow before 1841 to whom in 1853 their junior colleagues addressed the requisition suggesting the formation of an institute or society of accountants in the city. He was also an original member of the Glasgow Stock Exchange Association when it was formed in 1844.

He had been a partner of T. Gray Buchanan, another original member of both bodies, but at the time of the incorporation of the Institute was in partnership with Walter Mackenzie. The firm's offices were then at 66 St Vincent Street, and Aitken lived further west at 201 West Bath Street. His house there still exists.

On the formation of the Institute, Aitken became a member of the original council; but he had a greater interest and took a more prominent part in the affairs of the Stock Exchange Association of which he was chairman in the years 1865-1868.

Among other interests he was a local director of the Life Association of Scotland, and he was a Justice of the Peace for the Lower Ward of Lanarkshire and also for Ayrshire. He was also, although then retired from active business, chairman of Glasgow Royal Exchange from 1884 until his death.

He retired from business in 1870 but survived for another 20 years. During his retirement he lived in Largs, and when the town became a burgh was elected its first Provost. His house in Largs was afterwards acquired by the burgh and was used as the town's offices.

Robert Aitken's decision to spend his retirement in Largs may have been influenced by his interest in yachting—he was President of the Royal Northern Yacht Club.

R. EASTON AITKEN

b. 27-xii-1842 G 1870 d. 4-i-1922

R. Easton Aitken was a son of Robert Aitken, an original member of the Glasgow Institute.

After attending Glasgow University he spent some time in the offices of his father's firm of Aitken & Mackenzie. Thereafter he was employed for about three years in a mercantile counting house. He then decided to become a civil engineer, entered into a regular indenture of apprenticeship in that profession and served as an apprentice for five and a half years. During his period as a civil engineer he spent some time in Germany and he had experience of valuations of mineral and other properties and also of railway promotions, all of which he summarises in his application for membership of the Institute in the following way: "... business experience of a most varied description including railway and other parliamentary employment and actively engaged in the valuation of mineral and other property and ironworks to the value of over one and a half million pounds, frequently necessitating the investigation of business books to ascertain profits and having frequent reference to the principles regulating valuation by annuities."

On his father's retiral in 1870 he became a partner of Walter Mackenzie, who was then president of the Institute, and in the same year was admitted to membership. Further to qualify himself for his new career he returned to the University to take the Scots Law class.

Although he was at first engaged in the accounting side of his firm's business he was to become better known as a stockbroker. He had joined the Glasgow Stock Exchange Association in 1869 and he was three times chairman of that body; in 1889/92, 1898/9 and 1903/4.

R. E. Aitken took some active part in local government affairs and was appointed a Justice of the Peace for the City of Glasgow and for the county of Dunbartonshire. He was also prominent in the Volunteer movement, becoming Lieut-Colonel in the 1st Lanark Volunteer Corps, and the holder of the Volunteer Decoration.

He lived in Blythswood Square, Glasgow and was congregational treasurer and latterly an elder of Free St Matthews Church near by. A son, R. C. Seymour Aitken, also became a chartered accountant.

FINDLAY B. ANDERSON

b. c 1849 E 1872 d. 23-i-1927

At the time of his death F. B. Anderson was the senior surviving member of the Edinburgh Society and was then aged 78. His father, also Findlay Anderson, was a member of the Madras Civil Service. Findlay junior was educated at Edinburgh Academy and at Repton. After serving as an apprentice with Lindsay, Jamieson & Haldane he became a member of the Society and then in the following year was assumed as a partner in that firm.

He suffered from deafness and this caused him to devote most of his time to work which could be carried out within his own office. His deafness may also have been the reason why he declined nomination to the Society's Council. He had a reputation for always producing well written, clear and concise reports on any matters remitted to him.

Among his professional activities he was for many years up to 1900 a director of the Scottish Provident Institution and was later appointed auditor of that institution.

His recreational pursuits were varied and included at different times of his life cricket, skating, which he did with skill, golf, which he played with keenness but without great skill, and angling. He was also interested in photography and was an early motorist, at one time owning a steam car, but later graduating to a Rolls-Royce. In spite of his deafness he was very fond of music and had an organ installed in his home. Another, and more unusual, interest was conjuring at which he was expert.

Among his forebears was the Rev. David Anderson, Professor of Humanity at St Andrews University, who died in 1697.

Anderson died in his 78th year.

FRANCIS ANDERSON

b. 25-vi-1854 E 1878 d. l-xii-1908

Francis Anderson was also an apprentice with Lindsay, Jamieson & Haldane a few years later than Findlay B. Anderson. He was the third son of Francis Anderson, W.S. Like F. B. Anderson he had been at Edinburgh Academy. Shortly after his admission to membership he was appointed as Private Secretary to the Marquis of Bute. This appointment took him to London, and the early Chartered Accountants Official Directories give his address as 22A Queen Anne's Gate, London, S.W. Lord Bute died in 1900 and Anderson then retired to North Berwick, where he died in his mid-fifties.

H. K. ANDERSON

b. 1854 G 1876 d. 7-vi-1911

H. K. Anderson was the second son of William Anderson, C.A., one of the most notable of the early members of the Glasgow Institute. He was educated at Glasgow Academy and at Blair Lodge. He entered the office of his father's firm, Kerr, Anderson & Co., about 1871 and when admitted as a member of the Institute was already a partner in that firm. He had also in 1875 become a member of the Glasgow Stock Exchange Association.

He assisted his father in a number of important liquidations and other matters, but his own principal activity was in the management of estates and trusts.

Outside business he was keenly interested in athletic sports, especially, as a young man, in cricket, and in his twenties was convener of the Glasgow Academical Club cricket committee. He later took up golf and again took part in the administration of the game, being a member of the committee which was responsible for the arrangements for the amateur golf championship at Prestwick in 1911, the year of his death. He died at the comparatively early age of 57.

JAMES ANDERSON

b. G 1856 d. 6-i-1890

James Anderson was a brother of the better known William Anderson, one of the most notable of the original members of the Glasgow Institute. He appears as number 58 in the Institute's roll of members. At the time of his application for admission he stated that he had spent ten years with Kerr & Anderson and Kerr, Anderson & Brodie. He was apparently not a partner in the firm. The Glasgow Directory for 1855 does not list a James Anderson as an accountant but one of that name appears as a house factor. The occupations were at that time often combined but whether in the light of his statement about service with Kerr & Anderson this is our James Anderson seems doubtful.

James Anderson died rather less than two months after his elder brother.

WILLIAM ANDERSON

b. -ii-1817 G 1853 d. 13-xi-1889

William Anderson was in practice as an accountant in Glasgow from about 1840. He was one of the senior practitioners to whom the letter suggesting the formation of an association of accountants in Glasgow was addressed in 1853 and took a prominent part in the organisation of the Institute. He was one of the original members who did not submit formal applications for admission and was appointed as a member of the first Council of the Institute. He was also a member of the first committee appointed by the Council—a committee to deal with the revision of the bankruptcy laws, set up on 2nd December, 1853.

Anderson had been born in Kilmarnock in February, 1817 but his family appear to have removed to Irvine while he was still very young, for it was at Irvine Academy that he received his education and in the office of the Town Clerk there that he took up his first employment. That cannot have lasted long, for at the age of 16 he came to Glasgow and entered the office of James McClelland. This was in 1833 and after his training there he began as was then usual to practise on his own account and in 1842 entered into partnership with James and Henry Kerr as Kerr & Anderson. In 1853 John R. Brodie was assumed as a partner and the firm's name was changed to Kerr, Anderson & Brodie. These partnerships were the origins of Kerr, MacLeod & Macfarlan, now part of Deloitte & Co.

During the 1840's Anderson was largely employed in connection with new railway schemes and he built up a considerable reputation. In 1856, when Glasgow Corporation acquired the undertaking of the Glasgow Water Company, he was appointed by the Corporation to be one of the arbiters to fix the consideration and he was appointed to act in a similar capacity when later the Corporation acquired the Glasgow Gas Company.

In 1878 he was asked, along with Dr McGrigor, to examine the state of affairs of the City of Glasgow Bank. They reported on 5th October, 1878 that it would be advisable to wind up the business. In the liquidation which followed Anderson was one of the liquidators appointed. In the subsequent criminal proceedings against the directors of the bank James Muir, a partner of Anderson, was one of the chief prosecution witnesses. Earlier, Anderson had been involved in the liquidation of the Western Bank and in the litigation against Messrs Baird which followed that liquidation.

In 1870 he was elected President of the Glasgow Institute and on expiry of his normal term of three years was reappointed for a further term of three years. It was during his presidency that the Institute first acquired its own premises in West Nile Street, Glasgow. Because the Institute's borrowing powers were ill-defined the purchase of these premises was made in Anderson's name.

He was again appointed to the Institute's Council in 1885. Among interests outside the profession he was a director of the Merchants' House of Glasgow and of the Andersonian University in Glasgow. He was also a manager of the Ferguson Bequest Fund.

Like a number of the other original members of the Glasgow Institute he was also an original member of the Glasgow Stock Exchange Association.

He was a Justice of the Peace for the Lower Ward of Lanarkshire and also for Dunbartonshire.

His brother James Anderson was also an early, though not an original, member of the Institute. His two sons, W. J. and H. K. Anderson became members of the Institute in 1876, having trained in their father's office and become his partners in 1875.

W. J. ANDERSON

b. c 1852 G 1876 d. 1922

W. J. Anderson was the elder brother of H. K. Anderson and elder son of William Anderson. His early career was in close parallel with that of his younger brother. Before becoming a partner in his father's firm in 1875 he had served for four years as an apprentice and two years as a clerk with the firm. He, like his brother, became a member of the Glasgow Stock Exchange Association in 1875 and was admitted as a member of the Glasgow Institute in 1876, his name standing next before his brother's in the membership roll.

His interests lay mainly in the stockbroking side of the firm and he was chairman of the Stock Exchange Association in 1897-1898. In 1918, following a change in the rules of the Stock Exchange Association, the accountancy and stockbroking sides of the firm's business separated—the former continuing as Kerr, MacLeod & Macfarlan, while the latter took the name Kerr, Anderson, Dunn & Co.

W. J. Anderson retired from business within a relatively short time after the division of the firm.

During the 1914-18 war he rendered conspicuous service to the Red Cross Society and for this service was awarded the C.B.E. in 1918.

He was for many years honorary treasurer to the trustees of Park Church, Glasgow and was a Justice of the Peace.

He had four sons, all of whom were killed during the 1914-18 war. The eldest was a partner in his father's firm and was the only Scottish Chartered Accountant to be awarded the Victoria Cross—regrettably a posthumous award.

WILLIAM AULD

b. G 1853 d. 30-i-1885

William Auld was one of the senior accountants in Glasgow to whom the requisition suggesting the formation of an association was addressed in 1853. He was one of the original members of the Institute and a subscriber to the rules adopted under the 1855 Charter. He was, however, better known as a stockbroker than as an accountant and was three times chairman of the Glasgow Stock Exchange Association, his terms of office being in 1870-71, 1874-75 and 1878-79. He had become a member of the Stock Exchange Asociation on its formation in 1844.

His first partnership was with Andrew McEwan with whom he formed the firm of McEwan & Auld in 1836. On McEwan's death in 1866 he joined J. Wyllie Guild in a partnership known as Auld & Guild. This partnership was dissolved in 1877 and he was then joined by McEwan's son in a stockbroking partnership under the name of Auld & McEwan.

Auld was obviously for a long period a man of substance for as early as 1855 his residence was in Woodside Place in what was then a comparatively new section of Glasgow's West End. He was a Justice of the Peace for the Lower Ward of Lanarkshire.

JOHN MENZIES BAILLIE

b. 24-iv-1826 E 1854 d. 6-x-1886

John Menzies Baillie was the son of R. G. Baillie of Culter Allers an estate of some 4,500 acres in Peeblesshire and Lanarkshire. He was apprenticed to William Moncreiff and became his partner in 1849. In 1854 shortly after the formation of the Edinburgh Society he became a member and he continued to practise as Moncreiff's partner till 1880. In that year he succeeded to his father's estate and retired from business. In 1882 he built a new house in Scottish baronial style at Culter Allers but he did not long survive to enjoy his estate and this house as he died at the age of 60.

While in practice in Edinburgh he was a director of the National Fire & Life Insurance Co. of Scotland. He also acted for a time as auditor, presumably an honorary appointment, of the New Town Dispensary.

ROBERT BALFOUR

b. 24-vi-1818 E 1854 d. 14-viii-1869

Robert Balfour had been practising as an accountant in Edinburgh since 1842. He was a son of James Balfour, W.S., of Pilrig; his mother was Frances G. Blackie, who was the daughter of an Aberdeen advocate. He was educated at Edinburgh Academy and Edinburgh University, where he was successively Secretary and President of the Speculative Society. He was then apprenticed to William Paul, a well-known Edinburgh accountant, who predeceased the formation of the Society.

Balfour took a life-long interest in his old school and for 24 years was secretary of the Academical Club. After his death his friends established prizes for French and German in his memory. He played a leading part in procuring for the Academy the cricket and sports field at Raeburn Place and shared with two others—Kenneth Mackenzie, who was also to become a chartered accountant, and Thomas Cleghorn, the "whole pecuniary responsibility" for this. The ground was opened in 1854, after the formation of the Society but before the granting of the Charter.

Balfour set up in business as an accountant in 1842 in partnership with Patrick Brodie, who had also been trained in Paul's office. The partnership lasted only till 1844 when Brodie became secretary of the Scottish National Insurance Co., from which post he proceeded in 1846 to be manager of the Glasgow office of the British Linen Bank and then in 1860 to be general manager of the bank.

Balfour, who was also an actuary (F.F.A. 1868), was from 1846 Edinburgh Secretary of the City of Glasgow Life Assurance Co. In 1868 he became honorary secretary of the Faculty of Actuaries in the formation of which he had helped.

Balfour was married but, on the same day as he himself died, his only son died at the age of 17 from scarlet fever.

JAMES H. BALGARNIE

b. 1829 E 1855 d. 10-i-1879

James H. Balgarnie was a son of Robert Balgarnie, home farmer to the Marquis of Lothian.

After serving as an apprentice with Charles M. Barstow he set up in practice in 1850 at the early age which was then customary as few accountants then employed assistants of mature years. Following the formation of the Edinburgh Society he was admitted as a member in 1855 and was in practice till his death. In the previous year he was the auditor of the Philosophical Institution.

Balgarnie's son Norman also became a member of the Edinburgh Society in 1887, some years after his father's death, but died in 1902 at the age of 37.

ANDREW BANNATYNE

b. G 1862 d. 29-i-1885

In the year following his admission as a member of the Glasgow Institute, Andrew Bannatyne also became a member of the Glasgow Stock Exchange Association. At the date of his admission to membership of the Institute he had had seven or eight years' experience in the offices of accountants and stockbrokers but had not been in business on his own account. After serving for four years as an apprentice with J. Wyllie Guild he continued with him as a clerk for a further year. In 1860 he became a clerk with McEwan & Auld.

It would seem likely, therefore, that in 1862 he was between 22 and 25 years old. In the 1870's he was a partner in Bannatyne & White with offices at 4 West Nile Street, Glasgow. White was not, at any rate before 1879, a member of the Institute.

Bannatyne served on the Council of the Institute in 1882-1884.

HUGH B. BARCLAY

b. G 1870 d. 3-iii-1892

Hugh Barclay was associated with James Wyllie Guild for about ten years before becoming a member of the Institute. The latter part of that period was during the time when William Auld was a partner of Wyllie Guild and this may have been what led Barclay to become a member of the Glasgow Stock Exchange Association in 1869. Auld, although a member of the Glasgow Institute, was mainly interested in stockbroking. In 1870, when Robert Aitken retired from the firm of Aitken & Mackenzie, Walter Mackenzie assumed Aitken's son R. Easton Aitken and Hugh B. Barclay as partners and the firm was then known as Mackenzie, Aitken & Barclay. This partnership did not long continue as Barclay's health broke down and he retired in 1876.

JOHN BARRON

b. E 1854 d. 1-xi-1873

John Barron was one of the original members of the Edinburgh Society but nothing is known of his training or family background, nor is there any information about his professional activities save that he was depute clerk of tiends (an official of the Court of the Commission of Tiends).

CHARLES MURRAY BARSTOW

b. 11-i-1804 E 1854 d. 10-xi-1885

Charles Barstow was one of the most prominent of the first generation of Chartered Accountants. He was born at Earlston, the son of Captain Barstow of Kelso. After being educated in Yorkshire, he moved to Edinburgh where he was trained in the office of James Brown, who was later to be the first president of the Edinburgh Society. Then in 1828 at the age of 24 he set up in practice as an accountant on his own. His first partner was James Latta who had been his apprentice. He built up a substantial business, and accounting matters were frequently remitted to him by the Courts. When the Society of Accountants in Edinburgh was founded in 1854 he was one of the original members. He was an early member of the Society's Council and in 1869 he was elected as the third President of the Society, an office which he held until 1876. In the course of his presidency his partner, Latta, died. Subsequently Barstow assumed as a partner Robert Cockburn Millar who, like Latta, had been his apprentice. The firm then became known as Barstow and Millar, and continued to be so known though Millar retired from the partnership and set up on his own account. In fact the practice is still carried on in that name.

When Barstow relinquished the presidency in 1876 he was presented by the members with his portrait, a replica of which is in the Institute. The presentation was made at the only official dinner of the Society held between its foundation and the jubilee dinner in 1904.

The business which Barstow built up was largely associated with landed property and he was always interested in schemes for land improvement and in other developments of interest to landed proprietors, such as quarries, mines, canals and railways. He was also connected with water and gas companies, and in a different field was a director of The English and Scottish Investment Company of Canada Ltd.

His recreational activities reflected his interest in the land and the countryside. He was a good shot and a keen fisherman and was well-known in the hunting field as a follower of the Lothian hounds. He was the author of a book of reminiscences *Days with the Lothian Hounds*. He had a great interest in old Scottish characters and characteristics and had a store of reminiscences bearing on these. This was perhaps not surprising as he was a kinsman of Dean Ramsay whose book on the topic is well-known.

His only public service as recorded was as a Justice of the Peace which in those days was much more a matter of service than it is now.

DAVID BIRD

b. G 1877 d. 1913

When David Bird was admitted as a member of the Glasgow Institute he was probably in his early twenties, as he had been for fully three years with Mitchell & Watson, C.A., and then for a year and a half with David McCubbin, C.A. Following his admission as a chartered accountant, Bird set up in partnership with James Affleck. By the end of the century Affleck was dead and Bird had apparently retired as the Scottish Chartered Accountants Directory for 1899/1900 shows his address as 'The Beeches', Sandbank, an unlikely address from which to conduct an accountancy practice at that time. He earlier had an address in Bellshill.

ADAM E. BLACK

b. G 1877 d. 1893

Adam E. Black was a son of Rev. Dr Black, minister of Wellington United Presbyterian Church of Scotland, Glasgow. At the time of his admission to membership of the Glasgow Institute he had served five years with Moore & Brown. In

1878 or 1879 he entered into partnership with Alexander Fleming and they practised together until Black died when he was still a young man. Outside his professional work he was interested in the Volunteer movement and held the rank of major in the Lanarkshire Engineer Volunteers.

ALEXANDER BLACK

b. c 1798 G 1853 d. 8-ix-1880

Alexander Black was one of the original members of the Glasgow Institute and one of the relatively few to be born in the eighteenth century. He was among the men in practice in 1841 to whom the letter suggesting the formation of a society of accountants in the city had been addressed, but took little subsequent active interest in Institute affairs. He devoted all his attention to the stockbroking side of the activities of his firm (Black & Robson), having become a member of the Glasgow Stock Exchange Association in 1845. For the short period of four months in 1870, when he was already over 70 years of age, he was chairman of the Stock Exchange Association. He played some part in civic affairs and was a member of the parochial board of Glasgow City parish.

He lived to an advanced age but when he was 82 years old was killed in a railway accident at Pennilee near Paisley.

HUGH BLAIR

b. 27-xii-1844 E 1869 d. 20-viii-1906

Hugh Blair was the son of Hugh Blair, W.S., of Auchenreoch, Kirkcudbright. He was educated at Edinburgh Academy and at Rugby and thereafter became an apprentice with Watson and Dickson, both of whom were original members and had been in practice in Edinburgh for many years. In the same year that he was admitted as a member of the Society he passed the examinations of the Faculty of Actuaries, of which he became a Fellow in 1872. He served on the Councils of both the Society of Accountants in Edinburgh and the Faculty of Actuaries and was President of the former from 1901 to 1904. Among other services to these two professional bodies he was a member of the General Examining Board of the Scottish Chartered Accountants, Deputy Chairman of the Faculty of Actuaries and actuary to the Faculty's Widows Fund.

In 1874 he entered into partnership with James M. Macandrew, who had been a member of the Society since 1854 and who was also an original member of the Faculty of Actuaries. Macandrew preceded his younger partner as President of the Society and on demitting that office in 1889 retired from the partnership. The firm had an extensive practice and the partners of the firm were auditors of a number of charitable and educational institutions. Those with which Blair was particularly connected included Edinburgh Royal Infirmary, George Heriot's Trust, Edinburgh School Board and the Faculty of Advocates. He was also auditor of the Scottish Equitable Assurance Society, of the Clydesdale Bank, and of the Real Estate Security Co. Ltd.

The son of a lawyer, Blair had other family legal connections. Both of his brothers were members of that profession, one being Sheriff of the Lothians and Peebles, while his wife was the daughter of Sheriff Bell, of Banff, Elgin and Nairn. She and their family of two sons and one daughter survived Blair.

J. BLAIR

b. G 1869 d.

When J. Blair became a member of the Glasgow Institute he had been in business on his own account for five years. His training must have started not long after the incorporation of the Institute because prior to setting up in business he had been a clerk with William Mudie, C.A., for four and a half years and with Wink & Wight, C.A., for two years. Nothing is known of his subsequent career and his name does not appear in the first official Directory of Scottish Chartered Accountants for 1896/97 so presumably he was no longer a member then. His name does not appear in the list of deceased Scottish Accountants appended to Richard Brown's history.

ROBERT BLYTH

b. 1843 G 1872 d. 27-iv-1917

The son of a partner in a firm of muslin manufacturers and grandson of a Glasgow leather merchant, in his 'teens Robert Blyth became a clerk in the office of James McClelland. After about ten years' service he was rewarded with a partnership, the firm then adopting the name McClelland, Mackinnon and Blyth. While a member of that firm Blyth was the auditor of two Scottish banks and an Irish bank. In 1892 he was appointed manager of the Scottish Amicable Life Assurance Society. In the following year he became a Fellow of the Faculty of Actuaries. Whether previously acquired actuarial skill had led to his life assurance appointment, or whether that appointment led him to become an actuary is not clear. His next move is perhaps more readily understood; in 1895 he became general manager of the Union Bank of Scotland, an appointment which he held until his retiral in 1910. Already before joining the Scottish Amicable Life Assurance Society he had served a term on the council of the Glasgow Institute—from 1884 to 1886. He also held official positions in connection with the other two professions in which he was active. He served as President of the Insurance and Actuarial Society of Glasgow, and was also President of the Institute of Bankers in Scotland. He was well known as a writer and lecturer on banking, insurance and finance and contributed articles on these topics to various journals including *The Accountant's Magazine*. He was a member of the Merchants' House of Glasgow, a Justice of the Peace and active in various charitable associations.

Blyth was living in retirement at Balvenie, Skelmorlie when he died.

ARCHIBALD BORTHWICK

b. 1811 E 1854 d. 3-vii-1863

Archibald Borthwick was one of eight men present at the first meeting held to consider the formation of an association of accountants in Edinburgh. He acted as chairman of that meeting and was the mover of the resolution to proceed with the formation of an association designated in his resolution the "Institute of Accountants". He became a member of the first council of the Society.

The Borthwick family traced its descent from the eleventh century, when their ancestor, a Livonian Knight, came to Scotland in the train of the princess who married Malcolm Canmore. In the fifteenth century the then head of the family was created Baron of Borthwick (1452). The title fell into abeyance for a period but was revived in 1762. Ten years later it again went into abeyance and in the latter part of the nineteenth century the succession was the subject of a prolonged legal dispute which was not settled till after Archibald's death, when in 1870 his younger brother Cunninghame Borthwick of Ravenstone, Wigtonshire was adjudged to be the heir, and the title was revived in his favour. Cunninghame was the 20th in order of succession and the 11th baron in possession of the dignity. Archibald Borthwick had married in 1840 Mary Louisa Home who had previously been engaged to his elder brother Thomas, who died as a relatively young man. They had three daughters but no male heir so that the title when eventually revived fell to the third brother.

Archibald's father was Patrick Borthwick, the first manager of the National Bank of Scotland. Like many of the early members of the Society he was a pupil at the Royal High School. His classmates there included Archibald Campbell Tait, who became Archbishop of Canterbury; R. Murray McCheyne, another well-known divine though of a different complexion; and John Brown, the author and creator of *Rab and his Friends*.

After his attendance at Edinburgh University, where he was a student from 1826 to 1828, his father placed him in the office of J. A. Cheyne, W.S., a director of the National Bank of Scotland. Cheyne, though a member of the Society of Writers to the Signet, had from about 1820 designed himself as an accountant. In 1831 Cheyne was appointed manager of the newly formed Life Association of Scotland and having apparently been impressed by the ability of his young pupil took him with him to that institution as secretary and cashier. After three years Borthwick returned to accountancy and began to practise in Edinburgh in 1834. His brother Thomas, although not recorded in Richard Brown's list of deceased accountants, appears to have been his partner about this time. Archibald Borthwick's activities continued to alternate between accountancy and insurance. In 1838 he was concerned in the formation of the City of Glasgow Assurance and Reversionary Co., the second life assurance company to be founded in Glasgow, and moved to Glasgow as manager of that company. His absence from Edinburgh was not prolonged, for in 1839, his brother Thomas having died, he returned to Edinburgh and to accountancy.

Thereafter accountancy was his main interest, though he continued to be a director of the City of Glasgow Assurance Co., and also, as was then possible, acted as auditor of that company. His practice flourished and from 1846 to 1857 he had as a partner Samuel Raleigh who had been his apprentice.

In 1858 he assumed as a partner James Howden and in 1863, not long before Borthwick's death, J. A. Molleson, who had been an apprentice with the firm, also became a partner.

In 1858 Borthwick's youngest daughter died at the age of only eight and this loss led him to take, for the rest of his life, a very deep interest in the Hospital for the Poor Sick Children.

Although he had been active in the actual formation of the Society, Borthwick did not, thereafter, take any prominent part in its administration, though in 1854/1855 he was convener of a committee concerned with the formulation of the Society's Rules and Bye-Laws.

He died, after a varied and active career, at the age of 52.

J. T. BOWIE

b. 1-vii-1829 E 1859 d. 9-viii-1906

J. T. Bowie is one of those early members of the Society of Accountants in Edinburgh of whom little is known beyond the span of their years and the fact that they were accountants or, to be fully accurate, chartered accountants. Bowie lived to the respectable age of 77. At the age of 30 he was admitted as a member of the Society and presumably for the next forty years or more carried on his profession in a quiet and unremarkable manner. His address in the later years of his life and perhaps for a much longer period was 18 Northumberland Street, Edinburgh. Beyond that is silence, not broken by the notice of his death which appeared in *The Accountant's Magazine* for 1906.

ALEXANDER BRAND

b. A 1867 d. 1876

Alexander Brand was one of the twelve original members of the Aberdeen Society of Accountants. When the Society was formed Brand had apparently been in practice for about twelve years. Whether this indicated an age in the mid-thirties, as it might, or whether he had previously engaged in some other occupation is not known. Brand had an advertisement in the

1867/68 Aberdeen Directory showing him as specialising in advice on insurance and as agent for four insurance companies. He served on the Society's Council in 1869 and 1870 and the following year was elected President, an office which he held till 1873. His election to the Presidency might indicate a greater age than has been surmised, but the small number of members of the Society must be remembered, while, although some of the early chartered accountants survived to great age, others died in quite early life.

JOHN BREWIS

b. 1854 E 1879 d. ll-ii-1900

John Brewis was born at his father's seat Eshott Hall, Northumberland. His father was Thomas Brewis of that address. He was educated and received his professional training in Edinburgh. He first attended a private school in the city, and then proceeded to the High School and to the University. He served as an apprentice with Howden and Molleson. Thereafter he was for a period a partner with G. T. Chiene, Junior and John S. Tait.

In 1889 he was joined in partnership by his brother-in-law R. D. Rainie and they practised at first as Brewis & Rainie and later as Brewis Rainie & Boyd. Remits from the Courts brought Brewis into contact with the leading legal firms in the city and his business steadily grew. When Howden & Molleson moved their offices from 5 North St David Street to York Place, Brewis & Rainie took over the North St David Street offices.

As a young man Brewis was well known as an athlete and later was a keen angler and a good shot. His friends, it is said, saw him as, like his father, a type of the "fine old English gentleman". He did not, however, survive to merit the epithet "old" as he died in his middle forties. He had served as a member of the Society's Council from 1892 to 1896.

Another Brewis (Edward) was admitted as a member of the Society in 1893. He was perhaps a family connection of John Brewis as his address was Acton Hall, Felton, Northumberland.

FRANCIS A. BRINGLOE

b. 14-ix-1847 E 1871 d. 10-iv-1903

Francis Bringloe, the son of Francis J. Bringloe, W.S., was educated at Edinburgh Academy and Edinburgh University and was an apprentice to Lindsay Jamieson & Haldane. After qualifying he set up in practice and some years later was joined as a partner by J. Campbell Penney, who had also served his apprenticeship with Lindsay Jamieson & Haldane. They built up a good business but in 1890 Campbell Penney was appointed Accountant of Court and retired from the partnership. Bringloe then continued the practice in partnership with J. Maxtone Graham.

Bringloe served the Society in various capacities. He was a member of the Council from 1884 to 1888, was auditor from 1898 to 1901 and from then until his death was Collector of the Society's Annuity Fund.

Like many of his contemporaries he had a managerial connection with insurance, being manager of the Guarantee Association of Scotland Ltd.

Bringloe was an episcopalian and took a great interest in the affairs of The Scottish Episcopal Church. He died in his mid-fifties.

JOHN A. BRODIE

b. G 1853 d. 1879

John A. Brodie was one of a number of men who obtained their early training and experience in Edinburgh but who came to Glasgow while still young and made their professional careers there. He was for three years in the office in Edinburgh of William Moncreiff and then for a further three years accountant and cashier with the National Insurance Co. of Scotland. He was one of the signatories to the letter addressed to senior accountants in Glasgow suggesting the formation of a formal association of accountants in that city, and as he appears to have commenced business only shortly before he must have quickly made an impression on his Glasgow colleagues. Further evidence of his ready acceptance in the West is the fact that in 1853 he became a partner in Kerr, Anderson and Brodie, already as Kerr & Anderson a well established business. He was a partner in that firm till 1870.

JOHN WILSON BRODIE

b. 14-v-1851 E 1875 d. 7-i-1937

John W. Brodie was the elder son of Patrick Brodie, manager of The British Linen Bank. He was educated at Edinburgh Academy and was an apprentice with Kenneth Mackenzie. Among his classmates at the Academy were R. J. Torrie, who later became his partner in the well known stockbroking firm of Torrie, Brodie & Maclagan; W. Home Cook, who was also an apprentice with Kenneth Mackenzie and became prominent as an Edinburgh chartered accountant; and Robert Louis Stevenson. He became a member of the Society in 1875, having shared the Society's £30 fellowship in the preceding year. For a short time after becoming a chartered accountant he was in practice but already his interest in investment business and investment companies was emerging, as in 1878 he was manager of The Real Estate Security Co. Ltd.

About the same time (1877 to 1879) he was a president of the Speculative Society, the well known Edinburgh University debating society of which many young men later to attain prominence were members. He was also an active member of St Andrew Boat Club.

After a comparatively short term in practice he joined R. J. Torrie in partnership as accountants and stockbrokers. The emphasis was always on the stockbroking side and eventually the firm, by then Torrie, Brodie and MacLagan, became one of the leading Edinburgh firms of stockbrokers. Brodie was a director of a number of investment companies including the American and Second American Trust Companies and the Scottish American Investment Co. Ltd., of which he was a director from 1891 till 1933 and chairman from 1922 to 1926.

For the long period of 54 years he was secretary to the Chalmers Hospital and had also other charitable interests.

When he died he was the then senior member of the Society. He was survived by his elder son who was associated with him in business and by his widow and two daughters. His younger son, who won the Victoria Cross, was killed during the 1914-18 war.

W. P. WILSON BRODIE

b. 23-xii-1853 E 1877 d. 30-xi-1932

Wilson Brodie was the second son of Patrick Brodie, manager of the British Linen Bank. Like his elder brother John Wilson Brodie, C.A., he attended Edinburgh Academy, but he then went on to St Andrews University. As a young man he was distinguished as an athlete and for a time held the pole jump record.

He was apprenticed to A. Weir Robertson, the first secretary of the Society. His athletic prowess led to an interruption of his career, however, since as a result of a football injury he had to reside abroad for a considerable time. His health having recovered and his career resumed, he became Edinburgh manager of the Commercial Union Assurance Co., an appointment in which he continued until his retirement. After his retiral Brodie lived at North Berwick. So far as health permitted he enjoyed golf there and also at Muirfield. Whatever effect his football accident may have had on his health and on his career it does not seem to have shortened his life materially since he survived till only a month before his 79th birthday.

JAMES BROWN (1)

b. 1786 E 1854 d. 2-ii-1864

James Brown was the first president of the Society of Accountants in Edinburgh. He was the son of Rev. James Brown of Newbattle. His grandfather was also a minister, who had been Moderator of the General Assembly in 1777. The family could trace their descent from the Browns of Fordell Castle, Perthshire and Fairmount, Fife, back to 1250.

Brown was educated at Edinburgh High School and at Edinburgh University and was probably practising as an accountant by 1813. In 1816 he married and purchased the property at 94 George Street, where he lived till 1846, having his office for the greater part of that time on the ground floor of the house.

Brown's wife was a daughter of Colonel Wm. McKerrell of Hillhouse, Dundonald, Ayrshire, a property which had been in the McKerrell family for 400 years and to which Brown's eldest son James Adam Brown succeeded in 1853. James Adam Brown then adopted the name McKerrell Brown but he had no family to succeed him. Prince Louis Napoleon, afterwards Emperor of the French, stayed at Hillhouse in 1839 at the time of the Eglinton Tournament, the magnificent pageant promoted by the 13th Earl of Eglinton in which the Prince was one of the participants.

Before the formation of the Society Brown had already built up a large business, mainly involving the administration of Trusts and bankruptcies. He was responsible for the administration of many large estates, including that of Walter Campbell of Islay, who owned most of that island. He was also trustee for the creditors of Leith Banking Company, which failed in 1842. From 1825 he was auditor of the Edinburgh Life Assurance Company, of which in 1840 he became a director. In 1835 Brown formed a partnership with Charles Pearson and in 1847 the firm's office was transferred to 128 George Street, which had been Pearson's winter residence. Pearson had received his training in Brown's office and they were both original members of the Society, of which, like his former master and partner, Pearson was to become President.

Two of Brown's sons trained as accountants in their father's office. The elder, like his father, was an original member of the Society, but as it was about this time that he succeeded to the McKerrell property he does not seem to have pursued his accountancy career further. His second son John McKerrell never became a member of the Society and did not follow the accountancy profession, but two of his sons became chartered accountants, and the elder, James McKerrell Brown, was President of the Society from 1918 to 1922.

James Brown continued to practise till his death and also continued to be the Society's President, holding office for about eleven years. In addition to other business interests, of which some have been mentioned, he was a director of the Bank of Scotland.

He is recorded as having been a man of quiet tastes with the faculty of discarding business cares when he left his office or, as it was for much of his career, his desk, and he enjoyed spending his leisure hours with his family.

JAMES BROWN (2)

b. 21-xi-1853 E 1878 d. 1947

James Brown, later known as James McKerrell Brown, was the grandson of James Brown, the first president of the Edinburgh Society. He attended Edinburgh Academy from 1864 to 1871 where he distinguished himself as an athlete. He was the son of John McKerrell Brown, the second son of the first James Brown. This Brown served as an apprentice with Mansfield & Spottiswoode and later with F. & F. W. Carter. He became a member of the Society in 1878 after having been joint winner of the Society's £20 bursary in 1874. He spent a year with Moncreiff &

Gillies Smith before setting up on his own. His brother Henry H. McKerrell Brown was admitted to membership in 1887 and the two were subsequently in partnership in the firm eventually known as J. & H. McKerrell Brown & Gray. James Brown was president of the Society from 1918 to 1922. Considering his distinguished connections and services to the Society the information available about his professional career is remarkably scanty.

JAMES ADAM BROWN

b. 1817 E 1854 d.

James Adam Brown, one of the original members of the Edinburgh Society, was the eldest son of James Brown, who became the first President of the Society. He was educated at Edinburgh Academy and at Edinburgh University. Thereafter he went into the offices of his father's firm of Brown & Pearson and trained as an accountant. At the time of the formation of the Society he would be about thirty-six years old and as he became one of the original members he must have considered accountancy as his profession, but there is no indication either that he ever became a partner of his father, which would have been normal, or that he had begun to practise independently. In 1853 his grandfather, Colonel William McKerrell of Hillhouse, Dundonald, Ayrshire, died and James Adam Brown succeeded to the estate. He later assumed the surname McKerrell-Brown and presumably on his succession abandoned his career in accountancy, whatever that may have been. He married a daughter of Principal Hill of Glasgow but they had no family.

RICHARD BROWN

b. 17-viii-1856 E 1879 d. 24-v-1918

Richard Brown's name is familiar to all interested in the history of accounting and accountants in Scotland as the editor and part-author of the historical review *A History of Accounting and Accountants* (Edinburgh 1905; reprinted London, 1968), published at the time of the celebration of the jubilee of the granting of the first Royal Charters incorporating societies of accountants in Great Britain. His book also included the first annotated lists of early accountants in Scotland—chartered and pre-chartered. He was born about two years after the granting of the charter to the Edinburgh Society, at the farm of Kirkhouse, Dolphinton. His father, also Richard Brown, was a farmer there and his forebears had farmed in the same parish for upwards of two hundred years. Richard was educated at the local parish school and on his 16th birthday he made the change from country youth to young city gent and was apprenticed to Kenneth Mackenzie & J. T. Smith, C.A., both notable members of the still young Society of Accountants in Edinburgh. Brown, himself, was admitted as a member of that body at the age of 23, having in the previous year shown his exceptional capability by winning the Society's £30 fellowship. In 1880 Kenneth Mackenzie died and five years later Smith became manager of the Life Association of Scotland and retired from the practice of accountancy. Before Smith's retirement he allocated his professional work among members of his staff, including Brown, and recommended their services to his clients. Having thus succeeded to a part of Smith's business, Brown set up on his own account and in 1893 assumed as partners H. L. Usher and K. M. Gourlay. The firm of Richard Brown & Co. thus constituted carried on for upwards of 70 years. It then joined with Lindsay, Jamieson & Haldane as Haldane, Brown & Co., and the practice is now part of Arthur Young McClelland Moores & Co.

By 1891 Richard Brown's standing as a leading member of the Society was already recognised and in that year he became a member of the Society's Council. The following year he was elected as Secretary and Treasurer in succession to James Howden and William Wood respectively Secretary and Treasurer. He held these offices for 24 years until his election as President of the Society in 1916.

During this long period Richard Brown played a leading part not only in the progress of his own Society but in the development of the accountancy profession in Scotland. Among the first of the changes in which he was actively concerned was the re-arrangement of the examination system which followed the constitution of the Scottish Chartered Accountants General Examining Board in 1893. He was appointed to be the first secretary of that board and until 1916 he was, in that capacity, responsible for the whole of the examination arrangements. Evening classes for the apprentices connected with the Edinburgh Society were also started at his suggestion and he was involved in the setting up of *The Accountant's Magazine* in 1897, to which in succeeding years he contributed many editorial and other articles. He also contributed to the *Encyclopedia of Accounting* published in 1903.

When the jubilee of the granting of the Royal Charter to the Society of Accountants in Edinburgh came round in 1904, this, to quote from the Preface to the *History of Accounting and Accountants*, "suggested the propriety of writing an account of the origin and growth of the profession while it was still possible to ascertain the facts and describe the circumstances with some degree of fulness. The idea having been heartily approved of by the Scottish Societies of Accountants, the project soon expanded, and it was decided to include a history of Accounts, Auditing and Book-keeping". The help of a number of collaborators was secured these being, to quote again from the preface, "men engaged in active business, who had at the same time to attend to the daily demands of a somewhat exacting profession", and the result is a work of great interest and value to all their successors. The greater part of the work was done by Richard Brown and he also compiled an interesting bibliography of book-keeping and, with the assistance of Alexander Sloan, C.A., lists of deceased Scottish accountants which form appendices to the history.

A few years after the Scottish jubilee, there occurred the "majority" celebrations of the American Association of Public Accountants. Richard Brown attended these celebrations as one of the Scottish delegation and twice addressed those attending.

Apart from his work in building up and conducting a substantial practice and his official work in the administration of the Society's and the profession's affairs, Richard Brown had a wide variety of interests.

He travelled extensively in Europe, North Africa and North America. He took an active interest in Church affairs, was for seven years a representative from Selkirk to the General Assembly of the Church of Scotland, served on several Assembly committees including the Endowment Committee of which he was vice-convener. In 1910 he was the Church's auditor.

He retained his interest in the affairs of his native district and for many years was secretary of the Edinburgh Upper-Ward of Lanarkshire Association.

A man of musical and literary taste and ability he found a good deal of his recreation in books and music. He was a member of the Edinburgh Amateur Orchestral Society and played both violin and viola with that orchestra. His literary interests were especially concentrated on matters antiquarian and he was a keen student of local history. The Institute's present extensive collection of antiquarian books on accounting owes much to Brown's interest and to the nucleus which he provided for it.

In later years Brown had a country home at "The Hangingshaw", Yarrow, where he spent much time. He created there a rock garden in which he took a great interest and also enjoyed walking in the countryside and shooting.

All this work and service was crowded into a life of just over sixty years.

WILLIAM BROWN

b. G 1857 d. 13-vi-1889

In the year before he became a member of the Glasgow Institute, William Brown had become a member of the Glasgow Stock Exchange Association and had also gone into partnership with Robert McCowan, chartered accountant and stockbroker, in whose office he had been a clerk for the preceding ten years. In 1869 he became a partner of Alexander Moore and the firm practised as Moore & Brown until Brown's death, when the surviving partners amalgamated with Carson & Watson.

Brown was a member of an Institute Committee set up in 1867 to consider the use of the Institute's funds and proposals to form a widows' fund. He later served on the Council from 1876 to 1878.

W. S. BROWN

b. c 1851 G 1877 d. 15-i-1888

W. S. Brown, the Brown of Brown, Fleming & Murray, precursors of Whinney, Murray & Co., did not survive to see his name linked with that of Murray. At the time of his admission he was a clerk with Auld & Guild with whom he had then been for five years. He remained with that firm for a further year or two and then entered into partnership with J. Gibson Fleming, who became a member of the Institute in 1880, their firm being known as Brown & Fleming. Brown died at the early age of 36. In his short career he must have made a sufficient impact to make the continued inclusion of his name in the firm's style desirable.

B. R. BRUCE

b. A 1874 d.

Ben. R. Bruce was admitted as a member of the Society of Accountants in Aberdeen in 1874, having apparently been an apprentice with Robert Fletcher, one of the original members of the Society, from 1861 to 1865. Fletcher moved to London in 1868, and Bruce continued in the employment of James A. Murray, who had been Fletcher's partner. In 1874 Bruce also became a member of the Aberdeen Stock Exchange, and in the local directory for 1874/5 his name appears as carrying on business as an accountant and sharebroker at 37 Market Street and living at 11 Albert Terrace. His name is also included in the lists of members of both the Society of Accountants and the local Stock Exchange. Bruce's name does not appear in any other issue of the directory and it is not known whether he died shortly after having commenced business on his own account. A Mrs David Bruce seems to have lived at 11 Albert Terrace for some years before and after 1874; she presumably was B. R. Bruce's mother.

T. G. BUCHANAN

b. G 1853 d. 31-vii-1871

T. G. Buchanan was an original member of both the Institute of Accountants and Actuaries in Glasgow and, in 1844, of the Glasgow Stock Exchange Association. He had been in business since at least as early as 1841 and was one of those senior accountants to whom the letter suggesting the formation of an association was addressed in 1853.

In 1845 he was a partner of Robert Aitken at 3 Exchange Place, Glasgow and later was a partner in T. G. Buchanan and L. M. Kerr, Accountants and Stockbrokers at 157 Buchanan Street. About this time he lived at 5 West Regent Street, a short walk from his office. Although he took an active part in the formation of the Institute and was a member of the first council, his main interest would seem to have been the Stock Exchange. For the long period of 21 years from the formation of the Stock Exchange Association in 1844 till 1865 he was vice-chairman of that association.

Outwith his business interests, he was a director of the Buchanan Society.

HENRY BUDGE

b. 1835 E 1863 d. 1873

Henry Budge was born at Grantown, a son of Henry Budge who was an excise officer. He became a member of the Edinburgh Society at the age of 28 having trained with James Brown and Kenneth Mackenzie. His membership lasted just ten years, and he was only 38 when he died.

CHARLES CAIRNS

b. G 1854 d. 1883

Charles Cairns was one of that group of early members of the Glasgow Institute who received their early training in Edinburgh but spent the greater part of their business careers in Glasgow.

He moved from Edinburgh to Glasgow in 1846. By then, according to his letter of application for membership, he had had a legal education which would have entitled (his word) him to qualify as a member of the Society of Solicitors in the Supreme Courts and had considerable experience in the management of an extensive business in Edinburgh. Cairns does not in his letter of application say whether this extensive business was a legal or an accountancy business. He was presumably well enough known in Glasgow by the date of his application to rely on his experience in his own business as an accountant and stockbroker as justifying his fitness for membership. He was already a member of the Glasgow Stock Exchange Association, to which he was admitted in 1852, and was one of the signatories to the letter of requisition addressed by a group of junior to a group of senior Glasgow practitioners which led to the formation of the Institute. Although his business apparently prospered—he lived at a good West End residential address in 1855—this was more as the result of his activities as a stockbroker, to which he devoted most of his energies, than as an accountant. In 1865 being in arrears with his Institute subscriptions he ceased to be a member. At that time a number of members in apparently good standing allowed their membership to lapse in this way, rather than by straightforward resignation; most of these were men who devoted their attention to the stockbroking side of their businesses. Cairns continued to be a member of the Stock Exchange Association till his death, when he was probably in his sixties.

HENRY CALLENDER

b. E 1854 d.

Henry Callender, an original member of the Edinburgh Society, was a member till 1873 when he was excluded from membership. Presumably this was for non-payment of membership dues. A surprising number of early members were so excluded—surprising for two reasons: the annual subscriptions were small, and some at least of those whose membership terminated in this way were apparently respectable citizens, who might have been expected to avoid the ignominy of expulsion by resigning. It can only be surmised that for some reason they found that their membership was of less advantage than they had expected and so simply lost interest.

Callender was also an actuary and was for a time manager of the Scottish Life and Mercantile Insurance Co., and also an Edinburgh Director of the Scottish Imperial Insurance Company, whose head office was in Glasgow.

He took an interest in local government and was at one time Edinburgh City Treasurer.

ROBERT F. CAMERON

b. c 1853 E 1876 d. 15-iv-1929

Robert F. Cameron was the first chartered accountant to practise in Inverness. The business which he founded still flourishes there.

Robert Cameron was the eldest son of James Cameron, Balnahyle, Ross-shire.

As a youth he came to Edinburgh as an apprentice to Lindsay Jamieson & Haldane. Two years after his admission he returned to the North and in 1878 he started practice in Inverness where he built up an extensive business over the years. He was auditor of the Highland Railway Company and was also auditor of numerous public bodies. In spite of being so far from Edinburgh he continued to take an interest in the affairs of the Society and was elected as a member of the Council. Unfortunately, the deafness from which he suffered compelled him to resign before completion of the normal term.

Locally, he was a Justice of the Peace and was an elder in Inverness Parish Church. His favourite recreation was shooting.

Cameron lived to celebrate his jubilee as a member of the Society and died well advanced in his seventies.

JAMES R. CARPHIN

b. 22-i-1835 E 1857 d. 6-iv-1897

James Carphin was born on 22nd January, 1835. He was the son of George Carphin, commissary clerk depute. His grandfather had also been a commissary clerk. J. R. Carphin was educated at Edinburgh Academy and at Edinburgh University. He served as an apprentice under a regular indenture to R. E. Scott, his indenture of apprenticeship being one of the first to be registered with the Society. He practised as an accountant in Edinburgh till 1881 when he was appointed chamberlain of the Edinburgh Merchant Company. During his career he was for a time manager of the British Guarantee Association. He was also the founder and manager of the Scottish Fire Insurance Company which later amalgamated with the European Life Assurance and Guarantee Association and eventually became part of the Caledonian Insurance Company.

Carphin was married and had a family of two sons and five daughters. One of the sons, G. H. Carphin was also a chartered accountant; admitted in 1889.

D. S. CARSON

b. 1850 G 1875 d. 2-ii-1917

In his late teens, D. S. Carson went into the office of Kerr, Anderson, Muir & Main. In 1875 he was admitted as a member of the Glasgow Institute and shortly thereafter commenced to practise, being soon joined as a partner by Lawrence Hill Watson. Their firm of Carson and Watson, which was thus established, became by amalgamation in 1890 part of Moores, Carson & Watson, a firm prominent in Glasgow for well over half a century. Following further amalgamations it is now known internationally as Arthur Young, McClelland, Moores & Co.

Like many Glasgow accountants of his time, Carson was also a member of the Glasgow Stock Exchange Asociation, which he joined in 1890.

He was for very many years a director and chairman of Cassell Cyanide Co. Ltd. Another long-standing appointment which he held, but of a charitable nature, was as secretary of the Higginbotham Sick Poor Nursing Association, in which capacity he acted for 24 years.

Carson was for a term a member of the council of the Glasgow Institute. Two sons were also members of the Institute and partners in Moores, Carson & Watson. One of them was the last President of the Glasgow Institute before the amalgamation of the Scottish Societies in 1951.

D. S. Carson lived in Kilmacolm and was an elder in the Church there.

ROBERT CARSWELL

b. 1842 G 1872 d. 1923

Robert Carswell was for a long time a prominent and active member of the Glasgow Institute.

He was born at Duncarnock Farm, Newton Mearns in 1842 and at about the age of 15 he entered the office of Thomson & Jackson. He remained with them for 14 years but in 1871 started to practise on his own account. The following year he was admitted as a member of the Institute and about a year later was joined in partnership by Alexander Murray, who, although an older man than Carswell, had been employed by the latter, and who did not become a member until 1878. It is an indication of the relatively slow increase in the number of Glasgow Chartered Accountants at that time that though the admission dates of the two partners were separated by six years, their admission numbers were only separated by thirty, Carswell being number 105 and Murray number 135.

Carswell served altogether four terms of three years on the Institute's Council and at the age of 70 was elected President, which office he filled from 1912 to 1915.

He was a widely read man and accumulated a good personal library, so that it is not surprising to find that for a long period he was a member of the Institute's library committee. Until 1961 the Glasgow Institute Library included a large and varied collection of non-technical books which was then dispersed for reasons of space-saving and economy as it was not widely used by members.

For over 25 years, Carswell was session-clerk of Newton Mearns United Free Church. For a time he was chairman of the local Conservative Association and was also a member of Eastwood Parish School Board and a Justice of the Peace. He did not, however, take the same prominent part in local government affairs as his partner Murray.

In 1901 the two older partners were joined by John Lauder, admitted as a member in 1900, and latterly by James Carswell, Carswell's son, admitted in 1904, and the firm became known as Carswell, Murray & Lauder.

W. J. CARSWELL

b. G 1857 d. 1885

W. J. Carswell's name appears in the Glasgow Directory for 1855 as a house factor and insurance agent. He had become a member of the Glasgow Stock Exchange Association in 1845 but resigned his membership in the following year. He applied for membership of the Institute of Accountants and Actuaries in Glasgow shortly after its formation and before the granting of the charter. The council decided that his previous occupation was not sufficient to qualify him for membership and he was not admitted to membership until 1857. In his application Carswell had stated that he had been an apprentice and clerk to Richard Hall, writer in Glasgow, who was the law agent of the Clydesdale Bank and that in Hall's office he had been principally engaged on sequestrations and trust estates. After he commenced business on his own account, he must have interested himself mainly in factorage and insurance business. He is recorded as having been Resident Secretary in Scotland of the Provincial Insurance Co., Scottish Secretary of The Imperial Fire Office and Superintendent for Scotland of The Economic Life Assurance Society.

FREDERICK HAYNE CARTER

b. 24-viii-1817 E 1854 d. 3-ii-1886

Frederick H. Carter was the author of the first book on accounting to be written by a chartered accountant. The first edition of his book, *Practical book-keeping adapted to commercial and judicial accounting*, appeared in 1861, seven years after the author had been admitted as a member of the Edinburgh Society. The first edition of the book extended to 155 pages. It went through no less than six editions, the last of which, "revised and corrected" and also much extended by his son, ran to x plus 264 pages and was published in 1890. Unfortunately the Institute Libraries do not possess a copy of the first edition of this first book by a chartered accountant, but its library in Edinburgh has copies of the second, fourth and sixth editions.

Carter was trained by Keith & Horne a

firm which had been in existence since about 1820. He was later employed by William Law before commencing to practise on his own account in 1840. On the formation of the Society of Accountants in Edinburgh, Carter became a member. His first partner was Alexander B. Tawse who became a member of the Society and Carter's partner in 1855, but who died in 1858. Carter then continued to practise on his own until joined in 1869 by his son, F. W. Carter, who had become a member of the Society in 1868. The firm was then known as F. & F. W. Carter, but afterwards became Carter Greig & Co.

Frederick H. Carter was interested in the preservation and improvement of the amenity of his native city and was a member of the council of the Cockburn Association, whose object was, and is, to promote these aims.

Among professional appointments he held was that of auditor of the Scottish Union Insurance Co. He was also a Justice of the Peace.

FREDERICK W. CARTER

b. 25-ix-1846 E 1868 d. 1925

Frederick Carter was the eldest son of F. H. Carter, C.A. He was born in Edinburgh and was educated at Edinburgh Academy and Edinburgh University. He served as an apprentice with J. M. McAndrew, C.A., and the year after his admission to membership became a partner with his father. He had a long and successful professional career during which he gave distinguished service to the Edinburgh Society and to the community at large.

He first served on the Council of the Society from 1886 to 1890, served as an examiner from 1887 to 1893 when, on the institution of the General Examining Board of the Chartered Accountants of Scotland, he was appointed as one of the Edinburgh Society's representatives on the Board and continued to be a member until his death in 1925. He was President of the Society from 1904 till 1907 and on demitting office was again elected to the Council for a three year term. On the death of his successor, J. A. Robertson-Durham, in 1909 he temporarily resumed the presidency.

In the same year in which Carter became a member of the Society of Accountants he joined the militia. He served as an officer for nearly twenty years, retiring in 1887 with the honorary rank of Colonel.

In addition to his firm's audit practice, which was considerable, Carter was a director and chairman of several companies. He was also a Trustee of the Edinburgh Savings Bank. Two details about his audit connections are worthy of note. Between 1867 and 1924 he personally conducted in London 114 half-yearly audits of a well-known company; and in 1923 as a special mark of appreciation of the services of his firm as auditors since the formation of the Company, the Fife Coal Co. Ltd., at their fiftieth annual general meeting, voted them a special honorarium, perhaps not a unique but certainly a rare acknowledgment of an auditor's services.

The jubilee of the granting of a Royal Charter to the Society of Accountants in Edinburgh was celebrated during F. W. Carter's presidency and to mark the occasion he presented to the Society as a jubilee gift a Presidential badge.

After his father's death, F. W. Carter was joined in partnership by J. T. M. Greig and the firm took the name of Carter, Greig & Co., under which the practice continued for many years. It is now incorporated with that of Oswalds.

Carter had a wide rage of hobbies and recreations. He hunted, shot, fished and played golf. He also travelled widely in pursuit of another of his interests, photography; and he made a notable collection of Worcester porcelain.

He married Alexa Marion, only child of William Halliday, Lidderdale of Lochbank, Castle Douglas, and their only child, a daughter, married G. H. L. Foulis, the second son of Sir James Foulis, ninth baronet of Colinton.

THOMAS ROBERTSON CHAPLIN

b. E 1854 d. 1857

Thomas R. Chaplin was one of the original members of the Edinburgh Society. He had apparently been in practice for some years before 1854 as had his partner David Robertson Souter. There was probably some family connection between them as Souter had an uncle called Chaplin whose name also included Robertson. T. R. Chaplin did not long survive the incorporation of the Edinburgh Society.

GEORGE TODD CHIENE

b. 21-viii-1809 E 1855 d. 17-vi-1882

George T. Chiene was a Fifeshire man, the son of Captain John Chiene, R.N. He was educated in Crail and then at Edinburgh High School. After leaving school he trained with Messrs Paul & Mackersy. He was in business from about 1850, apparently having delayed setting up on his own account till a later age than was common among his contemporaries. A son and grandson were both members of the Edinburgh Society. Another son had a distinguished career as a surgeon. Like so many of the early Edinburgh accountants, G. T. Chiene had insurance and investment company connections. He was the auditor of Alliance Heritable Security Co. Ltd., and was manager of the Ancient Insurance Association of Scotland Ltd.

GEORGE T. CHIENE, Jnr.

b. 30-x-1844 E 1869 d. 5-ix-1900

George T. Chiene Jnr. was for a quarter of a century one of Edinburgh's leading accountants. He was the second son of George T. Chiene who was then about thirty-five years old; unlike many of his contemporaries Chiene Snr. does not seem to have embarked on practice on his own account until he was about forty. However that may be, he was obviously in a position to provide his family with a good education, and Chiene Jnr. first attended Edinburgh Academy and then the Universities of both St Andrews and Edinburgh. He was trained as an accountant with Lindsay, Jamieson and Haldane, the nursery of many notable early members of the Edinburgh Society. When he became a member of the Society, although his father was then in practice, he did not join him in business but at first practised on his own. Later he had as a partner for a short time John Brewis. This partnership was dissolved and later still Chiene took as a partner John S. Tait, who became a member of the Society in 1881, and so founded the well-known firm of Chiene & Tait.

Among other professional appointments Chiene was auditor of the National Bank of Scotland and of the Standard Life Assurance Co. He was also manager of the National Guarantee Association, and acted as factor for several estates in Fifeshire, a county with which he had family connections.

As a young man Chiene was a first class cricketer and a good football player. He was captain of the Edinburgh Academical Rugby Club in 1867-8. He was also a good golfer.

He served for two terms on the Council of the Society from 1880 to 1884 and from 1894 to 1898.

He died after a long illness and at a relatively early age at Lundin Links in Fifeshire.

ROBERT CHRISTIE, Jnr.

b. c 1819 E 1854 d. 24-iii-1874

Robert Christie Jnr. was one of the signatories to the petition for the granting of a Royal Charter to the Society of Accountants in Edinburgh. He also took a prominent part in the formation of the Faculty of Actuaries having been one of the Scottish members of the Council of the Institute of Actuaries. His father, an accountant and latterly manager of the Scottish

Equitable Life Assurance Society, was one of a number of accountants with insurance connections who before the granting of the charter were associate members of the Society. The rules adopted under the Charter provided for only one class of member, and about half of those whose main occupation was the management of an insurance company withdrew from membership. Christie Snr. was one of those who withdrew.

Robert Christie Jnr. had an altogether less remarkable career than his father, who among other appointments had acted in the unusual capacity of trustee for the creditors of the City of Edinburgh in 1833, when the city's finances were in disarray. He was for a time assistant secretary of the Edinburgh & Northern Railway Co., one of the many railway companies formed about the middle years of the 19th century. In 1862 after earlier amalgamations the company was absorbed by the North British Railway Company.

Christie Jnr. was later Edinburgh secretary of the Northern Assurance Company.

WIILIAM CHURCH

b. G 1857 d. 1-i-1887

William Church was a son of William Church, described as a manufacturer in Glasgow. He practised as an accountant in Glasgow from 1848. Prior to that he had had ten years' varied experience, in mercantile matters, possibly in partnership with a brother. He was probably in his later thirties and had been married for some years when he applied for membership of the Glasgow Institute. In addition to his accountancy business, or rather, perhaps as part of it, he was the local secretary in Glasgow for the Scottish Provident Institution, an appointment he appears to have held for at least twenty-five years. He was also an agent for the Insurance Company of Scotland.

He took no active part in Institute affairs, but it may give some indication of his personal interests to know that he was the honorary treasurer of the Glasgow Archaeological Society, and also a member of the Committee of Glasgow Art Union.

W. R. M. CHURCH

b. 1854 G 1877 d.

W. R. M. Church was a son of William Church. After spending four years in the office of Moore & Brown, C.A., and a further two years in his father's office, he was admitted as a member of the Institute. In his letter of application he stated "I desire to qualify myself by undergoing the examination to take place next week". Examinations were then still rather informal and there was no formal requirement of service as an apprentice.

Five years after becoming a chartered accountant Church became a member of the Glasgow Stock Exchange Association.

He appears to have been in practice in Glasgow for upwards of 40 years.

In the late 1870's, while he was in his twenties, W. R. M. Church served as a Lieutenant in the 4th Lanark Rifle Volunteers.

T. BENNET CLARK

b. 5-ii-1855 E 1878 d. 16-vi-1926

T. Bennet Clark was born at Alloa, the second son of William Bennet Clark who was Sheriff Substitute of Clackmannanshire from 1852 to 1876. Clark was educated in Alloa and then in Edinburgh at Edinburgh Collegiate School and at the University. He then became an apprentice with R. & E. Scott, who were relatives. During his apprenticeship he won the bursary awarded in connection with the Edinburgh Society's third year examination in 1874. Shortly after his admission, he was assumed as a partner in R. & E. Scott and in 1897 when E. E. Scott died he became the senior partner of the firm which had by then merged with C. & D. Pearson.

Clark served several terms on the Council of the Edinburgh Society. In addition to the professional appointments he was a director of the Scottish Equitable Life Assurance Society and of a number of other companies.

Outside his professional interests, Clark's main avocation was botany. He was for long a member, and for a term president, of the Edinburgh Botanical Society, and at his home at Newmills, Balerno, where he resided from 1895 to 1923 he created a notable garden. His botanical enthusiasm was shared by his only son, who became assistant to the Professor of Botany at Trinity College, Dublin.

Clark was a member of the Royal Company of Archers and had also an interest in a more modern form of ballistics, being an Honorary Vice-President of the Chartered Accountants Rifle Club of Edinburgh.

He took a prominent part in Freemasonry.

Mrs Clark was a daughter of T. C. Hanna, C.A., and a great-granddaughter of the eminent Scottish divine, Dr Thomas Chalmers.

Clark returned to live in Edinburgh in 1923.

WILLIAM HOME COOK

b. 5-x-1851 E 1878 d. 1928

William Home Cook was the son of John Cook, W.S., and a grandson of Walter Cook, W.S. He was at school at Edinburgh Academy and then went on to St Andrews University. At the Academy his classmates included R. L. Stevenson and John Wilson Brodie, who was later his fellow apprentice with Kenneth Mackenzie.

Cook's first professional partnership was with William R. Mylne, practising as Mylne & Cook. They had a large and varied business which included the audits of two of the Scottish banks and of a large insurance company. Cook was the auditor of Edinburgh Royal Infirmary and treasurer of the Sick Children's Hospital. He was also the auditor of the Highland and Agricultural Society.

Apart from the work involved in carrying on his busy practice Cook was also active in Society affairs. He served for four terms on the Society's Council and in 1913 was elected President. He was also an honorary president of the Edinburgh Chartered Accountants' Students Society.

Cook was very much interested in the development of accounting education and took a leading part in helping to raise funds for the establishment of a chair of accountancy in Edinburgh University.

Outwith his professional concerns, Cook was interested in outdoor pursuits and also had cultural interests. He was an original director of the Scottish Zoological Park and worked for the creation of bird sanctuaries. He was also a keen angler and a rifle shot. In 1914 he presented a trophy to the Chartered Accountants Rifle Club of Edinburgh, of which he was then honorary president. He played golf at several of the leading East of Scotland clubs, including North Berwick, Muirfield and Leven.

In addition to his outdoor activities, Cook was a keen musician. He was a member of the Edinburgh Amateur Orchestral Society and in 1898-9 was president of that society. Also interested in art, he formed a large collection of paintings.

Two brothers followed their father in the legal profession in which they both achieved distinction.

DAVID CORMACK

b. E 1854 d. 27-viii-1867

David Cormack was an original member of the Edinburgh Society. He was also a member of the S.S.C. Society. Against his name in Richard Brown's list of deceased Scottish Accountants appears

James Brown, C.A., first President (1853-64) of The Society of Accountants in Edinburgh

Thomas Mansfield, C.A., President (1864-68) of the Edinburgh Society

Charles Murray Barstow, C.A., President (1869-76) of the Edinburgh Society

Charles Pearson, C.A., President (1876-79) of the Edinburgh Society

Alexander Weir Robertson, C.A., Secretary (1853-63) and Treasurer (1863-79) of the Edinburgh Society

James Howden, F.F.A., C.A., Secretary (1863-92) of the Edinburgh Society
(He became President in 1892)

the date 1829. This is taken to mean that he has been traced as in practice at that date. The only other information about him is the date of his death. From these dates it may be deduced that Cormack was in practice for nearly forty years and so would be upwards of sixty years old when he died.

D. N. COTTON

b. 29-viii-1856 E 1878 d. -v-1934

D. N. Cotton, like so many of the early members of the Edinburgh Society was the son of a lawyer. His father was George Cotton, S.S.C. Educated at Edinburgh Academy, the son was apprenticed to F. & F. W. Carter. In the course of his apprenticeship, he shared in the £20 bursary awarded by the Society to the most successful candidate in the third year examination. After admission, Cotton commenced to practise on his own account. In his later years, he was joined in the practice by his son, G. M. Cotton, who became a member of the Society in 1907.

D. N. Cotton was a Liberal in politics and was for some time Secretary of the Liberal Club in Edinburgh. His church affiliation corresponded to his liberal politics for he was a member of the United Presbyterian Church. In fact he acted as auditor for that church and later, following the Union of 1900 with the Free Church of Scotland, of the United Free Church. He was also auditor of the Edinburgh Merchant Company.

His principal outdoor recreation was golf, which he played at Barnton and Musselburgh.

A keen musician, he was a gifted pianist and a student especially of Beethoven. In later life he would recall with interest and pleasure how in earlier days he had heard Anton Rubinstein and Sir Charles Hallé.

JAMES COVENTRY

b. E 1855 d.

James Coventry became a member of the Society of Accountants in Edinburgh in 1855, but resigned his membership in 1860. Beyond these facts nothing is known of him and his name is not included in Richard Brown's list of Scottish Accountants who died before 1905.

DAVID COWAN

b. G 1872 d.

David Cowan was one of the relatively small number of Glasgow accountants who migrated to the capital. When admitted as a member of the Glasgow Institute he had been for nearly six years with Auld & Guild, first as an apprentice and then as a clerk. He became a member of the Glasgow Stock Exchange Association in 1874 but resigned his membership in 1879. Perhaps it was about then that he removed to Edinburgh, where he became a partner in the stock-broking firm of Bell, Begg & Cowan.

Like a number of his young contemporaries, he was involved in the Volunteer movement and held a commission in the 1st Lanarkshire Rifle Volunteers.

In the *Scottish Chartered Accountants Official Directory* for 1899/1900 he is one of four Glasgow members with an Edinburgh address.

He may have retained some accounting connections for from 1878 he was joint auditor with Alexander Moore of the North British Canadian Investment Co. Ltd.

ROBERT C. COWAN

b. 21-iv-1836 E 1864 d. 19-viii-1898

Robert C. Cowan was a West of Scotland youth who trained as an accountant in Edinburgh, became a member of the Edinburgh Society and spent his professional life in Edinburgh. He was born in Ayr. His father, Hugh Cowan, was agent for the Royal Bank of Scotland there. Robert was educated at Ayr Academy and then went on to Glasgow University where he took an M.A. degree. He then moved to Edinburgh where he was for about 15 months in the office of Morton, Whitehead & Greig, W.S., and then an apprentice to Donald Lindsay and G. Auldjo Jamieson of Lindsay, Jamieson & Haldane. The decision that he should go to Edinburgh and to that particular office may have been reached because Lindsay was a director of the Royal Bank of Scotland, and, no doubt, knew and was known by Hugh Cowan, one of the bank's agents.

Cowan was for a time a partner of A. T. Niven, but thereafter practised on his own account until, shortly before his death, he took into partnership J. Tait Watson. Among appointments he held was that of auditor of the Scottish Heritable Security Co. Ltd.

He served on the Council of the Society from 1895 to 1898. Earlier, in 1878, he was, although a Glasgow graduate, a member of the committee of the Association for the Better Endowment of the University of Edinburgh.

WILLIAM COWAN

b. G 1853 d. 5-viii-1881

William Cowan was one of the original members of the Glasgow Institute of whom one would like to know more. He practised accountancy from 1845 and was one of those who joined in the request to senior accountants to take steps to form a society of accountants in Glasgow. At that time he was a partner of John Mackintosh, who did not become a member. In 1868 Cowan ceased to be a member of the Institute because of non-payment of subscriptions. Then in 1874 he became a member of the Glasgow Stock Exchange Association, but his membership lasted only five years.

In the Glasgow directory of 1855 he is noted as secretary to the Glasgow board of the Caledonian Insurance Co., and as living at Oakvale, Hillhead, from which it might be deduced that he occupied a respectable position in the city's business community.

ALEXANDER CRAIG

b. E 1855 d. -ix-1897

Alexander Craig, one of the early members of the Edinburgh Society, trained as an accountant with Mansfield & Spottiswoode, who were in practice for many years before the formation of the Society, of which Mansfield was the second President. Craig practised in Edinburgh.

ROBERT CRAIG

b. G 1857 d. 11-vi-1864

When Robert Craig was admitted as a member of the Glasgow Institute he had from 1854 been a partner in the firm of Thomson, Ritchie & Craig, one of the predecessor firms of Thomson, Jackson, Gourlay & Taylor. Prior to joining Ritchie and Thomson he had been for seven years a clerk with James Gourlay with whom Ritchie had also been employed for most of that time. James Gourlay was not the Gourlay who was later a partner in Thomson, Jackson, Gourlay & Taylor. Craig died at a comparatively early age.

T. A. CRAIG

b. G 1877 d.

T. A. Craig when admitted to membership of the Glasgow Institute had been for twelve years a clerk with J. Wyllie Guild and with his firm of Auld & Guild. He continued in their employment where, in the words of his later application, he "was in principal charge of the accounting department of the firm" for a year or two more, before setting up in practice.

He took a prominent part in Institute affairs and, after serving on the Council, was treasurer of the Institute from 1900 to 1918. He was one of the original representatives of the Glasgow Institute on the General Examining Board, when it was set up in 1893, and also an original member of the Joint Committee of the United Kingdom Chartered Institutes of Accountants which was constituted in 1902.

GEORGE L. CRAIK

b. G 1863 d.

George L. Craik had first served as an apprentice in the legal offices of Moncreiff Paterson Forbes & Barr for three years and then was for four years a clerk with J. W. & D. R. Guild, C.A. He appears to have attached little importance to his membership as already by 1868 he was so far in arrears with his subscription as to have his membership terminated. At that time a period of arrears of four years was allowed before expulsion.

JOHN CROMBIE

b. 1832 A 1867 d. 1898

John Crombie was a member of the Society of Accountants in Aberdeen for 31 years. He became a member on the formation of the Society, his name having appeared in the local directory as an accountant from 1858. He had, however, had a legal rather than an accountancy training in the office of Robert Dyce, an Aberdeen advocate. In the directory for 1851 he described himself as a writer. He was then only nineteen. Having decided that his metier was accountancy rather than law he took an active part in the affairs of the new society. He was a member of the Society's Council on five occasions and was President from 1879 to 1881. He was for a time a magistrate of the city, and was an active Freemason, holding a number of masonic offices.

Among his professional appointments was that of auditor of Aberdeen Music Hall Co. Ltd. and later of Aberdeen Theatre & Opera House Co. Ltd. He was also actuary and secretary of Aberdeen Mutual Assurance and Friendly Society, and manager of Aberdeen Co-operative Property Investment Co.

CHARLES CUNNINGHAM

b. G 1853 d. 30-iv-1861

Charles Cunningham was an original member of both the Glasgow Stock Exchange Association and the Institute of Accountants and Actuaries in Glasgow. He started business in 1843 and must have joined the Stock Exchange almost immediately thereafter. He cannot have been a very young man then, as he was elected to the committee of the Stock Exchange Association in 1844, but nothing is known of his earlier, or indeed of his later, activities.

He was a signatory of the letter which led to the formation of the Glasgow Institute.

Cunningham was a member of the Parochial Board of the city parish of Glasgow.

ALLAN CUTHBERTSON

b. G 1853 d. 19-i-1864

Allan Cuthbertson was a member of the oldest accounting family in Glasgow. His father, William Cuthbertson, has been described as the founder of the accounting profession in the city. Allan was in practice with his brother Donald for many years. The brothers were among those involved in the formation of the Glasgow Institute, were both original members, and Allan was elected to the first Council.

The brothers had their office for many years in Fife Place, West George Street, but whereas Donald in 1855 was living at 188 St Vincent Street, not far from the Institute's present Glasgow premises, Allan by then had moved west to Kew Terrace, at that time close to the western extremity of the city.

The firm, at first known as D. & A. Cuthbertson, eventually took the name D. & A. Cuthbertson, Provan & Strong, though this was not until after the death of the Cuthbertson brothers.

Allan Cuthbertson died about eleven months before his elder brother.

DONALD CUTHBERTSON

b. 1782 G 1853 d. 8-xii-1864

Donald Cuthbertson when he became one of the founder members of the Glasgow Institute had already been in practice for about forty-five years and was one of the oldest of the founders. This may explain why in spite of the eminent position he occupied in the profession in the city he did not at the age of over seventy become a member of the council of the new Institute or occupy any other official position in connection with it.

He was the son of William Cuthbertson, who in the Glasgow directory of 1757 was designated as "merchant" but who has been described as the originator of the accounting profession in the city. Donald was educated at Glasgow High School and at Glasgow University, at both of which establishments he earned distinction as a student.

He then entered his father's office and after some years of training became a partner in 1810.

He is the first chartered accountant known to have had a university degree in law, having graduated LL.B. at Glasgow, though several other early members of the Scottish accountancy societies had legal training. Successive changes in his address throughout his long and successful career indicate the changes in the social and professional conditions which were then in progress. In 1818 his business and residential addresses were the same—128 George Street. In 1845 the office address was somewhat further west at 100 Fife Place, West George Street, where it remained for a considerable number of years. In 1855 his residential address was 188 St Vincent Street, not far from the present Glasgow premises of the Institute, while his younger brother Allan had moved near to the western extremity of the built up area, at Kew Terrace, Great Western Road.

Indicative of another type of professional change is the fact that he was for a time director and also auditor of the Scottish Amicable Life Assurance Society. In 1855 also he was a director of the City of Glasgow Bank but he died many years before the catastrophic failure of that institution. He was also on the Glasgow boards of the North British Insurance Co., and of the Scottish Provincial Assurance Co.

He was the first secretary of the Royal Asylum, Gartnavel, and the firm of D. & A. Cuthbertson, Provan & Strong continued to hold that appointment.

Among his charitable interests Donald Cuthbertson was a director of the City of Glasgow Native Benevolent Association.

He also took some part in the public affairs of the city and was for a time a magistrate. Up to 1832 he was convener of the committee for managing the High School, of which in his youth he had been a pupil.

As a young man, Cuthbertson was active in another form of public service and in 1804 was a lieutenant in the Volunteers.

He died at the age of 82.

JOHN DALGLEISH

b. E 1873 d. 16-iv-1921

John Dalgleish was admitted as a member of the Edinburgh Society in 1873. He later seems to have moved to Glasgow because he was admitted as an honorary member of the Glasgow Institute in 1878. Later still he was in London, his address in the *Chartered Accountants' Official Directory* for 1899-1900 being 8 Frederick's Place, Old Jewry. He subsequently had other London addresses.

THOMAS DALL

b. 10-x-1826 E 1855 d. 20-iii-1880

Thomas Dall was born at North Berwick. He was much employed by Edinburgh Corporation being auditor of the Improvement and Police Departments, and Accountant-Auditor to the Municipal Department. He was also auditor of the Edinburgh County Prison Board.

He had as a partner Hugh Miller, who had been his apprentice.

FRANCIS DICKSON

b. E 1873 d. 12-viii-1900

Francis Dickson was first an apprentice with James Wyllie, who died in 1871. He then transferred his indenture to T. G. Dickson; no family connection is known. After qualifying, Francis Dickson commenced practice on his own account. He continued to follow the profession as a sole practitioner until his death.

JAMES JOBSON DICKSON

b. 24-xi-1811 E 1854 d. 4-xii-1891

James J. Dickson was born in Edinburgh, where his father—Rev. David Dickson, D.D., was minister of St Cuthberts. He was educated at the Edinburgh High School and University. He then trained as an accountant with Paul & Mackersy, a firm which had been in business in Edinburgh in the first half of the century but whose partners were both dead before the formation of the Society. Paul was the son of an earlier minister of St Cuthbert's and Mackersy was also a minister's son. Dickson began to practise in 1835. For a time he was a partner of Archibald Horne, but latterly was on his own. He was at one time auditor of the Caledonian Insurance Company. He also, though with no apparent direct Lanarkshire connection, was auditor of the Edinburgh Upper Ward of Lanarkshire Association.

For upwards of twenty years Dickson was a member of the Royal Company of Archers, and for most of these years he was a prizewinner in archery shoots.

T. G. DICKSON

b. 1819 E 1854 d. 28-vii-1905

Thomas Goldie Dickson was an original member of both the Society of Accountants in Edinburgh and the Faculty of Actuaries. He was the son of Walter Dickson, W.S., of Monybuie in Kirkcudbrightshire. After attending Edinburgh Academy and Edinburgh University, he was for a time in the offices of his father's firm of Dickson & Stewart, W.S. He then became an apprentice with Donald Lindsay, who had been in practice in Edinburgh as an accountant since 1823. His training completed he commenced to practise on his own account, but after some time joined forces with Henry G. Watson, who had been in practice from about 1825 and who was about forty years older than Dickson. Their partnership continued till about 1870 when Watson retired and Dickson continued to carry on the business in partnership with A. B. Armitage.

He was a captain in the Accountants' company of the Edinburgh Rifle Volunteers.

In the meantime in 1862, Dickson had married the Hon. Louisa Charlotte Addington, daughter of the second Viscount Sidmouth, and had established himself as one of Edinburgh's leading accountants. Among other professional activities he was a director of Scottish Drainage and Improvement Company, a company which provided loans for landowners who wished to improve their estates.

He was elected President of the Society in 1889 after having served on the Council. He was also a Trustee of the Society's Annuity and Endowment Fund. In the last year of his presidency (1892) his son Leonard W. Dickson, M.A., was admitted as a member of the Society and afterwards joined his father in the firm of T. G. & L. W. Dickson.

During Dickson's presidency the Society first acquired premises of its own when it purchased the property at 27 Queen Street, Edinburgh.

For many years, Dickson acted for the Earls of Elgin, and in 1893 the then Earl who, like his father, was Viceroy of India, presented him with a silver goblet, as a memento of the long family association. This was inscribed "Presented to Thomas Goldie Dickson, Esq., C.A., by Victor Alexander, Earl of Elgin in memory of thirty years friendship of two Viceroys of India 1893".

In 1903 L. W. Dickson was appointed manager of Standard Life Assurance Co., and the firm was dissolved. T. G. Dickson, who by then was over eighty, retired.

In addition to Thomas at least one other member of the Dickson family lived to a great age. The oldest brother was admitted as a member of the Society of Writers to the Signet in 1843 and survived all his six younger brothers. In 1905 when his youngest brother, Thomas, died he was the "Father" of the W.S. Society.

CHRISTOPHER DOUGLAS

b. 20-x-1827 E 1854 d. 3-ii-1882

Christopher Douglas was born and educated in Kelso. His father was Captain P. H. Douglas, R.N. He trained with Archibald Borthwick and was then in practice in Edinburgh. He was one of the original members of the Society but resigned in 1855 because he had gone to reside "permanently" in London. This "permanent" residence proved of short duration and he was re-admitted to membership in 1860 on payment of arrears of subscription for the intervening years. Douglas is the first person known to have been re-admitted after ceasing to be a member and his application for re-admission caused some concern as the Society's rules made no specific provision for such a case.

ROBERT H. DOUGLAS

b. E 1855 d.

Nothing is known of Robert Douglas save that he became a member of the Edinburgh Society in 1855 and ceased to be a member in 1887.

JOHN EDWARD DOVEY

b. 1849 E 1874 d. 15-ii-1918

J. E. Dovey was a son of the Minister of Charlotte Baptist Chapel, West Rose Street, Edinburgh and for nearly forty years he was treasurer of that Chapel. He was also treasurer of the National Bible Society of Scotland and of Edinburgh Industrial Brigade Home for Working Lads.

For his success in the Society's final examination in 1873 he was awarded the Fellowship, then granted to the most successful candidate.

From 1883 until it was amalgamated with the North British Railway Co., Dovey was secretary of Anstruther & St Andrews Railway Company, one of the numerous local lines which were promoted during the period, when the country's railway system was developing.

He served on the Council of the Society in the closing years of the century and in 1900 presented to the Society's library an early edition of a treatise on Italian book-keeping by Johannes Buingha published in Amsterdam, of which the first edition was published in 1627. At the time no other copy of this edition was known in this country.

Dovey's elder daughter—he had a family of two sons and two daughters—was a missionary in China.

He retired from business in 1916, two years before his death.

ALEXANDER DOWNIE

b. 1841 E 1865 d.

Alexander Downie is one of a number of early members of whom little is known.

he was the son of Alexander Downie, Official Searcher of Records, and was educated at Edinburgh Academy. He became a clerk in H.M. Register House and published a book on book-keeping. His name appears in the *C.A. Official Directory* for 1899-1900 but no address is shown. His name was removed from the roll of members in 1905.

DAVID DREGHORN

b. G 1853 d. 21-xi-1875

David Dreghorn was one of those Glasgow accountants in practice before 1841, who were approached by their younger colleagues to take steps for the formation of a society of accountants in the city. He took an active interest in the formation of the Institute, was a subscriber to the original rules and was elected a member of the first council of the Institute. Yet in spite of this initial interest and of the prominent position he held in the city, he ceased to be a member of the Institute in 1868 because he had allowed his subscription to fall into arrears. About the time the Institute was formed he lived in Govan, then outwith the Glasgow boundary and not yet the industrial area which it subsequently became, but he was a magistrate of the city. He was also for a time collector of rates for Govan parish. Among other public appointments which Dreghorn held was that of a Commissioner for Property and Income Tax and he was a member of the Board of Commissioners of Prisons for the county of Lanark. In the early days of the Volunteer movement he was a captain in the corps and later was honorary colonel of the 3rd Lanarkshire Rifle Volunteers.

Among charitable interests he was deputy chairman of the Glasgow Society for the Prevention of Cruelty to Animals, while his business interests included membership of the Glasgow Board of the Lancashire Insurance Company.

WILLIAM DREW

b. G 1862 d.

William Drew started his business career in the service of the Union Bank of Scotland where from 1843 to 1859 he was employed in the Accountant's department. During 1859 and 1860 he was in partnership with Alexander Ritchie, C.A., who died at the end of the latter year. On joining Ritchie, Drew became a member of the Glasgow Stock Exchange. When Ritchie died he carried on for a time on his own but later was a partner of T. B. Robertson in the firm of Robertson & Drew, who in 1866 had offices at 168 St Vincent Street. Robertson was not a member of the Institute.

In 1867, Drew was a member of a committee set up to consider the position of the Institute's funds and made a proposal for the setting up of a widows' fund. This proposal was never implemented though both the Edinburgh and Aberdeen Societies had such funds.

JAMES DRUMMOND

b. E 1872 d. 13-i-1920

James Drummond was employed by John M. Jumner, S.S.C., for two years before entering the office of James H. Balgarnie to whom after a further two years he became an apprentice. Although his apprenticeship expired in 1864 he did not become a member till several years later. Little is known of James Drummond's antecedents or professional activities. He was for a time treasurer of the Edinburgh Perthshire Association, so that it may be surmised that he had connections with that county. He moved to England before the end of the century and in 1900 his name appears in the official *Scottish Chartered Accountants Directory* under "London" but with no specific address. Some years later (1908/9) his address is given as being in Maidenhead, Berkshire. His name disappears from the directory in 1920.

T. B. DRYSDALE

b. E 1872 d. 16-xii-1914

T. B. Drysdale was the son of William Drysdale, Depute Clerk of Session. He spent a year in the office of Alexander Weir Robertson and then became an apprentice with Adam Gillies Smith. Although he trained and qualified as a chartered accountant in what had already become established as the normal manner, he never practised professionally. He lived successively at Cleish, Kinross-shire, at Dunfermline and at Colinton.

W. T. DUNCAN

b. G 1872 d. 12-iv-1885

W. T. Duncan spent some eight years in the employment of James Wyllie Guild and his various firms. For two of these years he was in charge of the accounting department of Auld & Guild. It may be presumed that "accounting department" was used in Duncan's letter of application for membership to distinguish it from the stockbroking side of the firm, which at that time was important, and not from the bankruptcy activities which also formed a large part of Wyllie Guild's business then. At any rate in 1870 Duncan was the author of a prize winning essay on bankruptcy law, the manuscript of which was retained in the Institute's library for many years.

Duncan became a partner of Maclean Brodie in the firm of Brodie & Duncan, but later joined Robert McCowan in partnership as McCowan & Duncan. McCowan died in 1880 and Duncan, after assuming as a partner R. D. Findlay, the firm's stockbroking clerk, did not long survive him, although he was still a young man.

From 1883 to 1885 he served on the Council of the Institute. His death took place at Troon where his father lived.

GEORGE DUNDAS

b. E 1854 d. -x-1870

Dundas served as an apprentice with Keith & Horne and became an original member of the Society so that he must have been practising in Edinburgh in the mid-fifties. He subsequently emigrated to New Zealand, one of the first of a band of migrant Scottish Chartered Accountants.

ALEXANDER DUNLOP, Jnr.

b. 18-xii-1835 E 1860 d. 24-i-1888

Alexander Dunlop's father was Alexander Dunlop of Clober. He was educated at Edinburgh Academy and in 1878 was a member of the committee of Edinburgh Academical Club. Dunlop was an apprentice with Archibald Borthwick and Samuel Raleigh. He became Assistant Accountant in Bankruptcy. He was the eldest of a large family of sons, most of whom pursued careers in the professions or in commerce outwith Scotland.

THOMAS DYMOCK

b. E 1876 d. 22-viii-1923

Thomas Dymock trained with Howden & Molleson and in 1873 took first place in the Society's intermediate examination and was awarded a bursary. He was one of the relatively few early members who never practised. For fully forty years until he retired in 1918 or 1919 he was the secretary of the Scottish American Mortgage Co. Ltd.

He was deeply interested in religious and philanthropic work in Edinburgh, especially in Edinburgh Sabbath Free Breakfast Mission in which he was associated with James McKerrell Brown, C.A., who contributed a memorial notice to *The Accountant's Magazine*.

ROBERT EASTON

b. G 1867 d. 10-vi-1884

Robert Easton dabbled in several professions. He first served for three years as a writer's apprentice. He then spent four years as a clerk in the Kilmarnock Branch of the Union Bank of Scotland before entering the employment of White & Gairdner where he was for nine years prior to his admission to membership of the Institute. Five years after his admission as a chartered accountant he became a member of the Glasgow Stock Exchange. He was taken into partnership by Peter White but latterly carried on business as Robert Easton & Co.

JAMES ELLIS

b. E 1873 d. 28-ix-1878

James Ellis was an apprentice of Howden & Molleson, who shortly after becoming a member of the Society removed to Dublin. He practised as an accountant there, his address being given in the Dublin directory from 1876 to 1878 as 19 St Andrew's Street—was this a sentimental link with the country of his origins or just mere chance? It is to be presumed that he was still a young man when he died.

GEORGE AULDJO ESSON

b. 13-viii-1813 E 1854 d. 13-iii-1888

George A. Esson came from the North and received his early training in Aberdeen before coming to Edinburgh in 1837, where he was employed by Donald Lindsay. In 1838 he became Lindsay's partner. The firm of Lindsay & Esson was a predecessor of Lindsay, Jamieson & Haldane and it is interesting to note that the most notable partner of that firm George Auldjo Jamieson, who was also an Aberdeen man, received his later training with Lindsay & Esson and shared with the latter the Christian names George Auldjo.

In 1856 Esson, who with his partners had become an original member of the Society, was appointed Accountant in Bankruptcy. He still held that appointment in 1878 when having reached the age of sixty-five he may have retired.

HENRY A. FINLAY

b. E 1863 d. 1872

Henry Finlay was a son of G. L. Finlay, W.S. He was an apprentice to F. W. Carter and shortly after his admission to the Society he resigned his membership, but later in the same year (1865) he was readmitted. Whether his resignation was connected with his contemplated departure for India is not known, but he proceeded there. After a short time he returned to Edinburgh before taking up an appointment with the Agra Bank in London. This he held only for a year or two before his death.

ALEXANDER FLEMING

b. c 1850 G 1878 d. 21-iv-1903

Fleming was for thirteen years a clerk with Black & Robson, C.A. After his admission to the Institute he became a partner with Adam E. Black and they carried on business as Fleming & Black. On Black's death, William Boyd became a partner with Fleming but the firm name remained unchanged, as it did till comparatively recently.

Fleming had a long and active connection with Wellington U.P. Church where Dr Robson, a brother of George Robson of Black & Robson, C.A., and Adam Black's father, Rev. Dr Black were successive ministers.

JOHN FLEMING

b. G 1853 d. 1866

John Fleming was in business as an accountant from 1844 and was one of those who joined in the approach to senior members of the profession to suggest the formation of a professional institute. He became one of the original members of the Institute, his number on the member's roll being 21. He was elected as a member of the first council of the Institute and was also appointed a member of the committee set up in December, 1853 to consider possible amendment of the bankruptcy laws. He was a bailie of the city.

Among his professional appointments he was joint auditor of the Scottish Savings, Investment and Building Society.

In 1862 his house in Sandyford Place was the scene of a notorious murder. A servant girl was killed in the house while the family were on holiday and a former servant of the family Jessie McLachlan was accused of the murder. Her trial created a great sensation at the time.

ROBERT FLETCHER

b. c 1818 A 1867 d. 12-vi-1883

Robert Fletcher was born in Edinburgh and was educated there. The earliest part of his business life was spent as a clerk in the office of the Provincial Insurance Company in Aberdeen. Then, about 1848, he appears to have become a sharebroker, being so described in the *Aberdeen Directory* for that year. By 1852 he had changed his description to accountant and in 1867, when he was a partner of James A. Murray, he became one of the original members of the Aberdeen Society. Murray was another of the twelve original members.

Shortly after the formation of the Society Fletcher moved to London, to assist in the reorganisation of the London, Chatham & Dover Railway. He established in London the firm of Robert Fletcher & Co. in which he had as a partner Roderick Mackay.

Fletcher continued his connection with the Aberdeen Society and was President from 1875 to 1877. In 1877 he admitted to his partnership in London W. B. Peat who had been a clerk with the firm from 1870. The following year Fletcher retired from the firm and Mackay became senior partner. On the formation of The Institute of Chartered Accountants in England and Wales in 1880 Mackay became a member of its first council. On his death in 1891 the firm was taken over by Peat and its name changed to W. B. Peat & Co. later to become part of Peat, Marwick, Mitchell & Co. thus renewing the earlier Scottish connection.

ROBERT FORMAN

b. 3-ii-1839 E 1862 d. 25-ii-1899

Robert Forman's father was a lawyer—J. N. Forman, W.S. He was educated at Edinburgh Academy and then served as an apprentice with William Moncreiff and John M. Baillie. After his admission to membership of the Society he became a partner of Andrew Paterson, who was eighteen years his senior. Paterson retired from the partnership and from business in 1890, but lived to survive his junior partner by exactly a year.

HENRY FORRESTER

b. G 1873 d.

A son of Robert Forrester, C.A., one of the early members of the Glasgow Institute, Henry Forrester began his training in his father's office. He later served, following his father's death but before his own admission to membership, with McClelland, Son & Co., and with McClelland, MacKinnon & Blyth. He later spent about seven years in association with his brother J. M. Forrester, who was an accountant and stockbroker, as their father had been. Henry Forrester also became a member of the Glasgow Stock Exchange Association in the same year in which he was admitted as a member of the Institute. He resigned from the Stock Exchange in 1879 but was re-admitted to membership in 1889.

ROBERT FORRESTER

b. G 1854 d. 16-xii-1866

After being for upwards of thirty years engaged in mercantile matters as a partner successively in the firms of Forrester, Ferguson & Wilson; Forrester, Ferguson & Co. and Robert Forrester & Co., Robert Forrester began business as an accountant and stockbroker about 1850. In 1853 he became a member of the Glasgow Stock Exchange Association and the following year was admitted as a member of the newly formed but not yet chartered Institute of Accountants and Actuaries in Glasgow. He resigned his membership of the Stock Exchange in 1863.

One son, Henry Forrester, was a chartered accountant and another, J. M. Forrester, was an accountant and stockbroker. The brothers were for some years in partnership.

Robert Forrester was for a time a member of the parochial board for Glasgow city parish.

JOHN C. FOULDS

b. G 1853 d. 15-i-1906

John C. Foulds was in business as an accountant and stockbroker from about 1840 or 1841 and was one of the senior practitioners who were invited to consider the desirability of promoting a society of accountants in the city. He became an original member of the Institute on its formation and was one of the signatories of the first rules. He was also, in 1844, an original member of the Glasgow Stock Exchange Association and in that year served on the Council of the Association. In 1857-1858 he also was a member of the Institute's council.

In 1855 he lived in Abbotsford Place, then a fashionable residential quarter, and carried on business at 22 Renfield Street as an accountant, stockbroker, factor and agent for insurance companies.

In 1873 he ceased to be a member of the Stock Exchange. This may have been connected with the fact that he lived latterly in the West Indies, where his wife had property.

JOHN CHARLES FRASER

b. E 1854 d. -ix-1864

Fraser, who was an original member of the Edinburgh Society, was an assistant to the Accountant of Court.

CHARLES GAIRDNER

b. G 1853 d. 18-ii-1899

Charles Gairdner began his career as an apprentice with James McClelland with whom he served for four years. He then spent two years as a clerk with Peter White and in 1845 became his partner. In the same year he became a member of the Glasgow Stock Exchange Association which had been founded in the previous year and of which his partner was one of the original members. In 1853, Gairdner was one of the younger accountants who petitioned their seniors to take steps for the formation of a professional association, while his partner was one of the deputation who attended the first meeting at which the matter was discussed.

In 1857 his position in the profession was so far established that he was appointed one of the liquidators of the Western Bank. Five years later he became manager of the Union Bank of Scotland. At that time he ceased to be a member of the Stock Exchange and in 1868, having apparently decided that continued membership of the Institute was unnecessary, his membership was terminated because of non-payment of subscriptions. This caused no breach with his fellow members for in 1877 he was invited to contribute to a series of lectures organised by the Institute. He also contributed papers to the Royal Philosophical Society of Glasgow.

Gairdner was a director of the Glasgow Chamber of Commerce and also of the Merchants House.

He was a yachtsman and a member of the Royal Northern Yacht Club.

THOMAS W. GALLOWAY

b. E 1873 d. c 1931

Not much is known of T. W. Galloway's career save that he spent many years in London, and survived to celebrate fully fifty years as a member.

JAMES GALT

b. G 1864 d. 23-xi-1889

Not until he had had nearly a quarter of a century's experience as an accountant did James Galt become a member of the Glasgow Institute. He spent about fourteen years as a clerk in an accountant's office and must have entered an accounting partnership at about the time the Institute was founded for at the time of his admission, he had been in practice as a partner of a member of the Institute for about ten years.

He was a partner of John C. Reid in the firm of Reid & Galt, who among other professional concerns acted as managers of Glasgow Heritable Securities Co. Ltd.

WILLIAM GARDNER

b. E 1867 d. c 1882

William Gardner was the son of John Gardner, S.S.C., and was apprenticed to Thomas Martin, C.A., one of the original members of the Edinburgh Society, having previously spent eighteen months in his father's office. Ten years after he became a member he went to India but did not long survive.

ARCHIBALD GIBSON

b. 1793 E 1854 d. 1869

Archibald Gibson was a son of an Edinburgh lawyer, also Archibald Gibson, a W.S. He practised in Edinburgh for many years first as a partner of W. S. Moncreiff, who was in business from 1800 till he died in 1864 and then with Moncreiff's son, J. S. Moncreiff. Gibson, like the younger Moncreiff, was an original member of the Society.

T. P. GILLESPIE

b. 22-ix-1855 E 1878 d. 1931

T. P. Gillespie was a son of Alexander Gillespie of Biggar Park, Lanarkshire. He was educated at Edinburgh Academy and was an apprentice with Dr J. Turnbull Smith, LL.D., C.A. He does not seem ever to have practised, but was manager of a paper mill at Longcroft, Linlithgow, having married a daughter of Thomas Chalmers of Longcroft. They had a family of two sons and two daughters, but both sons were killed in the 1914-1918 war. Gillespie latterly lived in England.

NINIAN GLEN

b. 1857 G 1877 d. 29-viii-1912

Ninian Glen was born at Morebattle, Roxburghshire, where his father was a minister. He was educated in Glasgow at the Collegiate School, then at the High School and finally at the University. He graduated as M.A., and B.Sc. at the age of 18, by which time also he had begun his accountancy training. This he obtained in the offices of McFarlane, Hutton & Co. Immediately after his admission to membership of the Institute he entered into partnership with P. H. Aikman, practising as Aikman & Glen. Over the years, Glen built up a high reputation in the city and he was regarded as one of Glasgow's ablest accountants.

In addition to serving for a term on the Institute Council Glen took an interest in the educational work of the Institute. He was a member of the General Examining Board from its formation in 1893 until his death. In 1892 he published a Manual of Actuarial Science which remained in use as the recognised text book on the subject for chartered accountant students for over thirty years. This book was based on a series of lectures which he had given under Institute auspices. He also took an interest in education generally, and when living in Bearsden, was a member of the New Kilpatrick Parish School Board.

A son of the manse, he was for some time the Honorary Treasurer of the Society of Sons of the Clergy.

W. H. GLYNN

b. E 1871 d.

Apart from the date of his admission as a member of the Edinburgh Society, following service as an apprentice with John M. Baillie, and the fact that he later went to London, nothing is known of W. H. Glynn. Indeed even the official chartered accountants directory, while it lists his name in the geographical section under London, gives no specific address for him. His membership ceased on 1st February 1905 but it is not clear whether that was the date of his death.

RICHARD GORDON

b. E 1854 d. -v-1865

Richard Gordon, one of the original members of the Edinburgh Society, was in business as an accountant in Edinburgh from about 1830. He was present at the meeting at which it was resolved to proceed with the formation of the Society.

JAMES GOURLAY

b. 1804 G 1853 d. 17-v-1872

James Gourlay was the son of Robert Gourlay, an ironmonger in St Andrews, where James was born. Robert Gourlay was convener of the seven trades of St Andrews. He died in 1811. His widow brought her family to Glasgow in 1819 just after James had left school.

The youth was first apprenticed to Kerr & Adam, described as smallwares manufacturers. On completing his apprenticeship he joined his elder brother who was in business in Paisley as a wholesaler in the firm of R. & J. Gourlay. James Gourlay's part in the business was mainly as a commercial traveller and he covered nearly the whole of Scotland by horse or gig. He was also for a time one of only two travellers who regularly went from Glasgow to Ireland. As a result of his experiences he founded in 1838 the Commercial Travellers Society of Scotland and became its first treasurer, an appointment which he retained until his death.

In 1841 he retired from the business and set up as an accountant in Glasgow. From the experience he had gained he was able to value and dispose of bankrupt stocks to advantage and he built up a good connection with the best Glasgow, London and Manchester wholesalers.

Gourlay took an active interest in civic affairs. He became a member of the Glasgow City Parochial Board in 1848 and of the Town Council in 1849. While a member of the Parochial Board he secured a reform in the system of assessment. He remained a member of the Board until 1855. He was appointed a magistrate of the city about a year after joining the council and he later played a very active part in promoting the Loch Katrine Water Supply Scheme.

While a magistrate he was for two years convener of the board of management for Glasgow High School. He was also a member of the board of commissioners of prisons for Lanark county, a director of Glasgow Royal Infirmary, chairman of the directors of the Glasgow Athenaeum and a vice-president of the Glasgow Fine Art Association.

In 1855 he became agent at the Lauriston branch of the Bank of Scotland, and seems to have resigned his membership of the Institute at about the same time. A son later became manager of the Bank of Scotland in Glasgow.

JOHN GOURLAY

b. c 1836/37 G 1870 d. 12-v-1897

John Gourlay was the son of another John Gourlay, a gunsmith. He did not serve a regular apprenticeship and indeed does not seem to have had any formal accountancy training. At some time in his twenties, he set up in the profession on his own account and in his letter of application for admission as a member of the Institute stated that he had "been engaged in the profession on his own account for six or seven years with experience of working of Bankrupt and Trust Estates".

Later Gourlay became a partner in Thomson, Jackson, Gourlay & Taylor, the firm adopting that style when in 1877 he joined the partnership.

From 1878 to 1880 Gourlay served on the council of the Institute, and in 1888 he published a pamphlet "A talk about Accountants' work". He was well known as an advocate of temperance reform, was an elder of the United Presbyterian Church and was secretary of the Glasgow Institution for Diseases of Women and Children.

In the last years of his life, Gourlay's health was poor and early in 1897 he went to the West Indies in the hope that the change of climate would effect an improvement. This did not materialise and after a short stay he returned and died soon after. He was survived by five sons, one of whom was a chartered accountant, and one daughter.

JOHN GRAHAM

b. 1828 G 1853 d. 14-xi-1904

Graham's father, Patrick Graham, was a grain merchant in Glasgow. John was educated at Glasgow High School and in his early twenties joined his uncle, a Mr Lang, as a partner in the firm of Lang & Graham, accountants and property insurance agents. Lang did not become a member of the Institute, but Graham was one of the first members who was not directly involved in the discussions which led to its formation.

He built up a successful business in which his brother and later two of his sons became partners. He acted as auditor of the Caledonian Railway Company and the county of Renfrew and was the Secretary of the New Club from its formation in the 1890s. The firm which he founded was the predecessor of Grahams, Rintoul, Hay Bell & Co., now Grahams, Rintoul & Co.

Graham took a prominent part in the affairs of the Institute. He served various terms on the council and was President in 1881-1884. He was also the first President of the Insurance and Actuarial Society of Glasgow.

Outwith the profession he was active in church affairs and in freemasonry. He was also active in the affairs of the Graham Charitable Society. He was a member of the Park Parish Church, Glasgow, but latterly spent much time at his residence, Broadstone, Stranraer, was an elder in Stranraer Parish Church and as such was for many years a well-known member of the Church of Scotland General Assembly. In freemasonry he was Provincial Grand Master of Lanarkshire for a long period until the year of his death, though his health for some two years prior to that had been indifferent.

Because of his Stranraer connection, he was a Justice of the Peace for the county of Wigton.

WILLIAM GRAHAM

b. G 1869 d. 23-xi-1908

William Graham was a younger son of Patrick Graham, grain merchant in Glasgow and a brother of John Graham, one of the Institute's early Presidents. He originally studied for the ministry, but abandoned his intention because of a throat infection. From 1863 to 1867 he assisted his brother as a clerk and then became his partner.

About 1884 he "inherited a competency" from an uncle and retired from J. & W. Graham, making over his interest to his nephews, Patrick and Charles, John's sons. He then purchased a property, North Erines, Kintyre and moved there presumably intending to lead a country life and follow pastoral pursuits of a different kind from those which had first attracted him. After a time, however, he found life in Kintyre too quiet, sold off his property and returned to Glasgow in 1899. From then until his death, he devoted his whole time to public and charitable work, mainly in connection with education.

From 1899 he was a member of Glasgow School Board and became convener of its Finance Committee and later of its Property Committee. He was also a member of the governing bodies of a number of educational institutions or trusts including the Logan & Johnston School of Domestic Economy (now the College of Domestic Science), the Glasgow Athenaeum and the Marshall and Buchanan Trusts and was treasurer of the Graham Charitable Society. Other charities on the Boards of which he served included the Glasgow Eye Infirmary, Home for Infirm Children and the Larbert Institution.

Like his brother, William Graham was an elder of the Church of Scotland, serving as such in Sandyford Parish Church.

He was never married, but lived with and was survived by a sister.

JAMES GRAHAME

b. c 1832 G 1866 d. 25-i-1917

James Grahame was the son of T. Grahame, W.S., joint keeper of the Register of Sasines etc. for Renfrew, Glasgow and Paisley. His first school was Dumfries Academy, but he afterwards attended Glasgow High School and Glasgow University. Before taking up accountancy he was for four years in the Inspectors' Office of the National Bank of Scotland in Edinburgh. He then joined his brother A. H. Grahame and after some years became his partner and at about the same time became a member of the Glasgow Stock Exchange Association. Not for a further seven years did he seek membership of the Glasgow Institute.

Soon after he became a member of the Institute he was appointed a member of the committee set up in 1867 to consider the Institute's funds and proposals for setting up a widows' fund. In 1873 he was elected to the Institute council.

Thomas Hill, a cousin of Grahame, was the chairman of the Caledonian Railway Company, and through this connection James was for a time very much involved in railway matters. Together the cousins were responsible for a scheme for consolidating the numerous preference stocks of the Caledonian Railway Company.

Grahame also took an active interest in politics. He was the founder of the Renfrewshire Liberal Association in 1873 and of the West of Scotland Liberal Association three years later, while the year following he was asked to help in forming the East and North of Scotland Liberal Association. Following changes in party alignments arising from the Irish Question, the West of Scotland Liberal Unionist Association was formed in 1886 and Grahame was appointed the first honorary secretary. Also arising from his political activities, he was appointed by the Earl of Lytton, who in 1887 was elected Lord Rector of Glasgow University, to be his assessor on the University Court and acted in this capacity throughout Lord Lytton's three year term of office. Probably of more direct educational importance was the assistance he gave in the formation of the Glasgow Association for the Higher Education of Women.

Grahame had also an interest in a number of charitable organisations and in this field as in politics and education he was something of an innovator being one of the founders of the Scottish Society for the Prevention of Cruelty to Children. He was a director of the Glasgow Royal Asylum for the Blind and President of the Perthshire Charitable Society.

For a long period he was a member of the Royal Company of Archers, and he was a recipient of the Diamond Jubilee Medal.

Many years before his death, Grahame retired from business and went to live in Fort Augustus.

THOMAS GRANT

b. E 1854 d. 1855

Thomas Grant, who was the son of Rev. Dr Grant of St Andrews, was the manager of Edinburgh Savings Bank. He died about a year after the formation of the Edinburgh Society of which he was one of the original members.

JOHN GRAY

b. A 1878 d. 1890

John Gray trained in the office of James A. Murray, one of the founder members of the Aberdeen Society, with whom he was employed for ten years. He was afterwards Murray's partner, but the latter died in the year following Gray's admission to membership of the society. Gray later practised in partnership with James Strachan as stockbrokers and accountants. Both were members of the Aberdeen Stock Exchange, but Strachan was not a chartered accountant.

JOHN K. GREIG

b. A 1876 d. 5-i-1902

John Knox Greig was the first youth to have a formal indenture of apprenticeship registered with the Aberdeen Society and one of the first two members to be admitted to the Society after examination. His father, William Greig, was a builder in Aberdeen, but had died before John began his apprenticeship with Marquis & Lunan. After qualifying Greig was for a time a partner of James Meston, but latterly he carried on practice on his own.

ARCHIBALD GRIERSON

b. G 1879 d. 19-iii-1905

Most of Archibald Grierson's business career was spent in the transport business. He was first accountant and cashier to the Greenock Railway Co. That company was dissolved and he then spent seventeen years as principal clerk in the registrar's department of the Caledonian Railway Co. At the time of his admission to membership of the Institute, he was in the office of Auld & Guild, C.A. He later returned to transport and went to London as secretary to the London Road Car Co. Ltd., where he seems to have spent the rest of his active business life.

D. RAMSAY GUILD

b. G 1855 d. 9-iii-1874

David Ramsay Guild was a younger brother of the distinguished Glasgow accountant James Wyllie Guild, but had by no means such a noteworthy career. Their father was a solicitor (S.S.C.). The sons both attended Edinburgh High School and University and then entered legal offices. D. R. Guild spent four years with Joseph Grant, W.S., before coming to Glasgow to join his brother. He was for a time in partnership with his brother and during this time he was, from 1860 to 1865, a member of the Glasgow Stock Exchange Association.

It is not clear when the association with his brother ceased, but it may have been when the latter was joined in partnership in 1866 by William Auld. In 1868, D. R. Guild ceased to be a member of the Institute.

JAMES WYLLIE GUILD

b. 1826 G 1853 d. 5-i-1894

James Wyllie Guild, who played a prominent role in the formation of the Glasgow Institute and was for many years one of the city's leading accountants, was, like a number of others who were prominent in the early days of the Institute, in fact an Edinburgh man. He was born in Arbroath, the son of a solicitor (S.S.C.) and educated and professionally trained in Edinburgh. After attending Edinburgh High School and University, he became an apprentice with Ivory & Mackenzie, accountants in that city, and then was for about three years in the office of a Writer to the Signet.

In 1848 Guild came to Glasgow and set up in business as an accountant there. His first partner was a Mr Knox, of whom nothing more has been learned. Thereafter he had a number of different partners and the practice was conducted under a variety of names. After a partnership of some years with his brother, D. R. Guild, he was joined in 1866 by William Auld, whose partner, Andrew McEwan, had recently died. McEwan & Auld had been predominantly a stockbroking rather than an accounting firm and stockbroking for a time formed a significant part of the activities of the new firm of Auld & Guild. Guild had been a member of the Glasgow Stock Exchange Association from 1860. The partnership with Auld was dissolved after about eleven years and Guild was joined by John Fisher and by A. A. Guild (a son), the firm taking the name of J. Wyllie Guild & Fisher.

Wyllie Guild built up a very extensive business covering all sides of the profession as it was then carried on. On the insolvency side he acted as liquidator of the Aberdeen Bank, and of the Edinburgh & Glasgow Bank, was one of the liquidators of the Western Bank and was Trustee on the estates of three of the directors of the City of Glasgow Bank following its failure in 1878. He was also concerned in numerous other insolvencies.

He was associated with the formation of various companies, including the Broxburn Oil Co., one of the early Scottish shale oil companies, and was auditor of that company, of the North British Railway Co., the Glenboig Fireclay Co., and other important industrial concerns.

He had a long professional connection with Glasgow Corporation which began when he was employed in relation to the acquisition of land for the formation of the West End Park; and had a high reputation as an expert witness on accountancy matters.

His association with company promotions was not uniformly happy. In 1873 he acted in connection with the introduction to the Glasgow Stock Exchange of the shares of a number of chemical companies, and questions were raised which gave rise to investigations by both the council of the Institute and the committee of the Stock Exchange. While the result was that Guild was cleared of any suggestion of improper conduct, the committees felt that not all of his actions could be approved, and in consequence he felt it incumbent on him to resign the presidency of the Institute, to which he had just been elected. His reputation, however, suffered no lasting damage and in 1878 he was again elected to the presidency.

Guild's services to the Institute were many and covered a long period beginning with his appointment in December, 1853 to the committee on bankruptcy law, the first committee set up by the new Institute. He was secretary from 1867-1873, president 1878-1881 and treasurer 1881 till his death in 1894. He also took a major part in the promoting of the formation of the Institute library and donated many books to it, though a library committee was not constituted until after his death.

He was president also of the Insurance and Actuarial Society of Glasgow for two years.

In his younger days, Wyllie Guild held a commission in the 1st Lanark Volunteers, but latterly books were perhaps his greatest interest outside his work. He built up an extensive library, which was dispersed some time before his death. When his library was sold the Institute purchased a number of books from it. Guild wrote on professional and other subjects and published a number of books and articles. These included an autobiographical fragment *My Web of Life* published in 1876 and he edited a collection of letters from Jane, Duchess of Gordon to Francis Farquharson, who was the third generation of his family to be involved as accountants with matters affecting Highland estates.

When the Social Science Association and the British Association met in Glasgow, Wyllie Guild was officially concerned in the arrangements for their meetings. For some years also, he was a member of the committee of management of the Art Union of Glasgow and of the council of the Glasgow Archaeological Society.

F. D. V. HAGART

b. 25-ii-1852 E 1878 d. 3-x-1897

F. Hagart was the son of J. V. Hagart, S.S.C. He was an apprentice with Thomas Scott, C.A., and Thomas Scott Jnr., C.A. He died at an early age.

JAMES HALDANE

b. 1831 E 1856 d. 30-x-1907

James Haldane was a son of James A. Haldane, a member of the ancient family of Haldanes of Gleneagles. After attending Edinburgh High School and University, he trained as an accountant with R. E. Scott. After becoming a member of the Edinburgh Society he spent two years in the office of his brother, who was a Writer to the Signet, to gain legal experience, and in 1858 became a partner with Lindsay and Jamieson, Haldane being then added to the firm name. A memoir of Donald Lindsay the founder of the firm (written by Haldane) was published in Volume 1 of *The Accountant's Magazine*.

In his early years with the firm he was especially concerned with the audit department and among audits for which he was then or later responsible were those of the Union Bank of Scotland, the Town and County Bank, the Scottish Widows Fund, the North British and Mercantile Insurance Co., and the Cardiff Railway Co.

Later professional appointments included a number of directorships, among these being membership of the boards of the Royal Bank of Scotland, the New Zealand and Australian Land Co., and the Arniston Coal Co.

As might be expected with a member of such a prominent family, Haldane had many notable family connections, professional and others. His father and an uncle, Robert Haldane, were pioneers of evangelical religion in Scotland in the early nineteenth century, though later Haldanes had different religious views. His mother was a cousin of Sir Walter Scott, and the Earl of Camperdown, who owned Gleneagles, was a second cousin. Two of his brothers were in the legal profession and a third in the medical. Of his sons, two followed the law, while the middle brother was a chartered accountant and, like his father, became President of the Edinburgh Society.

Haldane is said to have liked, when reporting profesionally on any matter, to present a concise report, simply and clearly written. He made it a part of his leisure pursuits to study law reports as a pastime, rather than as a matter of business; this no doubt assisted him in framing his own reports.

James Haldane served the Society as a council member, as collector of the Society's endowment and annuity fund and as president from 1895 to 1898. He also served the community in a variety of ways. He was a manager of Edinburgh Royal Infirmary and a Commissioner of Income Tax. For a number of years also he was the chairman of the Business Committee of the Scottish Episcopal Church. The services he rendered and his civic standing were recognised by his appointment as a

Justice of the Peace and as a Deputy Lieutenant of the City of Edinburgh.

In politics Haldane was a strong Conservative and was one of the founders and for a time chairman of the committee of the Scottish Conservative Club.

HARVEY HALL

b. c 1841 A 1871 d. 27-v-1931

Harvey Hall was the eldest son of John Hall, a wholesale cloth merchant and guild burgess of Aberdeen. He was educated at Dr Tulloch's Academy and at Aberdeen Grammar School. He then attended Marischal College from 1856 to 1859 where he graduated M.A. Like a number of other early Aberdeen accountants he combined legal and accountancy training. He served a law apprenticeship with Lachlan Mackinnon, advocate in Aberdeen, and was then for some time with Morton, Whitehead & Greig, W.S., in Edinburgh, where he continued his legal studies. Returning to Aberdeen he became a member of the Society of Advocates in Aberdeen in 1866. In 1870 he joined George Marquis in partnership and with him built up a substantial legal and accounting business. He acted as auditor of the Aberdeen Society of Advocates and was for a time auditor of Aberdeen Corporation accounts. He was also law agent for Aberdeen Savings Bank and a director of the Caledonian Insurance Company. He and James Tytler were joint auditors of Aberdeen District Tramways Company which was incorporated by Act of Parliament in 1872.

Hall was on the council of the Aberdeen Society of Accountants in 1873-4 and 1877-8 and was President from 1885 to 1887.

He did not seek to take any prominent part in public affairs but gave devoted service in church and charitable matters, including the Royal Aberdeen Hospital for Sick Children, the Aberdeen Deaf and Dumb Benevolent Society and the St Andrew's Society of Aberdeen. In the 1870's when the city was extending Hall took a special interest in the church extension movement in the new areas.

Another interest was the volunteer movement. Hall was an original member in 1859 of the 1st Aberdeen Rifle Volunteers, was commissioned in 1867, became a Captain in 1870 and retired with the rank of honorary major in 1884. He was present at the 1860 and 1881 reviews and as a veteran at the 1905 review and was one of the first holders of the Volunteer Decoration. He was a keen shot.

Hall was a man of artistic tastes and was interested in the Aberdeen Artists' Society. He also travelled extensively in Europe.

A. F. HAMILTON

b. G 1876 d. 27-vii-1906

Before becoming a member of the Glasgow Institute, Hamilton had been for about nine years a clerk with Aitken & Mackenzie and Mackenzie, Aitken & Barclay. These firms were stockbrokers as well as accountants and in 1878 Hamilton became a member of the Glasgow Stock Exchange Association. Thereafter "while not entirely discarding accountancy business, he devoted himself principally to the Stock Exchange" in partnership with James Outram with whom he became a partner in the firm of Outram & Hamilton. For some time, until shortly before his death, he was vice-chairman of the Stock Exchange Association. For the last two [illegible]f his life he had poor health.

DUNDAS HAMILTON

b. G 1853 d. 1864

Dundas Hamilton was one of the group active in promoting the formation of the Glasgow Institute and his name stands as number 18 in the roll of members. From 1846 he was in business in partnership with William McNaughton (number 17 in the membership roll) as accountants, stockbrokers and insurance agents—Hamilton was a member of the Glasgow Stock Exchange Association from 1845 till 1862. About 1860 there may have been a change in the nature of his business activities as in the 1861 list of Institute members, he is described as being of the Glasgow Gas Light Co., and the partnership with McNaughton appears to have terminated.

Hamilton's name does not appear in Richard Brown's list of deceased Scottish accountants though that of his partner McNaughton does.

T. C. HANNA

b. 22-vi-1837 E 1864 d. 23-xii-1910

Thomas Chalmers Hanna was the son of the Rev. William Hanna and a grandson of Rev. Dr Thomas Chalmers, from whom he derived his Christian names. He was educated at Merchiston Castle School, Edinburgh Academy and Edinburgh University and was then apprenticed to Samuel Raleigh, C.A. In 1868 he formed a partnership with William Wood. His son and Wood's nephew were later to continue this partnership after Wood had died in 1895 and Hanna had retired, also in 1895.

Hanna acted as auditor of the Free Church of Scotland for a time.

Like many of his accountant contemporaries he was a keen Volunteer. Another of his leisure activities was travel in which he engaged extensively.

WILLIAM HARDIE

b. 1857 E 1878 G 1900 d. 16-iii-1937

William Hardie was trained in Edinburgh but after qualifying he came to the West of Scotland and his professional life was spent there. He was the second chartered accountant to be a member of two of the Scottish bodies, the first being J. M. (later Sir John) Macleod, who, though his membership in Edinburgh post-dated Hardie's by two years, became a member in Glasgow in 1894.

Hardie was the son of a minister and had a distinguished career as an accounting student. He was apprenticed to Lindsay, Jamieson & Haldane and in 1875 won the Society's £20 bursary in the third year examination. He then went on to win the £30 fellowship award in the final examination in 1877.

He practised both in Greenock, where he lived, and in Glasgow. The firm which he founded in Glasgow, Hardie, Caldwell Ker & Hardie, still continues. In Greenock he was in partnership with R. H. Rowan, an Aberdeen member, as Hardie & Rowan.

In 1893 he published a *Manual of book-keeping for law agents with forms of trust accounts* and was also co-author with Alexander Allan of a *Manual of book-keeping by double entry*. The latter book was written mainly for traders (wholesalers and retailers).

Hardie was secretary and treasurer of Greenock Chamber of Commerce for forty years and the Chamber made him a life member in 1924.

ARTHUR HART

b. G 1873 d.

Hart served a four years apprenticeship with Auld & Guild and then remained with them as a clerk for a further three years. He had probably been employed on the stockbroking side of Auld & Guild's business for in 1877 he became a member of the Glasgow Stock Exchange Association. He took a share in the official work of both his professional bodies and in addition to serving on the Institute Council he was chairman of the Stock Exchange Association in 1899-1900.

As a young man he held a commission in the 1st Lanark Rifle Volunteers.

ALEXANDER HENDERSON

b. E 1855 d. 3-iv-1913

Alexander Henderson was the son of Thomas Henderson of Press, Berwickshire. He trained in Edinburgh with Maitland & Wood, predecessors of Wood & Hanna. He was one of the earliest Scottish Chartered Accountants to go to Canada and died in Montreal, where he had been for many years.

WILLIAM HENDRIE

b. G 1853 d.

William Hendrie is something of a mystery member of the Glasgow Institute. He was admitted in 1853, before the granting of the Royal Charter, and his letter of application for membership states that he had spent seven years with McClelland and Mackenzie and had then commenced business on his own account in May 1853.

A full list of the Institute's members in 1861 does not contain his name and indeed, apart from the fact of his admission to membership, nothing further has been traced. His name is not included in Richard Brown's list.

D. G. HOEY

b. G 1870 d.

From 1860 to 1866 D. G. Hoey was principal clerk with McEwan & Auld. After McEwan's death in 1866, Auld joined J. Wyllie Guild and Hoey carried on business on his own account. In 1873, after only three years as a member, he resigned from the Institute.

ARCHIBALD HORNE

b. 1795 E 1854 d. 30-viii-1862

Archibald Horne was one of the original members of the Edinburgh Society and had been in business as an accountant in Edinburgh from 1824. He was a partner of William Keith, who was in practice from about 1820 till 1852 and whose father had practised as an accountant from 1780 till his death in 1803. Horne also had as partners at different times, J. J. Dickson (another original member) and Robert Christie.

He was a director of the North British Railway Company and a member of the Edinburgh board of the City of Glasgow Life Assurance and Reversionary Co.

Horne was elected as a member of the first council of the Society and was again a member of council from 1856 to 1860.

A son, also Archibald Horne, served as an apprentice with his father but does not appear to have become a member.

ANDREW McD. HOUSTON

b.. G 1869 d.

Houston spent eight years in the office of McCowan & Brown, C.A., and at the time of his admission to membership of the Institute was about to become a partner in that firm. At the same time he became a member of the Glasgow Stock Exchange Association of which both McCowan and Brown were already members. In 1869, Brown became a partner of Alexander Moore and both the names McCowan & Brown and McCowan & Houston appear to have been used for the continuing business.

JOHN HOUSTON

b. G 1855 d.

John Houston became a member of the Glasgow Institute after having spent eight years with John C. Foulds, C.A. He then set up on his own account. He was one of the earliest members to be examined before admission. He became a partner with George McFarlane but did not remain in practice for long as he removed to London. In 1859 he tendered his resignation from the Institute, since, having become a member of the Inner Temple, he was of opinion that he was no longer eligible to continue his membership.

JAMES HOWDEN

b. 11-ix-1829 E 1854 d. 18-ii-1909

James Howden was for long one of Edinburgh's leading accountants. He was the son of Andrew Howden, W.S. Howden was trained in the office of William Wood, and like Wood, was also an actuary, being an original member of the Faculty of Actuaries.

In 1857, he became a partner of Archibald Borthwick. In 1863, the year in which Borthwick died, J. A. Molleson was assumed as a partner and the firm name became Borthwick, Howden & Molleson. The "Borthwick" was later dropped and for many years Howden & Molleson was one of Edinburgh's most notable accounting firms.

Howden had an extensive connection among banks and insurance companies. He was the auditor of the City of Glasgow Life Assurance Co., an appointment which he resigned on becoming a director of the Edinburgh Life Assurance Co. He was also secretary of the National Fire and Life Insurance Co. of Scotland, and auditor of the Royal Bank of Scotland, the Commercial Bank of Scotland and the Town and County Bank and a member of the Committee of Inspection of the Bank of Scotland.

James Howden contributed a number of papers to the Edinburgh Chartered Accountants Students' Society, and to *The Accountant's Magazine* (which appeared in 1897), among which were a memoir of his partner Archibald Borthwick and *The Profession in Scotland—a Retrospect* (Students' Society, 1893).

In his younger days, Howden held a commission in the Accountants Company of Volunteers and later, under a commission of a different kind, he was a Debt Commissioner under the Roads and Bridges (Scotland) Act, 1878.

His chief relaxation was walking and he also travelled extensively, visiting America twice and on another occasion voyaging to Ceylon.

In 1856 he married a daughter of John Shaw Stewart; she predeceased him by only a few weeks after more than fifty years of marriage. One of their sons, was also a chartered accountant, and a grandson, John M. Howden, D.L., J.P., C.A., was President of the Edinburgh Society from 1922 to 1925. James Howden himself rendered distinguished service to the Society. He was Secretary for nearly thirty years from 1863 to 1892 and President from 1892 to 1895.

He was for long an elder of Free St George's U.F. Church, Edinburgh and the high regard in which he was held can be gathered from an extract from an article which appeared in the *Scots Law Times* when he demitted office as president and which was reprinted in *The Accountant* for 2nd March, 1895.

"He is a conspicuous type of the high principled man of business whose individual integrity, sound judgment and strict sense of professional honour maintain the lofty standard of Scottish professional life. His clients find in him not merely a sound and cautious adviser, but a sympathetic friend."

C. H. HUGHES

b. 15-i-1847 E 1869 d. 17-viii-1914

C. H. Hughes was the third son of George Hughes, W.S. He was educated at Edinburgh Academy and was an apprentice with D. S. Robertson, C.A. In the mid-seventies he was in Liverpool but later went to London and at the time of his death was living at Staines.

JOHN HUNTER

b. 1801 E 1854 d. 1869

John Hunter was a son of Professor Hunter of St Andrews. He was a Writer to the Signet, as well as being a chartered accountant. From 1849 to 1866 Hunter was the Court of Session auditor.

JAMES HUTTON

b. 1838 G 1867 d. 4-i-1912

James Hutton was born in Perthshire and came to Glasgow as a youth. At the date of his becoming a member of the Institute, he was in the employment of George Macfarlane, C.A. For the preceding ten years, he claimed to have had the chief management of that business and for the last two of these years had had an interest in the profits, but without being a partner. On admission as a member of the Institute, he was assumed as a partner by Macfarlane. The firm subsequently became Macfarlane, Hutton & Patrick under which name it was long and honourably known in Glasgow.

Hutton served two three year terms on the Institute Council and in 1894 was elected President, holding that office till 1897. He retired from active business in 1907, having been senior partner of his firm since Macfarlane's death in 1880.

He was one of the accounting witnesses at the trial of the directors of the City of Glasgow Bank, and among audit appointments which he held at various times were those of auditor of the United Presbyterian Church and, following the union of 1900, of the United Free Church of Scotland, and of the Commercial Bank of Scotland. He also held a number of local government audit appointments, including various departments of Glasgow Corporation and the counties of Ayr, Dumfries, Wigton and Kirkcudbright.

Among Hutton's charitable interests were Quarrier's Homes, The Glasgow Asylum for the Blind and the Young Men's Christian Association.

One of his sons was a chartered accountant and a partner in Macfarlane, Hutton & Patrick and another was a professor at Queen Margaret College.

THOMAS JACKSON

b. 10-xii-1836 G 1877 d. 20-xi-1922

Thomas Jackson was born at Blantyre and came of a farming family. He retained throughout his long life a love of the country and its ways and in his later years spent much time at his Ayrshire home, Smithstone, Kilwinning. He came to Glasgow as a young man and at the date of his admission had already had a long experience of the profession and indeed had been a partner in the firm of Thomson & Johnston for eleven years. The name Jackson was not added to the firm name until 1873. Then in 1877 the name became Thomson, Jackson, Gourlay & Taylor and so remained for over ninety years. Thomas Jackson himself was a partner for 54 years, retiring only two years before his death.

Jackson rendered notable service to the Institute. He was several times a member of Council and was President from 1903 to 1906. He was also an original member of the joint standing committee of the United Kingdom chartered accountancy bodies, which was set up in 1902.

The Jubilee of the granting of the Royal Charter to the Institute was celebrated during Jackson's presidency and he was chairman at the banquet held to mark the occasion. He also represented the Institute at the similar function held in the previous year to mark the Jubilee of the Edinburgh charter. To mark the Jubilee he presented the Institute with a presidential badge.

His firm established a branch office in London in 1887, one of the first of the Scottish accounting firms to do so, and Jackson took an active personal interest in the London business. Later the two offices were conducted as separate firms, while maintaining close professional contacts.

Jackson was active in church affairs as an office bearer in St John's Parish Church and later as an elder in, and the original treasurer of, Hyndland Parish Church. He held the latter office for nearly fifty years. For 35 years he was treasurer of Glasgow Elders Association and he was president of that association from 1913 to 1915.

His eldest son was a chartered accountant and a partner in Thomson, Jackson, Gourlay & Taylor but unfortunately he was killed at Gallipoli in 1915 during the first world war.

ALEXANDER JAMIESON

b. 1-iii-1809 E 1854 d. 13-vii-1878

Alexander Jamieson was another of the fairly numerous band of early Edinburgh chartered accountants whose fathers belonged to the legal profession. He was the son of Robert Jamieson, W.S. Details of his early career are not known, but at the age of thirty he commenced business as an accountant on his own account. One of the original members of the Society, he served on the Council in the years 1870-1874.

GEORGE AULDJO JAMIESON

b. 1-v-1828 E 1854 d. 18-vii-1900

George Auldjo Jamieson, who became almost a legendary figure among the early Edinburgh chartered accountants, was in fact an Aberdeen man. He was the son of Dr Jamieson of Aberdeen, a doctor in the naval service, and was educated in his native city, graduating from Aberdeen University in 1846. He obtained his early training in the office of Messrs Chalmers, advocates in Aberdeen, and then migrated to Edinburgh, where he was with Lindsay & Esson, accountants. Esson, who shared the same Christian names as Jamieson, was also an Aberdeen man. All three, Lindsay, Esson and Jamieson, were original members of the Society. For a short time the three practised in partnership as Lindsay, Esson & Jamieson, but in 1856 Esson accepted a public appointment and in 1858 the two others were joined by James Haldane and the firm became Lindsay, Jamieson & Haldane.

Jamieson was one of the liquidators of the City of Glasgow Bank and held a wide range of professional appointments, including audits and directorships. He also acted as financial adviser and administrator to many large landed proprietors, so that he became widely known and highly esteemed as one of the most eminent accountants of his time. He was a director, among other companies, of the Royal Bank of Scotland, the North British & Mercantile Insurance Co. and the Arizona Copper Co., and about 1892 made a tour of America.

Although leading a very busy professional life, Jamieson somehow found time to engage in various forms of public service and rendered great services to the Edinburgh Society of which having been three times a member of Council he was elected President in 1882. He held that office for six years. On demitting office he was again appointed a Council member. For ten years before becoming President he acted as an examinator. During his presidency the Society's Endowment and Annuity Fund was constituted. On his retiral from the chair, he was presented with his portrait painted by Sir George Reid, P.R.S.A. and a replica was obtained for the Society's hall.

Among Jamieson's public services were membership of two Royal Commissions—on Company Law and on Mining Royalties. He was for a number of years a member of Edinburgh Town Council and was invited to stand for election as Lord Provost. He was also a commissioner of supply for the County of Edinburgh.

A Conservative in politics, Jamieson was for many years chairman of Edinburgh West Division Conservative Association and he stood as a candidate for the division in 1885.

So the catalogue of activities could be continued to embrace charities (the Edinburgh Association for Incurables benefited from his services); church affairs (maintaining his connection with his native city he was chancellor of the Episcopal diocese of Aberdeen); and learned societies (he contributed papers to the meeting of the British Association in Manchester in 1887 and was a Fellow of the Royal Society of Edinburgh. He also published other papers).

Active to the end Jamieson died suddenly in the New Club in Edinburgh.

A son became a member of the Society in 1889 but did not long survive his father as he died in 1902 from wounds received while serving as a lieutenant in the Scottish Horse during the Boer War.

WILLIAM JAMIESON

b. G 1854 d. 1855

William Jamieson, having been for some seven years with McEwan & Auld, began business on his own account about 1851. Although not actively associated with the promotion of the Institute he was one of the early members, in fact one of the first members not concerned with the actual promotion and formation of the new body, but he did not long survive.

He was a member of the Glasgow Stock Exchange Association, with which, of course, McEwan and Auld were closely involved, from 1852 to 1854.

HENRY KEITH

b. G 1873 d. 2-x-1897

Henry Keith was a son of the Rev. P. H. Keith, D.D., minister of Hamilton. He served an apprenticeship of four years with Moncreiff Mitchell, C.A., and then continued in his office for a further four years. In 1873 when he became a member of the Institute he also joined the Glasgow Stock Exchange Association and stockbroking became his main business.

DUGALD CAMPBELL KERR

b. E 1855 d. 1857

D. C. Kerr, son of Herbert N. J. Kerr of St Ann's Cottage, near Brechin, had been an apprentice with David Cormack, S.S.C., who was also an accountant and became one of the original members of the Society. It would appear that Kerr probably died young.

HENRY KERR

b. G 1853 d. 9-xii-1874

Henry Kerr's father, James Kerr, was one of Glasgow's very early accountants having carried on business as an accountant from about 1805. Henry served as an apprentice with his father and then continued as a clerk in his office for some time before setting up his own business in 1842 in partnership with William Anderson. He was the senior of the younger accountants, who made the approach to older practitioners which resulted in the formation of the Glasgow Institute and was a member of the delegation which met the seniors to discuss their proposals. Like so many of the original Glasgow Chartered Accountants, Kerr was also an original member of the Glasgow Stock Exchange Association. He served on the Institute Council in 1868.

Kerr and Anderson were joined by John A. Brodie in 1853 in the firm of Kerr, Anderson, Brodie & Co. This firm was the origin of both prominent accounting and stockbroking firms still in existence, though the former is now merged with Deloitte & Co.

THEO. E. KEYDEN

b. G 1870 d.

Keyden served for four years as an apprentice with Aitken & Mackenzie. Thereafter about 1865 he became a partner of Robert Strang, an accountant and stockbroker. Strang was probably, like Keyden's later partner, George Miller, more concerned with stockbroking than accounting, and Keyden became a member of the Glasgow Stock Exchange at about the time he joined Strang. Miller, although principally a stockbroker, was also a member of the Glasgow Institute, which he joined in 1869.

ROBERT C. KING

b. 1857 G 1879 d.

Robert King was a son of the agent of the Commercial Bank of Scotland at Kilwinning. He was for a number of years a clerk with McClelland, Mackinnon & Blyth, and was one of the first men to be admitted as an associate member of the Glasgow Institute, a grade of membership which existed for a number of years, but which never seemed to serve any particular purpose. He was so admitted in 1878, but when applying for full membership the following year expressed his intention of submitting himself for examination at the diet to be held in October, 1879.

He resigned his membership in 1896.

JOHN LAMB

b. 1850 E 1874 d. 24-xii-1916

John Lamb was born and educated in Edinburgh, where he was a pupil at Hamilton Place Academy and at the High School. He was apprenticed to Thomas Dall, C.A. After qualifying he was in practice for a few years until 1880 when he joined the Scottish Provident Institution as chief assistant. In 1885 he became a Fellow of the Faculty of Actuaries, having taken first place in the final examination of that body.

In 1890 he became the secretary of the Scottish Provident Institution and continued to hold that appointment till his retiral in 1912.

JAMES LATTA

b. 1821 E 1855 d. 13-iv-1874

James Latta was born in Renfrewshire, but was educated at Edinburgh High School and trained as an accountant in that city. He was apprenticed to C. M. Barstow and subsequently became a partner with him. His apprenticeship ran from 1837 to 1842 but was not discharged till thirteen years later when he decided to join the recently formed Society.

HENRY LECK

b. c 1825 G 1853 d. 20-ii-1890

Henry Leck was probably under thirty when he was admitted as a member of the Glasgow Institute shortly after its formation. He was one of the first members to be admitted who had taken no part in the negotiations for the establishment of the Institute. He was a country boy who came to Glasgow in 1841 and gained his first business experience in a mercantile counting house. Then after serving for seven years as an apprentice and clerk with William Anderson and his firm of Kerr & Anderson, Leck began business on his own account about 1849. In 1855 he was living in Renfield Street and had an office in Buchanan Street.

He dealt extensively in heritable property, perhaps one of last century's "whiz kids", and was so successful as to be able to acquire for himself the estate of Hollybush in Dalrymple Parish, Ayrshire. This appears as his address in 1878, and he died there twelve years later.

JOHN GRANT LESLIE

b. A 1867 d. 1874

Leslie was one of the twelve original members of the Aberdeen Society. His name appears in the local directory as an accountant as early as 1835.

He served on the Council of the Society in 1870-1871.

At one time he was a Sheriff, Commissary and J.P. Clerk Depute.

JOSEPH M. LIDDELL

b. c 1825 E 1854 d.

Joseph M. Liddell apparently changed the spelling of his patronymic, for his father is described as Joseph Liddle, S.S.C. He trained as an accountant with Donald S. Peddie who was in business from about 1831 and who also became an original member of the Edinburgh Society. Liddell then practised for a time in Perth, but returned to Edinburgh, where he was presumably practising when the Society was formed. In 1857 he resigned his membership on again leaving Edinburgh; his destination on this occasion has not been traced.

DONALD LINDSAY

b. 1796 E 1854 d. 17-xii-1876

Donald Lindsay was born in Forfarshire, and was a son of James Lindsay (Carnegie) of Boysack, Angus. He came to Edinburgh where he was trained with Alexander Pearson, W.S., and in 1823 set up in business on his own as an accountant. In 1838 he assumed as a partner George A. Esson and the business was carried on as Lindsay & Esson. Later George Auldjo Jamieson, who had had part of his training with Lindsay & Esson, became a partner. Esson retired in 1856 to take up a public appointment and when James Haldane joined the firm, then Lindsay & Jamieson, the style was changed to Lindsay, Jamieson & Haldane, under which the firm became one of the most prominent in Edinburgh. Lindsay retired in 1867 having been senior partner in all the firms with which he was connected.

From 1837 till his retirement he was auditor of the Scottish Widows Fund. He was also a director of the Royal Bank of Scotland for over twenty years and his connection with the bank continued after his retirement till 1871 as an extraordinary director.

He was auditor of the Edinburgh Society in 1867 and had been a member of the original Council of the Society.

He had the reputation of being able to isolate and to set out lucidly the precise problem to be tackled in any case, but left detail to others.

In his retirement, Lindsay went to live on the estate of Ardargie in Perthshire which he had taken. In these later years, his sight failed and, being unable to read, he took up knitting as a relaxation and used to carry on this activity while talking to friends.

J. WILKIE LOGAN

b. E 1864 d. 1901

J. Wilkie Logan was an apprentice to Archibald Borthwick and James Howden. Nothing is known of his subsequent career and while his name appears in the official directory of Scottish Chartered Accountants for 1899-1900 no address is given. He seems to have spent a number of years in London.

WILLIAM LOW

b. E 1854 d. -viii-1855

William Low was in business as an accountant in Edinburgh from 1827. He was one of the original members of the Edinburgh Society but did not long enjoy the distinction of describing himself as a chartered accountant, since he died in the year following the granting of the Royal Charter to the Society. Frederick Hayes Carter, one of the prominent early chartered accountants, was employed by Low before commencing business for himself.

ARCHIBALD LUMSDAINE

b. E 1866 d.

Archibald Lumsdaine was the son of John Lumsdaine, surgeon, Gilmerton. He was educated at George Watson's Hospital, Edinburgh, and the treasurer of the hospital signed Lumsdaine's indenture of apprenticeship to Henry Callender along with his father as cautioner. The indenture has other unusual features. It was originally for a period of four years, but because of a change in the Society's rules was extended for another year. Also, at a time when provision was normally made for payment of a premium to the master, which might or might not be returned to the apprentice in whole or in part as salary, Lumsdaine's indenture binds the treasurer of George Watson's Hospital to pay to Callender the sum of £40 by four annual instalments. The amounts so paid to be passed on to the apprentice as salary with additional sums of £5, £10, £15 and £20 in each of the years of service. The minute extending the period of service makes no mention of further salary!

It is a pity that with such an interesting start to his career nothing further has been discovered about Lumsdaine. In the list of members for 1870/71 his address is given as "Mansion House", Greenock, but though his name is still in the list for 1875/76 no address is given. He would seem to have died comparatively young, after a not very successful career as there is a record of an application to the Society by his widow for assistance.

ROBERT LUMSDEN

b. G 1862 d. 25-xii-1898

Robert Lumsden's connections and interests seem to have been largely in banking. He served an apprenticeship in the Bank of Scotland. Later he was Inspector of Branches in that bank, and from about 1858 he was engaged as one of the liquidators of the Western Bank of Scotland. In 1868 his membership of the Institute ceased as he had allowed his subscription to fall into arrears.

He was a Justice of the Peace for the Lower Ward of Lanarkshire.

WILLIAM LUNAN

b. c 1819 A 1867 d. 5-v-1903

William Lunan was another of the original dozen Aberdeen members. He was a member of the Society's Council in 1868-69 and President for the term 1877/79.

Lunan's father was parish minister of Kinnettles in Forfarshire and he had his early training with a Mr McDonald in Arbroath. He then went to Edinburgh where he was in the office of Donald Lindsay. Moving to Aberdeen, he became a partner of George Marquis, who had been in business as an accountant there from 1837. Lunan's own name appears in the local directory from 1851.

ALEXANDER MACHRAY

b. c 1838 A 1874 d. 11-v-1916

At one time a partner in the firm of Cochran & Macpherson, Advocates, Aberdeen, Alexander Machray later turned his attention exclusively to accountancy. He was on the Council of the Aberdeen Society in 1876 and 1879 and was President of the Society in 1889-90.

In his early years Machray served an apprenticeship of five years with Smith & Cochrane, advocates. Thereafter he was employed by that firm for eighteen years, for the last twelve of which he was in charge of the firm's books and accounts. When in 1874 he applied for membership of the Aberdeen Society he had just been assumed as a partner.

He had a great interest in music, especially choral music, and for over fifty years regularly attended Handel Festivals at the Crystal Palace, London, as a member of the chorus. For some time before his death, however, he suffered from poor health.

JOHN T. MAIN

b. G 1876 d. 7-vi-1896

John Main was a graduate of Edinburgh University and began his business career in that city, where for four years he was a clerk in the life department of the North British & Mercantile Insurance Co. Ltd. He apparently moved to Glasgow about 1874 and had been for a year and a half in the office of Kerr, Anderson & Muir, C.A., when he applied for membership of the Glasgow Institute. He became a member of the Glasgow Stock Exchange Association in 1878.

When he became a partner in Kerr, Anderson & Muir, the firm name was changed to Kerr, Anderson, Muir & Main.

James McClelland, C.A., first President (1853-64) of The Institute of Accountants and Actuaries in Glasgow

Peter White, C.A., President (1864-67) of the Glasgow Institute

Walter Mackenzie, C.A., President (1867-70) of the Glasgow Institute
(He had been Secretary, 1853-67)

William Anderson, C.A., President (1870-76) of the Glasgow Institute

George Robson, C.A., President (1876-78) of the Glasgow Institute

J. Wyllie Guild, C.A., President (1878-81) of the Glasgow Institute
(He had been Secretary, 1867-73)

Alexander Sloan, C.A., Secretary (1873-1909) of the Glasgow Institute
(He became President in 1909)

R. A. MAIR

b. 1847 G 1871 d. 14-iii-1898

Robert Mair served first as a clerk with Reid & Galt, C.A., for five years and then was for four years with Alexander Moore and his firm of Moore & Brown. He was the 100th member to join the Glasgow Institute. On admission he founded with Robert Reid, who did not become a member of the Institute until 1875, the firm of Reid & Mair, which is still active in Glasgow.

Mair was the son of John Mair, lace merchant, Glasgow.

Though he did not, because of health reasons, enjoy a long professional career, he built a successful practice. He was the secretary of Vale of Clyde Tramway Co., and also of Greenock Port Glasgow and Gourock Tramway Co.

His health caused his retiral in 1897 when aged only fifty and the following year he died at his residence, Barncliff, Cove.

JOHN MAITLAND

b. 1803 E 1854 d. 23-i-1865

John Maitland was the eighth son of Sir Alexander Gibson Maitland, Bart., of Cliftonhall in Kirkliston parish. About 1834 he set up in business as an accountant in Edinburgh. Later he had as a partner, William Wood, who began business about 1841, and, like Maitland, became an original member of the Edinburgh Society. In 1850, Maitland was appointed as the first Accountant of Court.

He was a member of the Council of the Society from 1860 to 1864.

A brother of John Maitland lived for some years at 29 Queen Street, Edinburgh, now part of Chartered Accountants' Hall, Edinburgh.

JOHN MANN

b. 1827 G 1853 d. 12-xii-1910

John Mann was the son of another John Mann, an artist craftsman, painter and signwriter, who died shortly after his son was born. His mother was the daughter of a farmer on the Colquhoun estates at Luss, but she did not return to the country on her husband's death and the young John was brought up by her in Glasgow in somewhat straitened circumstances. He left school at twelve years old and for three years was employed as a doctor's boy. He next became an apprentice to William Anderson, an accountant, whose office was in John Street, Glasgow. Having completed five years as an apprentice young Mann then became a clerk to Andrew Harvie and in 1850, some three and a half years later, he succeeded to Harvie's business, so that when he joined with other accountants in promoting the formation of a professional Institute he had had his own practice for about three years and was aged 26.

In 1862 Mann married Mary Newton Harrington, daughter of a Coldstream draper. They had a family of four sons and three daughters. Three of the sons earned distinction in separate fields. The eldest, who became Sir John Mann, C.A., had a long and notable career in accountancy, Ludovic Mann became an insurance broker and was the inventor of the loss of profits policy, while Harrington inherited his grandfather's artistic abilities and was a noted painter.

John Mann's long and successful career was not entirely free from alarms. He was the holder of 16 shares in the City of Glasgow Bank when it failed in 1878. This involved him in a liability of over £40,000 and he narrowly escaped bankruptcy. In 1881 he faced trouble of another kind when the Accountant in Bankruptcy reported that Mann had not complied with his statutory requirements and the Court removed him from the office of Trustee in four sequestrations. The Council of the Institute considered the circumstances in which this happened and impressed on Mann the need carefully to avoid for the future giving cause for similar censure. All his difficulties were overcome, however, and the business which he founded continues to thrive.

Outwith lively professional interests, John Mann had a long association with the Royal Philosophical Society of Glasgow, of which he was very many years honorary treasurer. He was also a director of the Glasgow Athenaeum. He was one of the founders of Glasgow Abstainers Union and of this organisation was also for many years treasurer.

He was a collector with a wide range of interests which covered coins, seals, stamps, medals, prints, autographs and archaeological curiosities.

Mann had a lively and enquiring mind and was always interested in new developments in the profession. He took a part in promoting the Western Friendly Society and in connection with that Society's affairs he acquired, about 1870, one of the earliest forms of calculating machine to help in handling actuarial calculations for the Society. This machine still exists in the offices of Mann Judd Gordon & Co.

He was also an early enthusiast for and teacher of Pitman's shorthand and made experiments with a system of shorthand of his own devising.

At the dinner held in 1905 to mark the Jubilee of the granting of the Royal Charter, John Mann was present, being then the sole survivor of the original members. The following year he was elected President of the Institute and held office till 1909.

THOMAS MANSFIELD

b. 3-iii-1800 E 1854 d. 20-vii-1868

Thomas Mansfield was the son of James Mansfield of Midmar, who was a banker. He commenced business as an accountant in 1825 and was later joined in partnership by Robert Spottiswoode. Both became original members of the Edinburgh Society. Mansfield was a member of the first Council of the Society and served as a Council member until 1859. He was again elected to the Council in 1863 and when James Brown, the first President, died in 1864, Mansfield was elected to succeed him and occupied the chair until his own death four years later.

He was a director of Scottish Union Fire and Life Insurance Co. and was a Justice of the Peace.

His son, Thomas John Mansfield, was an apprentice with his father's firm of Mansfield & Spottiswoode. He did not become a member of the Society until after his father's death, when he joined Robert Spottiswoode, the surviving partner, as a partner.

THOMAS JOHN MANSFIELD

b. 18-ii-1843 E 1871 d. 14-xi-1876

T. J. Mansfield was the son of Thomas Mansfield, accountant in Edinburgh, later, as one of the original members of the Society, chartered accountant. He served as an apprentice with his father's firm of Mansfield & Spottiswoode and was, after his father's death, a partner in the firm with Robert Spottiswoode. He died at the early age of 33.

GEORGE MARQUIS

b. c 1802 A 1867 d. 1874

George Marquis was born at Fochabers. He appears in the local directory as an accountant in Aberdeen from 1837. He had a succession of partners, including William Lunan, Harvey Hall and William Milne, of whom Lunan and Milne were also original members of the Aberdeen Society.

Marquis served on the Council of the Society on several occasions and was President for the years 1869-1871.

He was for a time auditor of Aberdeen Corporation accounts and was manager of Bon-Accord Property Investment Company, a company established in 1853.

Marquis was an elder in Trinity Free Church, Aberdeen.

DAVID MARSHALL

b. 3-iv-1830 E 1854 d. 30-v-1897

David Marshall was one of the younger original members of the Edinburgh Society. His father, William Marshall was a goldsmith and a director of the Life Association of Scotland. His grandfather, William Calder, had been Lord Provost of Edinburgh.

David Marshall, after attending Edinburgh High School, was apprenticed to Borthwick & Raleigh.

He was the clerk to the Commissioners of Income Tax for Edinburgh City. He also held directorships in various companies, including Edinburgh Fire Insurance Co., and the Scottish Plate Glass Insurance Co.

Marshall's son, F. A. Marshall, later became a chartered accountant and was in partnership with him.

JAMES MARTIN

b. 3-x-1846 E 1869 d. 18-i-1893

James Martin was a son of Thomas Martin, an original member of the Edinburgh Society. He served as an apprentice in his father's office and became a partner with him.

He was a member of the Council of the Society from 1885 to 1888.

THOMAS MARTIN

b. E 1854 d. 7-iv-1884

Thomas Martin trained with and was then in partnership with Alexander Low, who was in business as an accountant from 1832 till 1840 when he became manager of the Life Association of Scotland. Martin later became a partner of Samuel Raleigh. Both he and Raleigh had attended the first meeting in connection with the formation of the Society. He served twice on the Council of the Society and was a Council member at the time of his death.

Martin was the auditor of the Edinburgh Water Board Trustees.

His son, James Martin, was also a chartered accountant and in partnership with him.

W. C. MAUGHAN

b. 29-iv-1836 E 1860 d. 30-vi-1914

W. C. Maughan was the son of Capt. Philip Maughan of the East India Company's Naval Service. At the beginning of 1853 he became an apprentice to William Wood in Edinburgh. After becoming a member of the Society he practised for a short time in Edinburgh and then, perhaps because of his father's East Indian connections, received an appointment with the Bank of Hindustan in London. He did not remain there long, and in 1867 moved to Rome, where he was manager of an old established Scottish Bank—A. Macbean & Co. While in Rome he had a serious illness and this compelled him to retire from business. Most of his time, thereafter, was spent in travelling, writing and in public work and he lived to a good age.

He visited many parts of the world and was the author of several successful books; these included "The Alps of Arabia", "Roseneath Past and Present", "Annals of Garelochside", and several novels. For a time he lived at Roseneath, Dunbartonshire. While living there, he was for many years a member of the local School Board.

Maughan also took an active interest in politics and was twice a candidate for Parliament.

Returning to the East of Scotland he died at his home in Musselburgh.

GEORGE MELDRUM

b. 1812 E 1854 d. 12-x-1876

George Meldrum commenced business as an accountant in Edinburgh in 1842.

When the Edinburgh Society was formed he was one of the original members, having been one of the eight men who attended the inaugural meeting in A. W. Robertson's office.

He held appointments from the Free Church of Scotland.

JAMES MESTON

b. 25-ii-1821 A 1867 d. 6-viii-1892

James Meston was a country boy who made good in the City. He was born in Kintore, Aberdeenshire. He trained in Aberdeen in the legal offices of Blaikie & Smith, having previously spent some time in a mercantile establishment. In these early days he devoted his evenings to self-education and he so impressed John Smith (later to be the first President of the Aberdeen Society of Accountants), who was at the time President of the Aberdeen Society of Advocates, that Smith made him his confidential clerk. In the local directory of 1850, Meston was described as a writer, but in 1854 that description had been changed to accountant. In that year he left Aberdeen temporarily and spent the next three years in London.

When he returned to Aberdeen in 1857, Meston set up his own office as an accountant at 75 Union Street. At the same address Sir Alexander Anderson of Adam & Anderson had his offices. Anderson was one of Aberdeen's most prominent citizens and took a leading part in civic affairs (he was Lord Provost) as well as in commercial and industrial developments. His firm of Adam & Anderson were engaged on many important public schemes which included the erection of new corporation buildings, the acquisition for the corporation of Torry Farm and various railway projects. Meston impressed Anderson with his capacity and was employed by him on the "actuarial" work connected with many of these schemes.

James Meston might almost be called the founder of the Aberdeen Society. With William Milne he convened the first meeting to discuss the proposal and took by far the largest part in organising the society, so much so that he was voted a fee of 15 guineas for his services. He was also appointed secretary and treasurer of the Society and held these offices till his death. They continued to be held by partners of James Meston & Co., until the amalgamation of the Scottish Chartered bodies in 1951.

At a time when auditing did not form the large part of professional practice which it later attained, Meston held many important audit appointments not only in Aberdeen, but in London and in cities throughout Scotland and England. These included local authority audits, the audit of Aberdeen University and insurance and bank appointments. He was also Inspector of National Security Savings Banks for the Northern District of Scotland.

For a time, John K. Greig was a partner with James Meston, who later assumed Walter A. Reid, who had been his apprentice, and Andrew Davidson who was the son of the minister of Meston's native parish of Kintore.

When Aberdeen Chartered Accountants Students' Society was founded in 1886, Meston delivered the inaugural address, which was later published as a pamphlet.

Meston found his chief relaxation in holiday travel abroad and in the study of foreign languages. He was described after his death as "... a self-made man who rose from a comparatively humble station in life to a first place in the ranks of the professional men of the country" and also as a man of forceful character and indomitable perseverance with a temperament which made it impossible always to avoid collision with others but who was recognised as being invariably fair in controversy.

In a reminiscent speech dealing with his early association with Meston, Dr Walter Reid (as he had then become) recalled how his then senior had opposed the introduction of a copying press because—he was a heavy man—he could produce satisfactory copies merely by sitting on the letter book. He was not opposed to all technological progress, however, for Meston & Co., were among the first in the North of Scotland to instal the telephone, and the firm were pioneers in the use of columnar book-keeping.

He was for many years an office-bearer in the East Parish Church, but latterly was connected with the West Church. It may be noted that these congregations occupy separate portions of the same building.

In 1882 Meston underwent a serious operation and though he survived for another ten years his subsequent health was adversely affected. Two sons died in early manhood, but Mrs Meston and three daughters survived him.

ARTHUR WELLESLEY MILLAR

b. E 1871 d. -ii-1899

Arthur W. Millar was an apprentice of Henry Callender, C.A., but nothing is known of his later career.

ROBERT COCKBURN MILLAR

b. 1853 E 1877 d. 19-iv-1929

R. C. Millar was one of the earliest of what would now be called "academic accountants". He was an apprentice with C. M. Barstow and later his partner in Barstow & Millar and, though he subsequently left that partnership, the firm still continues under that name.

In 1876 Millar's performance in the final examination gained him a share of the Society's fellowship award.

For a time after leaving Barstow & Millar he practised on his own and then was joined by his brother, T. J. Millar, C.A., LL.B.

He was the first lecturer in the Practice of Commerce at Heriot-Watt College, now Heriot-Watt University, and was the author of various books and articles. The first of these, "The Accountant's Handbook of interest states, decimal calculations, consignments and joint accounts etc." was published in 1889. The title is an indication of the matters then occupying the attention of accounting theorists. Millar also contributed extensively to an Encyclopedia of Accounting published in Edinburgh in 1903 and many of his articles appeared in *The Accountant's Magazine*.

He had a high reputation as an expert witness and also for his skill in bankruptcy and liquidation work. In the latter field the most notable liquidation for which he was responsible was that of the Property Investment Co. of Scotland.

He held the appointment of Auditor of Edinburgh Parish Council and of the Burgh of Leith and was a joint auditor of the Clydesdale Bank. He was also a director of Edinburgh Savings Bank.

Millar served on the Council of the Society and was elected to the Presidency in 1910, holding office till 1913. He also represented the Society on the Scottish Chartered Accountants General Examining Board.

For forty-two years he was a member of the Edinburgh Chamber of Commerce and was chairman of the Chamber in 1907-1908.

His son, having first qualified as a chartered accountant, practised at the English bar. He had also two daughters.

GEORGE MILLER

b. c 1842 G 1869 d. 10-iii-1887

George Miller was trained with Aitken & Mackenzie, C.A., where, according to his letter of application for membership of the Institute he was latterly in charge, under Mr Walter Mackenzie of the accounting department of the firm. He was a partner successively of Theodore Keyden (as Miller & Keyden) and of

George Slimmon (as George Miller & Slimmon).

Miller became a member of the Glasgow Stock Exchange Association in 1868 and was mainly concerned with Stock Exchange business. Although only forty-five years old at the time of his death, he had retired several years before and was living on a small property which he had acquired in the country.

HUGH MILLER

b. 28-iv-1843 E 1868 d. 5-ii-1896

Hugh Miller was born in Edinburgh, a son of Robert Miller, a merchant there. He served as an apprentice with Thomas Dall, C.A., and then became his partner. Dall worked extensively for Edinburgh Corporation. Both men died in their mid-fifties.

JOHN MILLER

b. c 1815 G 1853 d. 23-ix-1894

John Miller was in business on his own account from the age of about thirty, having previously served for four years with an accountant in Glasgow. The nature of his other early business activity is not known. In 1846, the year after he started business on his own account, he became a member of the Glasgow Stock Exchange Association and he was mainly active as a stockbroker, firstly in partnership with James A. Ferguson and afterwards with his grandson William Quaile, C.A. (as John Miller & Quaile). That firm of which Miller's great-great-grandson, another William Quaile, C.A., became a partner is now merged in Kerr, Anderson, Miller Stevenson & Co., the Kerr Anderson part of which also had its origins with some of the early members of the Glasgow Institute.

Although mainly active as a stockbroker, Miller took a part in promoting the formation of the Institute and twice served on the Council.

JAMES MILNE (1)

b. c 1837 A 1873 d. 19-xii-1888

The early members of the Aberdeen Society included two men unconnected but bearing the same name, James Milne. Both became Presidents of the Society.

The elder James Milne was described in the local directory from 1856 to 1867 as a writer but thereafter as an accountant. He was a partner in the firm of Edwards & Macqueen, Advocates. It is an interesting point that although Milne did not become a member of the Society until 1873 he changed his designation to accountant in the year in which it was founded. At that time he was on the management committee of the Northern Agricultural Company.

He was twice a member of the Council of the Society and was elected President in 1887, but did not survive to serve the usual three year term.

JAMES MILNE (2)

b. c 1853 A 1877 d. 12-ix-1923

The younger James Milne was born in the parish of Drumoak, the son of Thomas Milne, farmer of East Quarter in that parish, and educated there. His father died when he was young and after spending two years in an advocate's office he was an apprentice with Marquis, Hall & Milne and remained with that firm until 1888 when he commenced practice on his own account. The Milne who was a partner at that time in Marquis, Hall & Milne was William Milne, who was one of the twelve original members of the Society. When he commenced practice, James Milne was appointed manager of Aberdeen Property Investment Building Society, an appointment which he retained until his death, thirty-five years later. He built up a large audit practice, in which he latterly had as a partner George Smith, and became a prominent member of the profession in Aberdeen.

He took an active part in the affairs of

the Society but apart from that did not concern himself in public affairs. He served on the Council of the Society, acted as librarian from 1895 to 1903, as a representative on the General Examining Board from 1896 to 1907 and was President from 1903 to 1907. He also instituted the James Milne prize fund for distinction in the final examination.

Milne was an office-bearer in Bon Accord United Free Church, Aberdeen.

He remained active to the very end of his life and was at his office on the day of his death.

WILLIAM MILNE

b. c 1832 A 1867 d. 9-ix-1906

Like the other two bearers of the name Milne, who were among the early members of the Aberdeen Society, William Milne became President of the Society. Also like a fair number of the early members, of whatever name, he had part of his training in legal offices.

He started his career with William Ross, Advocate, in Aberdeen, then moved to the office of John Blaikie, another advocate in Aberdeen. After that he moved to Edinburgh where he made his real initial entry to the accounting profession when he was employed by Lindsay, Jamieson & Haldane. Jamieson, of course, was like Milne an Aberdeen man.

Milne returned to Aberdeen and set up his own accounting business in 1863. He built up a wide connection and was involved in the audit of local authorities, Robert Gordon's College, the Aberdeen Savings Bank and the Great North of Scotland Railway Co., in addition to commercial work. He also acted as factor to the Marquis of Huntly.

For a time he was a partner in the firm of Marquis, Hall & Milne and then from 1897 he had as a partner Robert Milroy in the firm of Milne & Milroy.

With James Meston, Milne was responsible for convening the first meeting of Aberdeen accountants to consider the formation of a local society and he was one of the original twelve members. He served on the council at different times and was President in 1881 to 1883. He was the last survivor of the original twelve.

Milne was an office bearer in Queen's Cross United Free Church and took an interest in the affairs of Aberdeen Mechanics' Institute and in the Aberdeen Philosophical Society.

GEORGE T. MITCHELL

b. 3-ix-1812 E 1854 d. 19-vii-1894

George T. Mitchell was the son of Robert Mitchell of Airth. He was one of the original members of the Edinburgh Society, but resigned his membership in 1865, having left Edinburgh before then.

MONCREIFF MITCHELL

b. G 1854 d. 17-iii-1886

Although he was a very early member of the Glasgow Institute, becoming a member before the application for a Royal Charter was made, Moncreiff Mitchell took no part in the discussions which led to the formation of the Institute. Nor, except for one spell on the council, did he subsequently take any active part in Institute affairs.

He was in business as an accountant from about 1850. His early partner, Alexander Wylie, also became a member of the Glasgow Institute, but his next partner, A. F. Watson, was a member of the Edinburgh Society, who had migrated to Glasgow.

Mitchell became a member of the Glasgow Stock Exchange Association in 1858. He was a Justice of the Peace.

He appears to have prospered and was a member of the Royal Northern Yacht Club.

GEORGE MOFFAT

b. c 1840 G 1867 d. 16-i-1905

As a youth in his early teens George Moffatt entered the employment of Aitken & Mackenzie. After spending about eleven years in that office, he set up as an accountant in partnership with his brother John in 1865, in which year both brothers joined the Glasgow Stock Exchange Association.

John Moffatt retired from the firm but George carried on under the name of J. & G. Moffatt, which they had originally adopted.

He was on the Institute council in 1873.

JOHN MOFFATT

b. c 1837 G 1867 d. 26-iv-1911

John Moffatt was the elder brother of George Moffatt and was also in the service of Aitken & Mackenzie, when with his brother he decided to set up on his own account. Both brothers joined the Glasgow Stock Exchange Association and John became better known as a stockbroker than as an accountant. This may have been the reason why John left the partnership for he did not give up business activity, indeed, he was at business on the day before he died.

Shortly after joining the Institute he was appointed a member of the committee set up to consider the state and future of the Institute's funds. He became Vice-Chairman of the Stock Exchange Association of which at the time of his death he was the second oldest surviving member, having become a member in 1865.

JOHN F. MOFFATT

b. 19-ix-1840 E 1865 d. 9-iii-1921

John F. Moffatt was born at Doncaster where his father, William L. Moffatt, was an architect. J. F. Moffatt was educated at the Grammar School, Doncaster and the High School, Sheffield. His father having removed to Edinburgh he became an apprentice to A. T. Niven, C.A. He was later for a short time a partner with Niven, under the firm name of Niven & Moffatt; but for many years he practised on his own account.

He acted as manager of Scottish Heritable Security Co. Ltd., of which Niven was a director, and was himself a director of Alliance Assurance Company and of the Carron Grove Paper Co. Ltd.

Moffatt was on the council of the Society for a term at the end of the century.

He inherited from an uncle the estate of Eldon, Lasswade and was also the owner of a property at Glenisla, which he had purchased. His wife was a daughter of John McCulloch of the British Linen Bank.

Moffatt took an active part in church affairs and was session clerk and treasurer of Grange Parish Church.

JAMES A. MOLLESON

b. 1839 E 1860 d. 5-i-1902

James Molleson's father was a doctor in Forfarshire. His grandfather had been parish minister in Montrose.

He served as an apprentice with Borthwick & Raleigh and just before Borthwick's death in 1863 became a partner in Borthwick, Howden & Molleson, Howden having been a partner for some years. The firm continued for many years under the name of Howden & Molleson.

Molleson always took a great interest in the younger members of the profession, by whom his advice was greatly valued, and also in the training and examination of entrants to the profession. He was an examinator for the Society from 1882 to 1889 and after the formation of the General Examining Board in 1893 he represented the Edinburgh Society on that board. He was also on the council of the Society from 1890 to 1894.

Molleson's services as an expert witness were in great demand and he received many court appointments.

He was the honorary treasurer of the High School Commemorative Association.

In 1894 Molleson suffered from a severe attack of gout and his health never fully recovered thereafter.

HON. FRANCIS J. MONCREIFF

b. 27-viii-1849 E 1875 d. 30-v-1900

Francis Jeffrey Moncreiff was the fifth son of Lord Moncreiff of Tulliebole, Lord Justice Clerk. He was educated at Edinburgh Academy where he was awarded the Mitchell Medal for Mathematics in 1866 and where he also learned to play the game of rugby football, then in its early stages of development. After attending Edinburgh University, Moncreiff became an apprentice with Lindsay Jamieson & Haldane. During his apprenticeship his success both in study and on the sports field continued. In 1874 he was awarded a share of the fellowship then awarded by the Society to the most successful candidate in the final examination, having in the meantime been captain for some years of the Edinburgh Academical rugby team and played for Scotland in 1871, 1872 and 1873 in the first three international matches against England.

From 1875 to 1880 he was a partner with Adam Gillies Smith. He then set up another firm. In this he had as partners H. M. Horsburgh, who had been an apprentice of Smith and had also won the Society's fellowship, and T. P. Laird.

Perhaps not surprisingly, Moncreiff was extensively employed on court remits but he also had extensive connections in other fields. He was a director of the Bank of Scotland, Standard Life Assurance Co., and a number of other companies.

Moncreiff was a member of the Society's Council from 1881 to 1885 and from 1898 till his death. He was also collector to the Trustees of the Society's Endowment and Annuity Fund.

In addition to his skill on the football field, Moncreiff was also an excellent shot.

J. FORBES MONCREIFF

b. 5-vii-1847 E 1872 d. 1927

J. Forbes Moncreiff was a son of George Moncreiff, writer in Perth. Part of his early education was at Edinburgh Academy. Moncreiff was in practice in Edinburgh for many years in partnership with Mowbray Douglas, who became a member of the Edinburgh Society in 1880. The firm was known as Forbes Moncreiff & Douglas.

JOHN SCOTT MONCREIFF

b. 4-iii-1811 E 1854 d. 25-ii-1889

J. Scott Moncreiff was the fourth son of William Scott Moncreiff, an accountant in Edinburgh. Scott Moncreiff Senior began business as an accountant in 1800 when he was 34 and died in 1846. By that time his son John, who had followed his education at Edinburgh Academy by training as an accountant, was his partner. Another son, David, was also an accountant, but never became a member of the Society. John Scott Moncreiff was later a partner of C. W. W. Thomson. The firm which they founded became Scott Moncreiff, Thomson & Shiells, one of the leading Edinburgh accounting firms.

J. Scott Moncreiff was a member of the Council of the Society from 1868 to 1872. He had been one of the eight men who attended the first meeting in connection with the formation of the Society.

He was the auditor of the National Security Savings Bank of Edinburgh and was treasurer of the Institute for Relief of Incurables.

WILLIAM MONCREIFF

b. 28-ix-1813 E 1854 d. 31-viii-1895

William Moncreiff was the third son of James Wellwood Moncreiff, Advocate, who became Lord Moncreiff. He was educated at Edinburgh Academy and at the age of 29 he set up in business as an accountant in Edinburgh. His first partner was William Paul, who died in 1848. His next partner, John Mackenzie, had been trained by Paul and afterwards became Treasurer of the Bank of Scotland. He then had as partners, J. M. Baillie, who had been with him as an apprentice and who, like his master, became an original member of the Society, and A. G. Smith, C.A.

Moncreiff, in addition to being an original member of the Society, was a member of the first Council and served on the Council on three subsequent occasions.

From 1865 to 1889 he was Accountant of Court. By the latter year he was seventy-six years old so presumably he then retired.

He was, in early life, one of the founders of the Grange Cricket Club.

He was also a director of the Standard Life Assurance Co., and was a Justice of the Peace.

ALEXANDER MOORE

b. 1824 G 1857 d. 9-i-1913

Alexander Moore was born in Glasgow where his father was a surgeon but he spent part of his boyhood and youth in Belfast where he went, following his father's death, to live with an uncle. He had his first business experience in Belfast but returned to Glasgow about the age of fifteen. There he was employed in the counting house of William Easton & Co., Commission Agents. He remained with them for about eight years and then became a partner in another firm of commission agents. In his own words "progress was not very encouraging" so the partnership split up in June 1855 when "I set up as an accountant, for which I had long had a predilection". In the meantime he had had some practical experience of the trust work which was then a large part of accountancy practice for he had been appointed to take charge of the estate of the senior partner of his late employers. He also, before becoming a member of the Institute, attended the Scots Law class at Glasgow University.

Although his entry to the profession may seem to have been by a strange route, there is no doubt that when Moore set up as an accountant he had found his true vocation and he soon made his mark in his new profession.

Like many of his Glasgow contemporaries, Moore was also a member of the Glasgow Stock Exchange Association, which he joined in 1869. In that year also he formed a partnership with William Brown, C.A., who had already been a member of the Stock Exchange for several years. Brown died in 1889 by which time Alexander Moore, Junior, was a partner in the firm. The Moores then amalgamated their business with that of Carson & Watson, forming the firm of Moores, Carson & Watson.

Before that time, Moore had already established a high reputation and an extensive business. He had been trustee on the estates of two of the directors of the failed City of Glasgow Bank and as such had given evidence at the trial of the bank directors. He was concerned in the formation of Young's Paraffin Light & Mineral Oil Co. Ltd. in 1865 and of the Distillers Company Ltd. in 1877 and was auditor of both companies. Arthur Young, McClelland, Moores & Co., the successors of Moores Carson & Watson, are still auditors of the latter company. Moore was also one of the first auditors of Tharsis Sulphur & Copper Co. Ltd., and of the Clydesdale Bank and had other important audit connections.

In addition to his active professional commitments, Moore took a prominent part in the affairs of the Institute, though he was not active in civic affairs. He was a member of the Council of the Institute in 1881-1883, was President from 1884 to 1887, and auditor from 1890 to 1898. His son was also President, in 1915-1918.

Moore became an elder of Wellington Church in 1854 and was a generous supporter of the church and of many religious and benevolent institutions in the city. In

1904 to mark his jubilee as an elder he was the recipient of a presentation from the congregation.

Moore's wife, whom he married in 1852, was a daughter of Mr John McIntyre, a relative and business associate of Robert Napier, the early Clyde shipbuilder. Mrs Moore died in 1902, a few months after they had celebrated their golden wedding.

At the time of his death he was the oldest surviving member of the Institute.

He was interested in the fine arts and was secretary of the Art Union of Glasgow.

ALEXANDER MOORE JNR.

b. G 1877 d. 5-viii-1936

The son of Alexander Moore, Moore Junior served a four year apprenticeship with his father's firm of Moore & Brown. He became a partner in the firm and then in Moores, Carson & Watson.

He became a member of the Glasgow Stock Exchange Association in 1880 and many years later turned his attention more to stockbroking than accountancy.

Moore's chief interest was always his professional work, but as a younger man he was an officer in the Royal Engineers (Volunteers), retiring as a Major, and the holder of the Volunteer Decoration.

He rendered great services to the Institute, serving on the Council and from 1905 to 1915 as one of its representatives on the General Examining Board. In 1915 he was elected President of the Institute and held office until 1918.

The Joint Committee of the Councils of the Scottish Chartered bodies was formed about this time and Moore became the first chairman of that committee. In 1919 he presented through the joint committee the Moore Cup "for annual competition between the three societies in social sport. The nature and details of competition to be settled from time to time by the joint committee . . . and my desire is that the annual competition . . . should be of such character as will enable as large a number as possible of the members of the Societies to participate". The sport chosen as the field for competition was golf and the cup is now competed for by members of the Scottish Institute on a district basis.

After completing his presidential term, Moore was elected as treasurer of the Institute and held that office until 1924. In 1908 he had represented the Glasgow Institute at the celebrations to mark the 21st anniversary of the formation of the American Association of Public Accountants, and among other services to the profession he took an active part in promoting the Institute's Benevolent Fund.

As an accountant he acquired a special reputation as a negotiator and as an expert witness and his services in these capacities were in great demand.

After the 1914-1918 war, during which his only son died from wounds received at Gallipoli, Moore retired from Moores, Carson & Watson and formed the firm of Moore & Snodgrass, to which the stockbroking activities of the former firm were transferred; but he retained some accounting work in which he had a personal interest.

FRANCIS MORE

b. 31-iii-1838 E 1875 D. 16-x-1905

Francis More was born and educated in Dundee, where he was a pupil at the High School. After leaving school his early training was in legal offices, first with Reid, Herron & McLauchlan in Dundee and then with Duncan & Black in Edinburgh. He had reached an age at which at that time many men had founded their own professional businesses when he turned to accountancy in the employment of Lindsay, Jamieson & Haldane.

He became a partner in that firm in 1879 at a time when two of the firm's partners were involved as liquidators of the City of Glasgow Bank and pressure of work in the office was extreme.

More was of a quiet and unobtrusive disposition; of the type which would now be described as a "backroom boy". Notwithstanding that, he became a valued member of the firm and held many important appointments as auditor and as a director. He also rendered notable service to the Edinburgh Society.

He was a director of the Mersey Railway Co. and of the Scarborough and Whitby Railway, was auditor of the Cardiff Railway, and of the Royal and Union Banks and was one of the first to be appointed to audit the accounts of parish councils.

More was a member of the Council of the Edinburgh Society and from 1893 to 1903 one of the Society's representatives on the General Examining Board. He also took an interest in the affairs of the Edinburgh Chartered Accountant Students' Society and in 1900 succeeded his partner George Auldjo Jamieson as President of that Society. A paper on "Goodwill" which he contributed to the Society was published as a pamphlet and later revised and reprinted.

Outwith his professional work, More was honorary treasurer of the Edinburgh Auxiliary of the London Missionary Society, but, though repeatedly requested to do so, he declined to accept any church office.

His son Francis became a partner in Lindsay, Jamieson & Haldane and his second son was at the Scottish Bar. There were two other sons and two daughters.

PATRICK MORRISON

b. 7-viii-1825 E 1854 d. 20-x-1880

Patrick Morrison was born in Perth the son of James Morrison, who had founded the oldest accounting firm in Perth about 1827. Patrick began his training in his father's office and then moved to Edinburgh, where he was employed by Lindsay & Esson. About 1850 he began to practise in Edinburgh on his own account. He became a partner of A. T. Niven, but had to retire because of poor health.

WILLIAM MUDIE

b. G 1857 d. -ix-1904

Mudie was in business in Glasgow as an accountant from about 1845. He was the first member of the Glasgow Institute to pay the full admission fee of 50 guineas, earlier members having paid the reduced amount of 10 guineas.

He served on the Institute Council from 1882 to 1884. At about the time he was on the Council he was the manager of Scottish Savings Investment and Building Society. He resigned his membership in 1892. At that time he seems to have had some misfortune and to have been in straitened circumstances, because a donation of £25 was made to him from the Institute funds.

JAMES MUIR

b. 1839 G 1870 d. 8-xii-1898

James Muir was born in Glasgow where his father was "a much respected merchant". He was educated at the Collegiate Academy in Glasgow, an establishment run by a Dr Morrison, who subsequently practised at the English Bar. At this school he won the gold medal.

After spending a short time in his father's office, Muir went at the age of eighteen to the office of Kerr, Anderson & Brodie and remained with that firm for the rest of his life, a period of over forty years. In 1870, the year in which he became a member of the Glasgow Institute, he became a partner in Kerr, Anderson & Brodie, and also joined the Glasgow Stock Exchange Association.

He was frequently employed as an expert witness and was a witness for the Crown at the trial of the directors of the City of Glasgow Bank. He was a confident witness with a great command of language, his confidence fortified by the fact that he always prepared all detailed statements of evidence himself so as to be completely at ease during examination and under cross-examination.

Muir served more than once on the Institute Council. At the time of his death he was the senior partner of his firm.

In addition to his care for words and command of language he was a lover of art.

ALEXANDER MURRAY

b. c 1837 G 1878 d. 13-vi-1915

Alexander Murray was born at Rogart, Sutherland and educated there. As a youth he went to England and spent some years in business there, before returning to Scotland in 1865. He then came to Glasgow where he was first on the staff of the City of Glasgow Bank and then of the Glasgow Savings Bank. Only after this varied experience did he enter on an accountancy career, in the office of Robert Carswell, C.A. He became a partner of Carswell about 1873, before becoming a member of the Institute. The other partner of the firm of Carswell, Murray & Lauder was a much younger man, who did not become a member until 1900.

Murray was active in local government and became a recognised authority on local government finance. For some three years he was a member of Renfrew County Council and then in 1891 he was elected to Glasgow Town Council, of which he continued to be a member until 1910. He became City Treasurer and was the author of a number of papers on Glasgow Corporation Finance and Accounts which appeared in *The Accountant's Magazine* and in the Proceedings of the Royal Philosophical Society of Glasgow. In recognition of his public services, Murray was appointed as a Justice of the Peace and as a Deputy Lieutenant of the City.

He retained also an interest in his native county and district and was President of the Northern Highlands Benevolent Society and of the Glasgow County of Sutherland Association. He was also session clerk of Pollokshields West United Free Church and for over thirty years was appointed as a representative elder for Dornoch Presbytery to the General Assembly of the United Free Church.

Although much occupied with his extra-professional interests, Murray was entrusted with much important professional work.

DAVID MURRAY

b. -xi-1787 E 1854 d. 24-ii-1877

David Murray was already an elderly man when he became one of the early members of the Edinburgh Society. He had been in business since about 1826, having been trained in the Scottish Excise Office. That office was abolished in 1834 and Murray, who was then Deputy Controller of Excise for Scotland, thereafter devoted himself to his practice as a professional accountant. He was the last holder of the office of Deputy Controller for Scotland and another interesting link with the past was that he claimed to have spoken with a man who was alive when the Union of Parliaments took place in 1707.

His admission to membership of the Society, and that of William Myrtle, was in compliance with a wish expressed by the Lord Advocate that although they were not among the petitioners for the granting of the Royal Charter they should be assumed as members. A resolution to give effect to the Lord Advocate's wishes was unanimously approved by the Society on 29th December, 1854.

Murray was commissioner to the Earl of Fife's Trustees.

In 1904 his daughter presented to the Society a portrait enlargement made from a photograph of her father taken by O. Davis and in 1907 her executors presented to the Society a portrait of David Murray by W. Smellie Watson, R.S.A., a son of the first President of the Royal Scottish Academy but a less distinguished portraitist.

In 1905, when his last surviving daughter died there was set up under her will the David Murray Almonry Fund. The purpose of this fund was to provide for the erection of a number of cottages fot elderly men or women in decayed circumstances who had seen better days and to provide them with small annuities "but so as not to raise their total incomes above £50 per annum, excluding the value of the house". The Trustees of the Fund, which continues to operate, were to include a member of the Edinburgh Society of Accountants, and a member of the Institute of Chartered Accountants of Scotland is still appointed annually to act as a Trustee.

GEORGE MURRAY

b. E 1854 d. 19-iv-1884

George Murray, whose father was a minister at North Berwick, set up in business as an accountant in Edinburgh in 1835 and was one of the original members of the Edinburgh Society. From about 1864 he was in partnership with James Romanes as Murray & Romanes.

He was a member of the Council of the Society from 1876 to 1880.

Murray was a director of Standard Property Investment Co. Ltd.

JAMES ADAMSON MURRAY

b. A 1867 d. 1879

James A. Murray was one of the original twelve Aberdeen Chartered Accountants. His name appears in the local directory from 1857.

He served for three terms on the Council of the Aberdeen Society.

For a time he was in partnership with John Gray, who had trained with him and who was admitted as a member of the Society in the year before Murray's death. Earlier he had been a partner of Robert Fletcher, another original member of the Society, who removed to London in 1868. Murray was also a member of the Aberdeen Stock Exchange. He was the auditor of Aberdeen Heritable Securities Investment Co., one of the early local property investment companies.

ROBERT MURRAY

b. E 1854 d. 1870

Robert Murray trained with William Wood, C.A. He became assistant to the Accountant of Court, but from 1861 practised in Dundee.

He was a Trustee of Dollar Institution.

R. LEEF MURRAY

b. 31-v-1854 E 1877 d. 12-v-1916

Born the day after the petition for a Royal Charter had been signed by the 54 Edinburgh accountants who were then members of the Society, Murray was the son of William Murray, W.S. He was at Edinburgh Academy and then served a regular apprenticeship with Kenneth Mackenzie and J. Turnbull Smith.

After his admission to membership he was for a short time in Ceylon. He soon returned home, however, and from 1879 was in the service of the North British & Mercantile Insurance Co., until he retired in 1898 at an early age.

Murray was something of an athlete, being a fencer, gymnast and skater. It is recorded that, so far did the habits of these days differ from those of ours, he engaged in the last mentioned activity clad in a black coat and silk hat. He was also interested in music.

DOUGLAS MURRIE

b. E 1875 d.

Beyond the date of his admission and the fact that his membership extended to fully half a century, little or nothing is known of Douglas Murrie's activities. He appears to have practised in Edinburgh and latterly lived in Portobello.

WILLIAM R. MYLNE

b. c 1843 E 1869 d. 1927

W. R. Mylne was the son of James Mylne, W.S. He was at Edinburgh Academy from 1853 to 1860. He was an apprentice with William Moncreiff.

After some years of practice, as an accountant, Mylne assumed as a partner Wm. Home Cook and for a time the partnership was known as Mylne & Cook. Later the firm name became Wm. Home Cook & Coy. Mylne's son, James Mylne, who became a member of the Society in 1901, was a partner in that firm.

WILLIAM MYRTLE

b. 31-v-1818 E 1854 d. 22-iv-1902

William Myrtle was born in Edinburgh, the son of John Myrtle. He began business as an accountant in 1851. He was one of two men—the other was David Murray—who, though they were not members of the Society originally or parties to the petition for a charter, were admitted to membership at the special request of the Lord Advocate. Their admission was approved unanimously at the meeting of the Society held on 19th December, 1854. The reason for the Lord Advocate's interest is not known.

J. M. MACANDREW

b. 31-i-1818 E 1854 d. 2-ix-1911

J. M. Macandrew was born in Edinburgh, the son of John M. Macandrew, S.S.C., and was educated at the High School and University there. After being in the office of Francis Burke for a time he became an apprentice with Keith & Horne. Before this, however, Macandrew had shown a desire for a more active life than that of an accountant. He had an early wish to join the navy and in pursuance of that desire he, at the age of ten, ran off to Glasgow with John Tytler. Tytler's ambition for an active life was so far fulfilled that he became a general, but Macandrew had to settle for a sedentary career.

He was in business as an accountant from 1843 and he was one of 14 men who in January 1853 met and resolved to set up a society of accountants in Edinburgh. Earlier he had been a member of the Institute of Actuaries and when the Scottish members of that Institute formed the Faculty of Actuaries in 1846 he became an original member of that body.

In the early days of auditing Macandrew had an extensive audit practice, including the audits of many educational and charitable institutions, among them Edinburgh Merchant Company, of which he was the accountant and actuary, Heriot's, Stewart's and Gillespie's Trusts and Edinburgh Royal Infirmary. He was a joint auditor of the Clydesdale Bank and was the actuary for the Widows Fund of the Faculty of Advocates. He was also a director and treasurer of the Philosophical Institute of Edinburgh.

In 1874 Macandrew formed a partnership with Hugh Blair. He retired in 1888 and thereafter spent much of his time in London.

When he died he was the last of those who had attended the initial meeting at which the formation of the Society was resolved upon.

WILLIAM McBEAN

b. E 1860 d. 7-xii-1878

William McBean was an apprentice of J. M. Macandrew. He practised at one time in Dundee and later in Edinburgh.

He was the secretary and cashier of the Chalmers Hospital, Edinburgh.

JOHN C. McCALL

b. G 1875 d. 6-iv-1888

John C. McCall was from 1865 an apprentice and then a clerk with J. & W.

Graham, C.A. He subsequently became a partner in J. & W. Graham & McCall.

In 1884 an address which he had given to the Insurance and Actuarial Society of Glasgow was reprinted in pamphlet form from the transactions of the Society under the title "The Art and Practice of Account keeping". Some of the general comments he made are still of relevance. For example, he queries why it is "that so many are ignorant of the true value of figures and their relationship to each other, that they are frequently so used or so interpreted to express other than that which is fact", and provides for answer "I apprehend one reason is . . . that we . . . are guided too much by rules and too little by reason".

In 1888 McCall was elected to the Institute Council. He was then in poor health and went to the Mediterranean to seek recuperation. He died in Gibraltar from injuries received when he fell over a cliff during his holiday.

A. S. McCLELLAND

b. 1836 G 1870 d. 19-iii-1909

A. S. McClelland was the younger son of James McClelland, the first President of the Glasgow Institute. The joint lives of himself and his father covered the whole of the 19th century, his father having been born in 1799.

After being for some time as a youth in his father's office, McClelland was engaged for a time in mercantile business, and he was also local manager of the Phoenix Assurance Co. Returning to accountancy he became a partner with his father in 1866 in which year his elder brother, who had been a partner of the father, died.

One of the first important professional appointments which he received was as joint liquidator of the Western Bank.

He built up a large connection particularly in the iron and steel industry, then in a period of rapid expansion. He became a director of a number of companies in this and allied industries, including the Steel Company of Scotland, Coltness Iron Company, Dalmellington Iron Company, Clydebank Engineering and Shipbuilding Company, James Dunlop & Company and others. He was a director of the Glasgow Royal Exchange Newsroom. As a result of his wide experience of the industry, McClelland was called on to advise British shareholders on iron and steel properties in the United States and in Canada and visited these countries to inspect properties on their behalf.

McClelland was a member of the Council of the Glasgow Institute and in 1900 he was elected President, holding that office for the normal term of three years.

In 1887 he contributed a paper on "American Currency" to the proceedings of the Royal Philosophical Society of Glasgow.

Apart from his extensive business interests, McClelland led a quiet life and had a country home at Keiltour, Methven, Perthshire. He took no part in public affairs. Twice married, he was survived by two daughters.

JAMES McCLELLAND

b. 18-i-1799 G 1853 d. 24-x-1879

The name of James McClelland is in every sense one of the first names among the Chartered Accountants of Scotland. He played a prominent part in the formation of the Glasgow Institute, was its first president and did a great deal for the development of the Institute and of the profession.

McClelland was born in Ayr and educated at Ayr Academy. He came to Glasgow as a youth and was apprenticed to James Kerr in 1815. He remained with Kerr until 1824 when he set up in business on his own. For the four years from 1828 to 1832 he had a partner, Bogle, but then again for nine years he was on his own. Until 1900 there were numerous other changes in the partnership, before and after James McClelland's death, and his sons James McClelland, Jnr., and A. S.

McClelland were successively his partners. From 1901 to 1958 the firm was known as McClelland, Ker & Co. and it is now part of Arthur Young McClelland Moores & Co.

McClelland when he first started business issued a circular setting out the types of business which he was prepared to undertake. This was common procedure at that time. Most of the business specified related to insolvency, estate management or debt collection and there was no mention of auditing or taxation, though he did offer to keep and balance account books of merchants, manufacturers, shopkeepers etc. On the basis of the work then commonly undertaken by accountants, McClelland built up a substantial business and also a sound reputation so that when the question of forming a professional society of accountants in Glasgow was raised, it was natural to turn to him for leadership. He was appointed the first President of the Institute in the founding of which he had been active and he held office for eleven years, the same period as that for which James Brown, the first President of the Edinburgh Society, held office and much longer than any of their successors.

In 1860, James McClelland removed to London and retired from active professional life, though he still retained some business interests in Glasgow, including a directorship of the Glasgow and South Western Railway Co., which he held from 1852 to 1870.

Outwith the profession he took an interest in educational affairs and was one of the managers of the Andersonian University, which after intervening changes in title and function is now Strathclyde University. He was also a trustee of the Glasgow Athenaeum.

He made a serious study of bankruptcy law in which he suggested important changes. His suggestions were included in a pamphlet "Practical Suggestions for the Amendment of Portions of the Bankrupt Law of Scotland" published in 1863. In 1869 he published another pamphlet "Origin and Present Organisation of the Profession of Chartered Accountants in Scotland" which gives an interesting account of the early years of the profession as its development was seen by one who participated in and helped to direct it.

On his retirement McClelland made a journey to the Far East and published on his return "An account of a journey to India and the East".

He died in London at the age of 80 and the following year a bust of him by Moodie was presented to the Institute by his family.

JAMES McCLELLAND, JNR.

b. c 1831 G 1855 d. 29-iii-1866

James McClelland Junior served with his father's firm, then McClelland & Mackenzie, as an apprentice for four years and for about two further years as an assistant. In 1855 he became a partner with his father under the firm name of James McClelland & Son. There were two other changes in the partnership and in the firm name before he died at an early age in 1866.

James McClelland, Jnr., was, like his father, a Justice of the Peace.

ROBERT McCOWAN

b. G 1853 d. -iii-1880

Robert McCowan was in business as an accountant from about 1845. Earlier he had been employed by Robert Lamond, a solicitor. He was also a stockbroker and became a member of the Glasgow Stock Exchange Association in 1852. He was one of the young practitioners who were active in promoting the formation of the Institute.

McCowan was a member of the first committee—on the bankruptcy law—to be set up by the Institute just after its formation. He was later treasurer of the Institute from 1864 to 1880. In 1871-72 he was Vice-Chairman of the Glasgow Stock Exchange Association.

His firm were joint auditors with E. E. Scott, C.A., of Edinburgh, of the National Bible Society of Scotland. Other charities in which he was interested were the Glasgow Asylum for the Blind and Glasgow Royal Infirmary of both of which he was a director. He was secretary of Glasgow Agricultural Society.

McCowan also took some part in civic affairs and was a member of the Parochial Board of Glasgow city parish.

COLIN McCUAIG

b. 25-viii-1839 E 1864 d. 5-viii-1904

Colin McCuaig was for two years in the office of A. K. Morrison, S.S.C., before becoming, at the age of twenty, an apprentice with Mansfield & Spottiswood, C.A. After qualifying as a chartered accountant, he entered the service of the Scottish Union Insurance Co., and, having in the meantime become a Fellow of the Faculty of Actuaries, he became that company's actuary in 1890 and held that position till his death.

He was appointed as an examiner by the Society in 1891 and, on the formation of the General Examining Board in 1893, became one of the Society's representatives on that board. He was also a Trustee of the Society's Endowment Fund.

In his youth, McCuaig was a noted boxer and a golfer. Later in his life he acted as secretary and treasurer to Edinburgh Harmonists' Society.

DAVID McCUBBIN

b. G 1853 d. 4-v-1870

David McCubbin was a subscriber to the requisition addressed to senior members of the profession which led to the formation of the Institute. He had been in practice from 1847 and must have acquired some reputation as he was appointed to the committee appointed by the Institute in December 1853 to consider the amendment of the bankruptcy law. At that time he had an office towards the upper end of Buchanan Street and lived not far away in Bath Street.

ANDREW McEWAN

b. G 1853 d. 11-vi-1866

Andrew McEwan was one of those who were subscribers to the original rules and constitution of the Glasgow Institute. He had earlier been one of the original members of the Glasgow Stock Exchange Association also. He had received his training in the office of James McClelland and began business on his own account in 1834. From 1836 he carried on business as accountants and stockbrokers in partnership with William Auld.

McEwan was the first auditor of the Institute and held that office for many years. He had been selected to succeed Peter White as President of the Institute but died before his formal election to office. He had also served on the Council of the Stock Exchange Association. His partner, Auld, was better known as a stockbroker than as an accountant and in spite of McEwan's official activities on behalf of the Institute, the firm were predominantly brokers.

McEwan was a director of the Scottish Amicable Life Assurance Society.

GEORGE MACFARLANE

b. c 1809 G 1853 d. 1881

George Macfarlane was in practice from 1847 and was one of the group who took steps to promote the formation of an institute of accountants in Glasgow.

Macfarlane was for a short time a partner with John Houston, who went to London where he became a barrister.

He was a member of the Insurance and Actuarial Institute of Glasgow and in the local directory for 1855 uses the designatory letters M.I.A.G. These were possibly then of as much, or perhaps more, local significance than the recently introduced C.A.

His partnership with James Hutton which commenced in 1867 was the origin of the firm of Macfarlane, Hutton & Patrick, which continued for many years.

Hutton was on the Institute Council in 1868.

He had an interest in chess and was an extraordinary director of the Glasgow Chess Club.

ALEX. McINDOE

b. c 1856 G 1879 d. 28-ix-1919

Alex. McIndoe was one of the comparatively few who entered the membership of the Glasgow Institute through the grade of associate member which existed for some years. About 1872 he entered the office of Kerr, Andersons, Muir & Main, C.A., and in 1878 was admitted as an associate of the Institute. He became a member of Glasgow Stock Exchange Association in 1881. In 1893 he contributed a paper "On the report of Lord Herschell's Committee on Indian Currency" to the Royal Philosophical Society of Glasgow.

He was a partner in the firm of MacPhee & McIndoe.

KENNETH MACKENZIE

b. 17-vii-1812 E 1853 d. 16-ix-1880

Kenneth Mackenzie was the son of Richard Mackenzie, W.S., Deputy Keeper of the Signet, of Dolphinton, Lanarkshire. His elder brother, John Ord Mackenzie, W.S., succeeded to the Dolphinton estate of upwards of 3,000 acres in 1850. Kenneth Mackenzie was a pupil at Edinburgh Academny from 1824 to 1828 and after training as an accountant commenced business in 1837. Before the formation of the Edinburgh Society he had as partners Holmes Ivory, who died in 1855, and William Speirs, who was Mackenzie's partner for four years and was one of the early managers of Scottish Amicable Life Assurance Society. Later partners were George Todd, C.A., and J. Turnbull Smith, C.A.

Mackenzie was treasurer of the Edinburgh Society from its formation until 1863 and was thereafter twice a member of the Council.

He was also treasurer of the Edinburgh Academy and an active member of the Academical Club. He, with Robert Balfour, another original member of the Society, was one of the small group of Academicals who in 1854 assumed financial responsibility for the provision of the cricket field at Raeburn Place, Edinburgh, one of the first and at the time by far the largest of school playing fields in Scotland.

He was an associate of the Institute of Actuaries and his insurance connections included National Reversionary Investment Co., of which he was a Scottish director, Accident Insurance Association of Scotland Ltd., of which he was a director, and Edinburgh Life Assurance Co., of which he was auditor.

He was a director of the Royal Maternity Hospital, treasurer of the Royal Dispensary and Vaccine Institution and honorary treasurer of Edinburgh Original Ragged Industrial School Association.

WALTER MACKENZIE

b. 23-iv-1817 G 1853 d. 24-i-1898

Walter Mackenzie was the only man ever to serve two separate terms as President of one of the Scottish associations of Chartered Accountants, though three others have been President of The Institute of Chartered Accountants of Scotland after having occupied the chair of their local society before the amalgamation. He is also one of a small number of presidents whose sons in turn came to occupy that office.

He was a Dunbartonshire man, the son of Robert Mackenzie of Caldarran, who was a sufferer from asthma and died when his son Walter was only eight. Walter was educated at Dumbarton Academy and then, at the age of fourteen, proceeded to Glasgow University where for three sessions he attended classes in Latin, Greek, Mathematics and Philosophy. In 1835 he went to the office of James McClelland and in 1841 was assumed as a partner by McClelland, 18 years his senior. He was invited to become the manager of the Glasgow branch of one of the Scottish Banks but decided that he would prefer to remain in the accountancy profession. In 1855 McClelland assumed his son James McClelland, Jnr., as a partner and Mackenzie retired from the firm and formed a new partnership with Robert Aitken.

This partnership lasted till 1870 when Aitken retired and his son, R. Easton Aitken, and Hugh B. Barclay became partners. Six years later, Barclay in turn retired and Mackenzie's son Robert, afterwards Sir Robert, joined the partnership. In 1893 Walter Mackenzie himself retired, though he remained an officer of the Institute until his death.

Walter Mackenzie was an original member of the Glasgow Stock Exchange Association and his firm had a large stockbroking business, all the early partners being members of the Association. Indeed during each of Walter Mackenzie's terms as President of the Institute one of his partners, during the first term, Robert Aitken, and during the second term, R. Easton Aitken, was chairman of the Glasgow Stock Exchange Association.

Mackenzie's services to the Institute were many: he was secretary from 1853 to 1867, President from 1867 to 1870 and again from 1890 to 1894 and treasurer from 1894 to 1898. Any gaps between the holding of these offices were largely filled by membership of the Council. On completion of his second term as President, he was presented with his portrait.

Mackenzie had a large and varied professional practice. He undertook much bankruptcy business, one of his most notable appointments in this field being as liquidator of the European and Australian Royal Mail Co. He had also great experience in railway work and was at one time auditor of five railway companies, including two of the main Scottish companies, the North British and the Glasgow & South Western. In association with James Wyllie Guild, who was at the time joint auditor, he carried out a complete investigation of the finances of the North British Railway Co.

He was for a time chairman of Glasgow Royal Exchange and was a director of the Liverpool, London & Globe Insurance Co.

In 1888 Mackenzie and Wyllie Guild were the joint treasurers of the Glasgow International Exhibition.

In 1852 Walter Mackenzie married his cousin Elizabeth Campbell, a daughter of Sheriff Alex. Campbell of Barnhill, Dunbartonshire. Their son became a chartered accountant and in 1920-1922 as Sir Robert C. Mackenzie, K.B.E., C.B., D.L., followed his father as President of the Institute.

In 1873 Mackenzie purchased the estate of Edinbarnet in Dunbartonshire. The house which he built there was burned down but he rebuilt it immediately.

In his later years his health was not so good as earlier and he spent some of the winters in the South of France. While health permitted, he was a keen angler.

He was also a good churchman and was an elder in Park Church, Glasgow and in Old Kilpatrick Church, near his home at Edinbarnet. He presented a pulpit to the latter church.

Mackenzie took no direct part in civic affairs, but he was a Justice of the Peace for both Dunbartonshire and Lanarkshire.

GEORGE B. McKIM

b. G 1879 d. 14-viii-1915

George McKim was for about five years in the office of Reid & Mair, C.A., and then from around 1877 in practice in Glasgow in partnership with his elder brother Thomas.

He served for a term on the Council of the Institute and was also one of the Institute's representatives on the General Examining Board.

Politics claimed much of his time, though he never aspired to the parliamentary field. He was connected with the administration of the first Glasgow International Exhibition in 1888 and was also a member of the executive of the first East End Exhibition, from the surplus on which the People's Palace on Glasgow Green was built.

Music was another interest and McKim had a long connection with Glasgow Choral Union, of which he was in succession secretary and president.

THOMAS McKIM

b. c 1851 G 1879 d. 4-vii-1904

After twelve years as a clerk with Black & Robson, Thomas McKim joined his brother George in 1877 and set up in practice as accountants as T. & G. B. McKim. Two years later the brothers applied for membership of the Glasgow Institute and were admitted in 1879, their numbers on the membership roll being 140 and 141 respectively.

Thomas McKim took a great interest in Sunday School work and was for many years honorary treasurer of the Scottish National Sabbath School Union. He was, however, of a retiring nature and took no part in Institute or other public affairs.

WILLIAM MACKINNON

b. G 1867 d. 7-v-1891

William MacKinnon was employed in the office of Dugald McPhail & Co., cotton spinners. This firm failed in 1856 and, in connection with the winding-up, MacKinnon met James McClelland. McClelland, impressed by his ability, engaged him under a five year service contract. On the expiry of that contract, MacKinnon was given an interest in profits and at a later date became a partner, the firm name from 1872 being McClelland, MacKinnon & Blyth. The name MacKinnon continued to figure in the title until 1900, though William MacKinnon had then long been dead.

MacKinnon was a member of the Institute Council from 1879 to 1881. On his death in 1891 a special resolution of regret was passed by the Council.

J. L. McKIRDY

b. G 1853 d. 1856

J. L. McKirdy had been in business since 1844, first as a partner in Carrick & McKirdy and then on his own account. In 1846 he became a member of the Glasgow Stock Exchange Association. He did not long survive after the foundation of the Institute of which he was an original member. The only Carrick noted among the early accountants was in business from 1820 to 1840, according to the directory, so McKirdy may merely have succeeded to his name. Nothing further is known of him and he may have been one of those who at that period had their careers cut short by an early death.

DAVID McLAGAN

b. 9-x-1824 E 1854 d. 30-iii-1883

David McLagan was the son of Dr David McLagan. He was educated at Edinburgh High School and at the age of 16 he entered the employment of the Scottish Union Insurance Co. His career was rather that of insurance official, than accountant, something not entirely unusual among the early members of the Edinburgh Society. At 23 he became manager of the Insurance Company of Scotland. Then in 1862, having in the meantime joined the newly formed Society of Accountants in Edinburgh, he went to London as secretary to Alliance Assurance Co. His absence from Edinburgh was not prolonged. In 1866 he returned there as manager of Edinburgh Life Assurance Co.

McLagan was also an associate of the Institute of Actuaries.

DAVID MACLEAN

b. G 1870 d.

David Maclean was in business as an accountant and stockbroker from 1864 in partnership with his brother William. They were the sons of William Maclean, one of the original members of the Glasgow Institute.

WILLIAM McLEAN

b. G 1853 d. 19-ii-1893

William McLean was in business as an accountant and stockbroker in Glasgow from about 1842. He became a member of the Glasgow Stock Exchange Association in 1845 and for many years he was the secretary of the Association. Although he took an active part in promoting the formation of the Institute he did not thereafter play any part in its administration. He was well known in connection with a number of civic activities.

Two sons were chartered accountants and stockbrokers.

WILLIAM McLEAN, JNR.

b. G 1869 d. 15-ix-1893

William McLean, Jnr., was a son of William McLean, C.A., but like his father was more involved in Stock Exchange affairs than in accountancy. He did, however, serve a term on the Institute Council.

He was in partnership with his brother David from about 1863 as accountants and stockbrokers and in that year became a member of the Glasgow Stock Exchange Association. He was chairman of the Association in 1882-83 and again in 1885-86.

Although the brothers had similar business interests to their father they were never directly concerned in his business.

William McLean, Jnr., was interested in a number of charities and was a director of Glasgow Royal Infirmary and of the Glasgow Highland Society.

He survived his father by only a few months.

ROBERT MacNAIR

b. 17-iv-1855 E 1879 d. 21-v-1904

Robert MacNair was the eldest son of Rev. Dr James MacNair, minister of Canongate Parish Church. He was educated at Edinburgh Academy and as a youth he spent four years in the office of Scottish National Insurance Co., before becoming an apprentice with A. & J. Robertson, C.A.

Shortly after he became a member of the Society he joined the Edinburgh Stock Exchange. Thereafter he devoted his attention to stockbroking almost exclusively.

As a young man he was well known as a cricket and football player, and played cricket for Scotland against Australian and English elevens. For some years before his death, under the age of fifty, he was in poor health.

Possibly because he was known as a stockbroker rather than as an accountant, his name is not included in Richard Brown's list of Scottish Accountants deceased before 1905.

WILLIAM McNAUGHTON

b. G 1853 d. 5-ii-1864

William McNaughton was in business in Glasgow as an accountant from 1846 in partnership with Dundas Hamilton. They were both signatories to the letter requesting the senior accountants in the city to consider the formation of an association of accountants. McNaughton was a member of the original Committee or Council of the Institute. The partnership seems to have been dissolved about 1856 and Hamilton later became secretary of Glasgow Gas Light Co.

ARCHIBALD McNICOLL

b. G 1853 d. 19-iii-1894

Archibald McNicoll was in practice in Glasgow from 1848. He had previously spent six years as an apprentice and clerk in an accountants office. He was for a short time a member of the Glasgow Stock Exchange Association.

After becoming a member of the Institute he was appointed a member of the committee set up in December 1853 to consider possible amendments to the bankruptcy law.

He went to London in 1854 and seems to have remained there until his death 40 years later.

JAMES McOMISH

b. G 1878 d. 18-ii-1891

James McOmish was for five years a clerk with McCowan & Houston, C.A., and for four years with Thomson, Jackson, Gourlay & Taylor before becoming a member of the Institute. He was afterwards in partnership with his brother John, who became a member of the Institute in 1886, practising as J. & J. McOmish.

DAVID MacRITCHIE

b. 16-iv-1851 E 1877 d. 15-iv-1925

David MacRitchie was the youngest son of W. D. MacRitchie, M.D., of the East India Company's service, and Elizabeth, elder daughter of John MacRitchie, Writer. He was educated at Edinburgh Southern Academy, Edinburgh Institution and Edinburgh University. He trained as an accountant with C. & D. Pearson, C.A., but after his admission as a member of the Society did not practise at all.

MacRitchie was associated with almost every Edinburgh society that had for its object the intellectual life or the betterment of the poor and needy of the city. He was especially interested in antiquarian and ethnological subjects and published several books as well as contributing to scientific journals, to encyclopedias and to magazines. Among his books were "Ancient and Modern Britain", "The Gypsies in India", "Fauns, Fairies and Picts", "Scottish Gypsies under the Stewarts" and "The Savages of Gaelic Tradition".

MacRitchie was a confirmed bachelor but a great favourite in Edinburgh society.

He was, as might be expected in a man of his interests, a Fellow of the Society of Antiquaries of Scotland.

WILLIAM W. NAISMITH

b. c 1856 G 1879 d. 27-ix-1935

William Naismith was one of the few men who became members of the Glasgow Institute having first been admitted as an associate. He was also one ot the first to become an associate. He served a five year apprenticeship with McClelland, MacKinnon & Blyth and when applying for admission stated his "desire to qualify by undergoing the examination to be held on 16th October, 1879". He was already an associate at that time.

Naismith spent his whole business career with the County Fire Office and retired about 1915.

After his retiral he gave much of his time to the affairs of various missionary societies and was on the committees of a number of such societies. He was also Western Treasurer of the National Bible Society of Scotland.

He was a keen walker and mountaineer and so late as 1934 when he was 78 published a book on "Islands of Scotland" in which he dealt with his subject from the hill climber's angle. Naismith was also interested in antiquities, was a Fellow of the Society of Antiquaries of Scotland, and contributed a number of papers to that society's transactions.

A. T. NIVEN

b. E 1854 d. 1918

A. T. Niven was a son of the manse and had many family connections in the ministry. His father was parish minister of Balfron and his two grandfathers, one great grandfather, an uncle and two brothers were all ministers. One of his brothers was Moderator of the General Assembly of the Church of Scotland in 1906. He himself was an elder of the church for the remarkably long period of over 60 years.

He founded the firm of A. T. Niven & Co. in Edinburgh. Among those who trained in his office was G. A. Touche, later Sir George Touche, who founded the firms of G. A. Touche & Co., in London and Touche, Niven & Co., in New York. Niven's son, John B. Niven, was a partner in the latter firm, and all three firms are now incorporated in the international firm of Touche, Ross & Co.

Niven was secretary or director of a number of Edinburgh companies in connection with one of which he set a most remarkable record. This was the Edinburgh Railway Access & Property Co., which he helped to promote in 1853 and of which he was manager and secretary until his death. The objects of the company were to provide easier access between the Old and the New Towns by the formation of Cockburn Street. Niven attended 66 successive annual general meetings of the company.

In 1904 Niven was one of only three original members of the Edinburgh Society who were able to attend the Jubilee Dinner and from 1912 he was the sole survivor of the original members.

He was for 53 years a member of Edinburgh Presbytery and was interested in a number of religious societies, including the Scottish Protestant Association, of which he was honorary treasurer, and the improbably named Scottish branch Society for Irish Church Missions to Roman Catholics, of which he was honorary secretary.

At the Society's Annual General Meeting on 7th February, 1912 it was resolved to send to Niven a special message of greeting and congratulations, he being then the sole survivor of the original members of the Society. A few years later, in 1915, when, to mark the 60th anniversary of his ordination as an elder of the church, Niven was entertained to a luncheon and a presentation made to him, he was able in his reply to claim that he was the senior chartered accountant in the world.

ERIC M. NOBLE

b. E 1871 d.

Eric M. Noble was the son of the Rev. Andrew Noble, minister of the Free Church of Scotland at Louden, Ayrshire. He was a member of the Edinburgh Society for only four years. Admitted to membership in 1871, after serving an apprenticeship with Richard Wilson, C.A., he resigned in 1875.

JAMES J. OGILVY

b. E 1854 d. -iv-1876

Beyond the fact that he had been in business as an accountant from 1849 nothing is known of James J. Ogilvy's career.

JOHN OGILVY

b. 8-vii-1830 E 1855 d. 1894

John Ogilvy, son of John Ogilvy of Forfarshire, served as an apprentice with David Robertson Souter, Inchewan, who was in practice from about 1832. Nothing is known of his subsequent career except that he seems to have returned to his native area and probably practised in Dundee.

JOHN S. OGILVY

b. E 1854 d. 12-xii-1871

John S. Ogilvy was one of the original members of the Society, having attended the second meeting of promoters at which the resolution to proceed with the formation of the Society was passed. As with other early members bearing the same surname, no details of his career (beyond the fact that he emigrated to Australia) are known.

ARTHUR O'KELL

b. G 1877 d.

Arthur O'Kell was for seven years an apprentice and then a clerk with McClelland Son & Co., and the successor firm of McClelland, MacKinnon & Blyth. After admission to the Institute he was a partner with Alexander Finnie Young in the firm of O'Kell & Young.

ROBERT L. OLIPHANT

b. 5-iii-1841 E 1864 d. 12-i-1866

Robert L. Oliphant was a son of Robert Oliphant, W.S., of Rossie, a property near Forgandenny in Perthshire, which had been in the Oliphant family since 1583. Young Oliphant attended Edinburgh Academy from 1850 to 1852 then went to Loretto and subsequently to Edinburgh University, where he took an M.A. degree. He was then apprenticed to George Auldjo Jamieson and was admitted as a member of the Edinburgh Society at the age of 23. He died, however, only two years later.

DAVID E. OUTRAM

b. G 1853 d. 23-x-1893

David E. Outram was one of those who participated in the movement to promote the formation of a professional association of accountants in Glasgow. His early experience was obtained in the Bank of Scotland in Edinburgh, where on his own report he had up to 1845 been "employed in every department". He then came to Glasgow and set up as an accountant and stockbroker and he became a member of the Glasgow Stock Exchange Association in 1847. He took no active part in the management of the Institute but was chairman of the Stock Exchange Association in 1881/1882. He had an interest in chess and was an extraordinary director of Glasgow Chess Club.

DAVID F. PARK

b. 20-x-1848 E 1873 d. 11-v-1921

David F. Park was born at Tynefield, Dunbar, the son of David Park of Hedderwick and his wife Mary Irving Scott.

After schooling at Loretto and Edinburgh Academy he became an apprentice with R. & E. Scott, C.A. He also qualified as an actuary and was a Fellow of the Faculty of Actuaries.

The whole of Park's professional career was spent with Credit Foncier of Mauritius in London, whom he joined as an accountant in 1875 and from whose service he retired in 1908. Not long after going to London, he was in 1878 prizeman for the Gilbart Lectures on Banking at King's College, London. He was also the author of a treatise on Bank Accounting.

Park was twice married. Each of his wives was the daughter of a man with Indian connections. The first was the daughter of John Balfour, who was Inspector General of Hospitals H.M. Indian Army, while the second was the daughter of Thomas C. Glover, C.E., Bombay. The only son of the first marriage predeceased his father, but three children of the second survived him.

The estate of Blegbie in East Lothian belonged to the family, and in his early days Park hunted regularly with the Lothian Hounds. He was a Fellow of London Zoological Society and was especially interested in birds. After his retiral he returned to Scotland. He was latterly a keen golfer and in addition to being a member of the Royal and Ancient Club was a member of two leading English golf clubs—Royal St George's and Royal Wimbledon.

John Smith, C.A., first President (1867-69) of The Society of Accountants in Aberdeen. This portrait hangs in the Hall of The Society of Advocates in Aberdeen, of which John Smith was twice President
(Portrait by Sir George Reid, P.R.S.A.)

George Marquis, C.A., President (1869-71) of the Aberdeen Society

Alexander Brand, C.A., President (1871-73) of the Aberdeen Society

James A. Sinclair, C.A. (later 16th Earl of Caithness), President (1873-75) of the Aberdeen Society

Robert Fletcher, C.A., President (1875-77) of the Aberdeen Society

William Lunan, C.A., President (1877-79) of the Aberdeen Society

James Meston, C.A., Secretary and Treasurer (1867-92) of the Aberdeen Society

ANDREW PATERSON

b. 1821 E 1855 d. 25-ii-1900

Andrew Paterson was a pioneer of heritable investment companies. At one time also he was extensively employed on remits from the Courts and was trustee in some large sequestrations.

He was the manager of Heritable Securities & Mortgage Investment Association Ltd., from its formation in 1862, immediately after the passing of the 1862 Companies Act, until his retiral in 1890.

ANDREW M. PATERSON

b. E 1854 d. 1861

Andrew M. Paterson commenced business as an accountant in 1852, and on the formation of the Edinburgh Society became one of the original members. His whole business career, however, was relatively short.

ROBERT PATERSON

b. c 1850 G 1877 d. 11-v-1918

From about the age of fifteen Paterson was an apprentice with Alexander Moore, C.A. He remained with Moore's firm of Moore & Brown until he became a member of the Institute. He then formed a partnership with Joseph F. Newlands as Paterson & Newlands. Newlands was not a member of the Institute and seems to have been a son of William Newlands of T. & W. Newlands & Co., merchants.

Paterson took a prominent part in civic and public affairs. He was a member of Glasgow Town Council and of the City Parochial Board and a Justice of the Peace. He was also a member of the Board of Management of Glasgow Royal Infirmary and a Governor of the Technical College. A Liberal in politics, he stood as a Parliamentary candidate for the College division. He gave up his public work about 1903.

For the long period of 32 years, Paterson held a commission in the 5th Argyll & Sutherland Highlanders (Volunteers) retiring with the honorary rank of lieutenant-colonel.

He was an elder in St Enoch's United Free Church.

CHARLES PEARSON

b. 1803 E 1854 d. 17-x-1884

Charles Pearson was the founder of a notable family of Edinburgh chartered accountants, which even earlier had other professional members notable in their own spheres and later had other similar connections.

His father, David Pearson, was Depute Secretary to the Board of Excise and his father in turn had been Secretary of the Scottish Board of Excise. When Charles was a boy the family lived opposite Sir Walter Scott. Charles Pearson was educated at Edinburgh High School and University. He then trained as an accountant with James Brown, who became the first President of the Society. Pearson later became Brown's partner.

The offices of Brown & Pearson from 1835 to 1847 were at 94 George Street, where Brown had lived since 1816, with the offices on the ground floor. In 1847 the firm moved to 128 George Street, where Pearson had his winter residence. A former apprentice recalled that, when Pearson lived at 128 George Street, the dining room was used as such for breakfast and dinner, but between, during the business day, was the cash room.

In 1863 Pearson's eldest son, David Pearson, who had become a member of the Edinburgh Society the previous year, became his partner. Brown died the following year. After Charles Pearson's death, the firm of C. & D. Pearson amalgamated with R. & E. Scott under the latter name.

Charles Pearson gave notable service to the Society. He was an examiner for 18 years, served for three terms on the Council and was President from 1876 to 1879. His son followed him in the presidential chair nearly 20 years later. Charles Pearson was a director and auditor of Standard Life Assurance Co. Ltd., at a time when such a dual appointment was possible. He was also a director of Heritable Securities & Mortgage Investment Association Ltd. The firm of C. & D. Pearson were agents for Chartered Mercantile Bank of India.

Two of Pearson's younger sons were in the legal profession and one of them became a Court of Session Judge.

DAVID PEARSON

b. 1-x-1838 E 1862 d. 17-xi-1926

David Pearson was a son of Charles Pearson, who had been in practice in Edinburgh from 1835. He was educated at Edinburgh Academy and University and then became an apprentice with his father, by then a chartered accountant. In the same year as he was admitted as a member of the Society, David Pearson became a Fellow of the Faculty of Actuaries.

David Pearson became a partner of his father in 1863 and they carried on business as C. & D. Pearson. Following the death of Charles Pearson in 1884, C. & D. Pearson amalgamated with R. & E. Scott, the partners of the newly constituted firm which carried on under the latter name being David Pearson, T. Bennet Clark and John Dalziell.

David Pearson, like his father, became President of the Edinburgh Society, serving in that office from 1898 to 1901.

David Pearson's son, Charles, was also a chartered accountant as were two members of the next generation of the family.

For many years Pearson was one of the managers of the gardens on the banks of the Water of Leith. He took a great interest in the birds which came there and compiled a list of them.

He was a member of the Royal Company of Archers for some years and was also a Justice of the Peace.

DONALD S. PEDDIE

b. E 1854 d.

Donald Peddie was the second son of Rev. James Peddie, D.D. He commenced business in 1831, after having trained with David Paterson who practised as an accountant in Edinburgh for some years, but left about 1829 to take up a position with the Treasury. Peddie was one of the original members of the Edinburgh Society, but resigned his membership in 1883. He may then have retired from business.

J. CAMPBELL PENNEY

b. 18-vii-1851 E 1877 d. 25-ii-1920

J. Campbell Penney was the son of Lord Kinloch, a Court of Session Judge. He was educated at Edinburgh Academy and St Andrews University. He served as an apprentice with Lindsay, Jamieson & Haldane and after qualifying became a partner of Francis A. Bringloe, who had also been with Lindsay, Jamieson & Haldane but was some five years older than Penney. Bringloe and Penney built up a good business and then in 1890, the Judicial Factors (Scotland) Act, 1889 having combined the offices of Accountant of Court and Accountant in Bankruptcy, the latter was appointed Accountant of Court.

Penney married a daughter of Mr Gresham Gourlay, and his brother-in-law, K. M. Gourlay, was also a chartered accountant, to whom Penney's middle son, Colin, was apprenticed. J. Campbell Penney had five sons, three of whom served in the Forces during the 1914-1918 war, all winning the M.C. During that war Penney was appointed Custodian of Enemy Property in Scotland. The family connection with the accountancy profession continued in the next generation.

He was an excellent shot and a good golfer and was a member of the Royal & Ancient Club, the Honourable Company of Edinburgh Golfers (Muirfield) and the Burgess Golf Club. While at school and university he was a notable rugby player, and in 1870 was involved in the formation of the Edinburgh Wanderers Club.

Penney was an elder in St Stephens Church.

JAMES POLLARD

b. 24-v-1845 E 1873 d. 26-ix-1901

James Pollard was born in Dublin but spent nearly all his life in Edinburgh. Before entering on a formal apprenticeship to John Scott Moncreiff he had been for some years in the office of his firm then Scott Moncreiff & Thomson. He began practice almost immediately after the expiry of his apprenticeship and was joined in a year or two by his brother, William Pollard. They had a good business but James Pollard devoted a great deal of his time to civic affairs. He was a magistrate of the city of Edinburgh and was convener of the town council's public health committee. He took a very direct interest in the work of that committee and was a constant visitor to the City Hospital where it was said that he knew every patient, nurse and servant. He also visited hospitals and similar institutions on the Continent, especially in Germany where, as he had an excellent knowledge of German, he was able to learn personally a great deal about their organisation and methods. Pollard was a widely read man and a good speaker and he published a number of papers on public health and other matters as a result of his experience at home and abroad. Those included a study of the government of the city of Berlin. Pollard was a fellow of the Royal Statistical Society and of the British Economic Society.

Towards the end of his life, George Bird, who became a member of the Society in 1898, was assumed as a partner and it is indicative of James Pollard's standing in the profession that, after his death when the partnership was carried on by his brother William and Bird, the firm name adopted was James Pollard & Bird.

Pollard was a member of the Council of the Society from 1894 to 1898. He was secretary of Edinburgh Chamber of Commerce, and his firm were the managers of Alliance Heritable Security Co. Ltd.

WILLIAM POLLARD

b. c 1851 E 1875 d. 9-v-1905

William Pollard was an apprentice to Charles W. Thomson, C.A., to whose partner his elder brother, James, had been apprenticed. The brothers practised in partnership as J. & W. Pollard until James Pollard died when, George Bird having been previously assumed as a partner, the firm name became *James* Pollard & Bird.

William Pollard was a captain in the Edinburgh City Artillery Volunteer Corps.

CHARLES PRENTICE

b. E 1868 d. 23-ii-1892

All that is known of Charles Prentice is that he was the son of John Reid Prentice who lived at 6 Warriston Crescent, Edinburgh and that before becoming a member of the Edinburgh Society he had been an apprentice of George Murray, one of the original members of the Society.

JAMES PRINGLE

b. E 1870 d. 30-viii-1926

Pringle was born at Elgin where his father was minister of the United Presbyterian Church. He attended Elgin Academy and then, for two sessions, Aberdeen University. Coming to Edinburgh, he was apprenticed to R. & E. Scott. After becoming a chartered accountant, Pringle became a member of the Edinburgh Stock Exchange in 1873 and also qualified as a Fellow of the Faculty of Actuaries in 1874.

He did not practise as an accountant, but became a partner in John Robertson & Co., Stockbrokers, and also acted as a director of a number of companies. He retired from his stockbroking firm in 1896. During his lengthy retirement he travelled extensively and made two trips round the world.

He was for 34 years chairman of Scottish Lands and Buildings Co. Ltd., and was a director of the Scottish New Zealand Investment Co. For three years he was a member of Edinburgh School Board and he took an interest in church affairs and in the temperance movement.

Pringle could not be described as an outdoor sportsman, but he was a keen walker until his mobility was restricted by rheumatism. His other recreation was chess.

On his death Pringle left large charitable bequests mainly connected with his native town of Elgin. The principal of these, a fund which is still in existence, was a large sum to be administered by Elgin Town Council, the income from which is divided among Presbyterian, Congregational and Baptist ministers in the County of Moray.

MOSES PROVAN

b. G 1862 d. 21-ii-1871

From about 1846, Moses Provan was chief clerk with D. & A. Cuthbertson, reputedly the oldest firm of accountants in Glasgow. The story of his admission to membership of the Institute is somewhat confused. His letter of application for membership was dated 15th December, 1856 and was addressed from D. & A. Cuthbertson's office. The application was approved but Provan apparently did not in fact take up his membership and pay his admission fee till 1862. When he did so the fee paid was ten guineas, the sum originally fixed, and not 50 guineas which was the rate current in 1862.

Provan was a captain in the 5th Lanark Rifle Volunteers in the 1860's. He was also a director of the Glasgow Athenaeum.

He became a partner with his former employers and the firm's name eventually was D. & A. Cuthbertson, Provan & Strong.

Provan succeeded his senior partner as secretary and treasurer of Gartnavel Hospital.

ROBERT RAINIE

b. 7-xii-1818 E 1860 d. 29-iii-1882

Robert Rainie was the son of William Rainie who was an accountant in Edinburgh from 1832 to 1850 and he was trained in his father's office. His grandfather, David Rainie, had been Dean of Guild in Aberdeen.

Robert Rainie, who was also an actuary, was the secretary of the Life Association of Scotland. His son, R. D. Rainie, was also a chartered accountant and was a partner of John Brewis, C.A., who was his brother-in-law.

SAMUEL RALEIGH

b. 8-i-1815 E 1854 d. 26-vii-1882

Samuel Raleigh was an apprentice and later a partner from 1846 to 1857 of Archibald Borthwick. Later, with Borthwick and his future partner Martin, he was among the eight who attended the inaugural meeting of the Society in A. W. Robertson's office.

Raleigh was one of the liquidators of the Western Bank. He was an actuary as well as a chartered accountant and from 1859 till his retiral in 1881 was manager of the Scottish Widows Fund.

The first committee appointed by the newly formed Society was on the bankruptcy law, and Raleigh was convener of that committee. He also served the Society as an examinator from 1855 till his death.

GEORGE RAMSAY

b. 1809 E 1854 d. 1887

George Ramsay was a son of Thomas Ramsay and a grandson of Sir James Ramsay of Banff.

He commenced to practise as an accountant in Edinburgh in 1838. He was also an actuary and was manager of the Scottish Union Insurance Co.

PATRICK RATTRAY

b. c 1844 G 1868 d. -v-1914

Patrick Rattray commenced practice on his own account in Glasgow in 1867, having spent four years as an apprentice and a further four years as a clerk with Alexander Moore, C.A. He was afterwards in partnership for a few years with John Wilson, C.A. and after that partnership was dissolved had as a partner his brother, David Rattray (G 1881). This partnership later became Rattray Brothers, Alexander & France, and eventually part of Coopers & Lybrands. Patrick Rattray retired about 1909 and then lived in Dunblane.

He was a prominent Clyde yachtsman and owner at different times of a number of vessels of various sizes including the steam yacht "Colonsay" and, for one season, the famous cutter "Bloodhound" which had originally belonged to the Marquis of Ailsa. In 1892 Rattray was Rear-Commodore of the Royal Clyde Yacht Club.

JOHN C. REID

b. G 1853 d. 6-viii-1894

John C. Reid was employed for ten years by James Gourlay. Among his fellow clerks was William Tolmie and in 1852 these two became partners in Tolmie & Reid, when Gourlay relinquished the greater part of his business to them. Afterwards, Reid was in partnership with James Galt as Reid & Galt.

Reid was one of those who suggested to the senior accountants in Glasgow that the formation of a professional association would be desirable. He served on the Council of the Institute from 1868 to 1870.

He was secretary and deputy treasurer of the Commercial Travellers' Society of Scotland, which had been founded by James Gourlay.

ROBERT REID

b. c 1843 G 1875 d. 3-iii-1907

Robert Reid was a native of Kirkintilloch. He practised in partnership with R. A. Mair as accountants from about 1871. The firm of Reid & Mair, C.A., still carries on in Glasgow. Robert Reid's younger son was senior partner of the firm for many years.

Reid's original training was in legal offices in Edinburgh and Glasgow, and he was for a time in the legal department of the City of Glasgow Bank. This early training and experience especially equipped him to deal with the insolvency work with which he was mainly concerned when he came to practise professionally.

Reid served twice on the Council of the Institute and although of a rather retiring disposition became well-known in business circles in Glasgow. He was a Justice of the Peace both for Dunbartonshire and Lanarkshire.

WILLIAM REID

b. G 1856 d. 1863

At the time of his admission to membership of the Institute William Reid was in the employment of White & Gairdner, C.A. He spent about ten years in all with that firm. A short time before his death he resigned his membership.

ARCHIBALD JOHN RENNIE

b. A 1876 d. 1885

Archibald J. Rennie served as an apprentice with George Marquis. Following this he had been in practice in Aberdeen for fully five years before he became a member of the Society and he was almost immediately elected to the Society's Council, of which he was a member in 1877 and 1878.

His name is not included in Richard Brown's 1905 list of deceased Scottish accountants though he was dead before the end of the century and must have been well known in Aberdeen. He was Vice-Chairman of Aberdeen Co-operative Property Investment Company, auditor of Aberdeen Theatre and Opera House Co. Ltd. and a joint auditor of Aberdeen & District Tramways Co.

WILLIAM RICHARDSON

b. A 1876 d. 1885

William Richardson was the son of William Richardson, keeper of the Aberdeen Courthouse. He served under a regular indenture of apprenticeship with James Meston, and was later Meston's clerk and cashier. He was one of the first two men to be admitted as members of the Aberdeen Society after examination.

His name does not appear in Richard Brown's list, and nothing is known of his career. He was probably in his early thirties when he died.

ALEXANDER RITCHIE

b. G 1853 d. 15-xii-1860

Alexander Ritchie was in the employment of James Gourlay from 1847 to 1852. When Gourlay gave up his practice in 1852, Ritchie apparently did not share in the disposal of it, or at any rate not to the same extent as John Reid and William Tolmie, his fellow clerks. He did, however, then become a partner with James Thomson in Thomson & Ritchie. While employed with Gourlay, Ritchie had been engaged mainly on bankruptcy work. In 1859 he became a member of the Glasgow Stock Exchange Association.

ALEXANDER WEIR ROBERTSON

b. 21-i-1819 E 1854 d. 17-i-1879

Alexander Weir Robertson came from a family of lawyers and founded a family of chartered accountants. His father, James S. Robertson, was a Writer to the Signet as his father in turn had been, and one of James Robertson's brothers, Patrick, was a judge. A. W. Robertson's two sons were chartered accountants, as were a grandson and a great grandson.

A. W. Robertson was educated at Edinburgh Academy and was then apprenticed to Archibald Bruce. His indenture was transferred to Patrick Cockburn, but this cannot have been because of Bruce's death as he survived till 1849. Cockburn, however, died in 1837 and the young apprentice was transferred to Donald Lindsay to complete his training. He set up on his own account in 1842.

Robertson acted as secretary to the committee which promoted the formation of the Society. The meeting at which it was resolved to proceed with the scheme was held in his office. He was the first secretary of the Society, holding that office until 1863. He then became treasurer and retained that position until his death.

Robertson's father was a director of the Scottish Widows Fund and he himself had some insurance connections. It was perhaps his father's advice or influence which prompted him to become a Fellow of the Faculty of Actuaries as well as a chartered accountant. Two insurance companies of which he successively acted as manager—Experience Life Assurance Co., and Minerva Life Assurance Co.—were taken over by the Standard Life Assurance Co.

In the early days of his practice, Robertson acted in a large number of remits from the Courts.

His two sons, James A. Robertson-Durham and Patrick C. Robertson, both became partners in A. & J. Robertson, the latter not until after his father's death.

His wife was a daughter of Rev. John Ramsay of Gladsmuir, who was notable among other things as a curler.

CHARLES ROBERTSON

b. E 1855 d. -x-1903

Charles Robertson was a son of Major Robertson of Kindace, Ross-shire, but was educated partly in Edinburgh at the Academy. Although he became a member of the Society in the early days of its existence, having been an apprentice with Maitland & Wood, Charles Robertson had little interest in accountancy. He was in business for a short time only and then retired to the family estate of Kindace, to which he succeeded in 1868 and where he lived for many years. He was a Justice of the Peace and a Deputy Lieutenant of Ross and Cromarty.

J. A. ROBERTSON-DURHAM

b. 15-vi-1848 E 1870 d. 1909

J. A. Robertson was the son of Alexander Weir Robertson, the first secretary of the Edinburgh Society. His great grandmother, Janet Durham, was the heiress of Boghead and Foulshiells, Linlithgowshire, which were in the hands of her husband, Alexander Weir, in right of his wife. About the end of the century, Robertson succeeded to the estates and assumed the additional surname of Durham. He was educated at Edinburgh Academy and trained as an accountant in his father's office. He later became his father's partner in the firm of A. & J. Robertson.

The liquidators of the City of Glasgow Bank employed young Robertson on investigation work. In 1880 he made his first appearance in Court as an expert witness and thereafter his services in that capacity were constantly in demand.

Robertson-Durham also had a large audit connection which included two of the main Scottish banks, the Church of Scotland and many large companies. He was a director of the Commercial Union Assurance Co., and other companies and was manager of the Scottish Reversionary Co.

In 1884 he visited America to report on the affairs of the Arizona Copper Co. Ltd.

In addition to his multifarious professional activities, Robertson-Durham was also active in public affairs and church matters. From 1890 to 1896 he was a member of Edinburgh Town Council, from 1905 to 1907 he was a member of Bathgate Parish Council and at the time of his death he was a County Councillor for the County of Linlithgow. He became an elder of St Stephen's Church in Edinburgh while still under thirty and for a period of twenty years he represented Crail at the General Assembly of the Church of Scotland.

To the Society too he rendered notable service and in 1907 was elected President. He died before his term of office was complete

In 1874, like many other early Edinburgh accountants, he became a Fellow of the Faculty of Actuaries. Earlier than that he had been a member of the University Boat Club and won many trophies during the period 1869 to 1874. He was also a member of the Speculative Society at the same time as R. L. Stevenson.

Another of his interests was the Volunteer movement. He was commissioned in 1871 and 20 years later retired as a Lieutenant-Colonel. In the meantime he had become a member of the Royal Company of Archers.

Robertson-Durham was one of the first to make Saturday a regular day of leisure. He never attended at his office on that day. Until 1899 he spent most of his leisure time at Gullane, being a keen golfer.

He was a member of several Golf Clubs and in the early nineties was captain successively of the Gullane and Luffness Clubs.

After he succeeded to the Linlithgowshire estates he spent much time there.

In late life, following the example of his grandfather, the Rev. John Ramsay of Gladsmuir, he became a keen curler and was Vice-President of the Royal Caledonian Curling Club in 1903.

His eldest son was his partner for ten years.

JAMES CONSTABLE ROBERTSON

b. 1849 G 1878 d. 28-ii-1932

J. C. Robertson was the son of a farmer in Strathardle. As a youth he went to Dundee and trained as an accountant in the office of William Stiven. Stiven, although he had been in practice from 1856, like the majority of the Dundee practitioners of the time, did not become a member of any of the chartered bodies until the nineties, when a number of them were admitted to membership of the Glasgow Institute under a special rule. The career of his apprentice, Robertson, took a different course and he was the first Dundee practitioner to join the Institute, though even by 1878 he had had 14 years' experience in accountants' offices in Dundee, Bristol and Glasgow. Dundee always looked on him as its own and in 1923 he was entertained to a public dinner to mark his 60th anniversary as an accountant in the city—the reckoning obviously being from the commencement of his service with Stiven.

From 1873 to 1875 he was a partner in Kerr, Anderson & Co., in Glasgow, but in the latter year Robert Moody Stuart, a member of the Edinburgh Society who had commenced practice in Dundee in 1869, invited Robertson to return to that city as his partner, thus originating the firm of Moody Stuart & Robertson.

Robertson had a number of family connections with Dundee. An uncle, Donald Farquharson, was for 30 years Police Treasurer, and Finlay Farquharson, another uncle, was for an even longer time cashier in the city treasurer's office. Robertson, himself, was for seven years a member of Dundee Town Council during which he was, in 1917, City Treasurer, and he was also a member of the School Board. During the 1914-1918 war he was chairman of the National War Savings Committee for Dundee and his services were recognised by the award of the M.B.E.

Professionally he had a large and varied practice. Moody Stuart had been the first auditor of the Dundee Water Commission, and Robertson succeeded him in this appointment, to be succeeded in turn by his son. From its inception about 1882, he was the secretary of the Texas Land and Cattle Co., and repeatedly visited the United States on that company's business. Like other similar companies, this company was eventually wound up but, unlike many of the others, the liquidation produced a satisfactory return for the shareholders. He was also a director of British Canadian Trust Ltd., and auditor of a number of large Dundee investment trusts.

A zealous church worker, Robertson was for 40 years Sunday School superintendent and for a long period session clerk of Ogilvie United Free Church.

He was twice a member of the Council of the Glasgow Institute.

His son, Lewis F. Robertson, succeeded him as senior partner of Moody Stuart & Robertson. His eldest son predeceased him by over ten years.

LAURENCE ROBERTSON

b. G 1855 d. 31-xii-1893

Laurence Robertson was the son of a banker of the same name, who was manager of the Royal Bank of Scotland in Glasgow. He served for four years as an apprentice with McClelland & Mackenzie and then remained with them for a further two years before setting up his own business in which he was joined as a partner in 1859 by his brother, R. Hope Robertson. The firm were mainly known as stockbrokers, and both brothers were chairmen of the Glasgow Stock Exchange Association, Laurence on three occasions.

In spite of his Stock Exchange interests, Laurence Robertson was also active in the administration of the Institute and served twice on the Council. He was largely responsible for placing the system of examinations on a satisfactory basis before the establishment of the General Examining Board. He was also active in matters relating to the Institute's rules and suggested the introduction of the grade of associate member which existed for a number of years.

When a committee was set up in 1867 to consider the use of the Institute's funds and the question of a Widows' Fund, Laurence Robertson was appointed convener.

R. HOPE ROBERTSON

b. G 1862 d. 7-i-1903

Hope Robertson was a chartered accountant by virtue of his membership of the Glasgow Institute but he had a legal training and his professional career was spent in stockbroking. His father, Laurence Robertson, was manager of the Royal Bank of Scotland.

He served a five-year apprenticeship in the legal offices of Bannatyne & Kirkwood and then spent two years as a clerk with Dundas & Wilson in Edinburgh. In 1859 he became a member of the Glasgow Stock Exchange Association and entered into partnership with his brother, Laurence.

He was twice chairman of the Stock Exchange Association, first in 1892-93 and again in 1900-01.

Robertson was a member of the Royal Northern Yacht Club and for a time was secretary and treasurer of the club. He was also treasurer of the Glasgow Highland Society.

Unlike his brother, Hope Robertson took no part in Institute affairs.

He was an elder in Free College Church, Glasgow.

T. C. ROBERTSON

b. c 1847 G 1877 d. 1-iv-1887

At the time of his admission to membership of the Institute, T. C. Robertson had been for seven and a half years a clerk with Macfarlane & Hutton, C.A. A few years afterwards he began business on his own account, but he died suddenly in St Enoch Station, Glasgow, at the early age of 40.

T. EATON ROBINSON

b. c 1848 G 1878 d. 9-ix-1926

T. Eaton Robinson was born in Yorkshire, but came to Glasgow as a boy and was educated there. After attending Glasgow University he entered the office of John Gourlay. He had been with him for ten years and subsequently for fully a year with Thomson, Jackson, Gourlay & Taylor when he applied for and was admitted to membership. In 1883 he was appointed City Accountant, and the next year became City Registrar of Glasgow. When he retired in 1923 he had thus been in the service of the Corporation for 40 years.

Robinson was for 29 years an officer in the Volunteers, serving in the 17th (Accountants) company of the 1st Lanarkshire Rifle Volunteers. He retired from the service with the honorary rank of major, and was the holder of the Volunteer Decoration. He was interested in various charities and for over twenty years was honorary secretary of the Widows Friend Society of Glasgow.

Robinson was married and had two sons, the younger of whom was killed in action in 1916.

GEORGE ROBSON

b. c 1801 G 1853 d. 2-ii-1881

George Robson was a partner in Black & Robson and began practice in 1849. He was one of those active in the formation of the Institute. In 1853, also, he became a member of the Glasgow Stock Exchange Association.

He built up a large clientele whose confidence and respect he commanded. He also had the respect and confidence of his fellow members of the Institute, who elected him as President in 1876. Ill health, however, compelled him to resign the presidency before completion of his full term of office. At the same time he resigned his membership of the Institute.

Robson was a brother of the well-known preacher, Dr Robson of Wellington Street U.F. Church.

J. H. W. ROLLAND

b. 17-xi-1848 E 1871 d. 31-xii-1917

J. H. W. Rolland was born near Sydney, N.S.W., where his father, Dr Rolland, who had gone to Australia for health reasons, was farming. Dr Rolland died while his family were still young, and Mrs Rolland returned with them to this country. J. H. W. Rolland was educated at Christ's Hospital, London and at Edinburgh University. He then served his apprenticeship as an accountant with Lindsay, Jamieson & Haldane, C.A., and it is interesting to note that part of his apprenticeship fee was paid by the Governors of Christ's Hospital. Shortly after becoming a member of the Society, Rolland was assumed as a partner by G. T. Chiene, C.A.

In 1880, by which time he had also qualified as an actuary, he was appointed Edinburgh secretary of the Standard Life Assurance Co. In 1892 the company moved him to London as their general secretary and he eventually became manager in London. When for health reasons he was compelled to retire in 1912 he continued to live in London, though he spent most of his winters abroad.

Until his health prevented this, Rolland spent most of his holidays shooting or golfing in Scotland. He liked to keep alive his Scottish associations and was always pleased to welcome old Scottish friends at his home in Chelsea.

Rolland had a family of one son and three daughters, the son being a chartered accountant in London.

CHARLES S. ROMANES

b. c 1852 E 1877 D. 1922

Charles Romanes was born in Russia. He came to Edinburgh as a young man and studied at Edinburgh University before becoming a member of the Society. In 1878 he was secretary of the Scots Law Society.

In 1884 he formed a partnership with C. J. Munro which, under the name of Romanes & Munro, established for itself a prominent place in the profession in Edinburgh. Romanes is reported as having been untiring in his attention to business.

Romanes was greatly interested in antiquities and antiquarian lore. He was a Fellow of the Society of Antiquaries of Scotland and treasurer of the Scottish History Society. He published books and papers on antiquarian subjects including "A History of the Dallas family" and "The Cauls of Norfolk". In pursuit of his historical interests he carried out excavations at Coldingham Priory near his country house, Buckingbarn, Coldingham, and he bought the ancient Norham Castle.

Romanes was a Justice of the Peace for Berwickshire.

JAMES ROMANES

b. 1837 E 1864 d. 24-iv-1914

James Romanes was the third son of John Romanes, a writer and bank agent in

Lauder. He first attended the local school but then went on to Edinburgh High School and Edinburgh University.

Returning to Lauder he was for a time in his father's office before beginning a regular apprenticeship with Lindsay & Jamieson (later Lindsay, Jamieson & Haldane). Soon after becoming a member of the Society he joined George Murray and for a time they practised as Murray & Romanes. After Murray died in 1884 the firm name was changed to Romanes & Aitchison, R. S. Aitchison having joined the partnership some years before.

Romanes and his partners had a good practice with many important audits and he was also involved in the liquidation of some large companies. He was a director of several companies and as a director of the Scottish American Mortgage Company for 30 years paid many visits to the United States.

Romanes was fond of country life, was a keen shot and angler and spent much of his time at his property, Harewood Glen, Selkirkshire. Later, he lived in Melrose where he indulged his interest in horticulture, showing his produce successfully both locally and in Edinburgh. He also became a member of Melrose Town Council, a Commissioner for Income Tax for Roxburghshire and a Justice of the Peace for Selkirkshire.

Earlier in his life he was a member of No. 6 (Accountants) Company of the Queen's Rifle Volunteer Brigade and was present at the Royal Review in 1860.

He served on the Council of the Society from 1893 to 1897.

Among his other attributes Romanes was credited with a special gift for story telling and possessed a great fund of humorous anecdote.

PETER RONALDSON

b. 14-viii-1848 E 1870 d. 3-xii-1914

Peter Ronaldson was born in County Tipperary but was brought up in Edinburgh and at the age of 16 became an apprentice to Howden & Molleson, C.A. After his admission to the Society he qualified as a Fellow of the Faculty of Actuaries in 1872.

He was particularly interested in and knowledgeable about matters connected with land and the country and contributed an article on Farm Book-keeping to the Encyclopaedia of Accounting published in 1903. A partner in the firm of Ronaldson & Flett, he acted as actuary to the Edinburgh Reversionary Co., and he was a director of the Commercial Union Assurance Company.

Not long before his death, Ronaldson was called on to act as arbiter in a somewhat unusual case. This arose from the annexation of Broughty Ferry by the City of Dundee. As a consequence of this offices previously held by the Chief Constable of Broughty Ferry were extinguished and their holder claimed compensation. It fell to Ronaldson as arbiter to determine the appropriate compensation.

For 23 years Ronaldson was an officer in the Haddington Rifle Volunteers, retiring with the rank of major.

He was an office-bearer in the United Free Church of Scotland. For about thirty years he was a member of Edinburgh Chamber of Commerce, and he served on the Council of the Society from 1898 to 1902.

His death took place in rather tragic circumstances, while he was accompanying a son who was in the Canadian Forces to the railway station during the early months of the 1914-1918 war.

WILLIAM ROSS

b. c 1845 E 1869 d. 24-xii-1914

William Ross, a son of John Ross, S.S.C., was admitted to membership of the Edinburgh Society after having been an apprentice with Kenneth Mackenzie, C.A. He spent some seven or eight years in practice in Edinburgh and then went to the Far East. He was the first chartered accountant to go to Japan, but he went not as an accountant but as a merchant. He was in business as a merchant in Yokohama until after the end of the century, when he retired. He subsequently lived at Minehead, Somerset. He had family connections in the legal profession and for a time his address was c/o J. & J. Ross, W.S.

WILLIAM RUSSELL

b. E 1854 d. -xi-1871

William Russell spent nearly half a century in practice in Edinburgh, having set up in business in 1825. He was an original member of the Society.

WILLIAM SAUNDERS

b. E 1871 d.

Beyond the date of admission to membership of the Edinburgh Society, nothing is known of William Saunders' career. His father was William Saunders, S.S.C., and William Junior was an apprentice with the first secretary of the Society, A. Weir Robertson.

ROBERT SCOBIE

b. G 1853 d. 1857

Robert Scobie was in practice from 1847. For ten years before then he was a clerk and cashier with Alexander Rankin & Co., wholesale warehousemen.

Although when the Institute was founded he had been practising as an accountant for six years, he was apparently not well known among the city's accountants. Consideration of his letter of application for membership was postponed for a few weeks to enable enquiries to be made as he was not personally known to any member of the Institute's original Council.

For about ten years he was a member of a partnership under the name of Flint & Scobie.

DAVID SCOTT

b. 22-xii-1830 E 1855 d. 5-v-1898

David Scott was the son of Andrew Scott, W.S. He served as an apprentice with D. S. Peddie, but not a great deal is known of his subsequent career. He was auditor of, among presumably other companies, the Property Investment Company of Scotland Ltd., and he was joint treasurer of the National Bible Society of Scotland.

He was a member of the Council of the Society from 1879 to 1883.

EBEN E. SCOTT

b. 3-v-1839 E 1861 d. 10-vi-1897

E. E. Scott was the son of R. E. Scott, C.A., trained in his father's office and then became his partner.

Father and son took their Christian names from two of their Roxburghshire forebears, the well-known divines Ralph and Ebenezer Erskine.

The firm of R. & E. Scott, which later amalgamated with C. & D. Pearson, had an extensive connection among financial concerns and Eben E. Scott was a director of the Scottish Provident Institution and of a number of public companies.

He had a number of charitable interests and was a director of Donaldson's Hospital. He was also joint auditor of the National Bible Society of Scotland with Robert McCowan, C.A., of Glasgow and was a Church of Scotland elder.

In 1869 he became a Fellow of the Faculty of Actuaries and in 1870 published a book of tables of logarithms to five places. He was on the Society's Council from 1887 to 1891.

RALPH ERSKINE SCOTT

b. 27-xii-1804 E 1854 d. 7-v-1887

R. E. Scott, a member of the first Council of the Society, was in practice from about 1836. After some 25 years on his own he was joined by his son and the business continued as R. & E. Scott. R. E. Scott built up a substantial connection and he was a director of a number of insurance and other companies. One of these was the Edinburgh and Leith Gas Light Company.

Apart from his business connections Scott was a Trustee of the Dollar Institution and was on the Board of the National Bible Society of Scotland.

He served on several occasions on the Council of the Society and was President from 1879 to 1882.

He had originally been trained with David Paterson, an early Edinburgh practitioner, who left the city in 1829 to take up a Treasury appointment.

THOMAS SCOTT

b. 26-vi-1797 E 1854 d. 1883

Thomas Scott was one of the comparatively few early members who were born before the end of the 18th century. He was the son of a minister of Newton. After training with James Brown he began to practise in 1823. His son later joined him in business. Scott was a member of the original Council of the Society and altogether served five terms on the Council.

THOMAS SCOTT, JNR.

b. 1833 E 1855 d. 24-iv-1910

Three Thomas Scotts appear in the early membership lists of the Edinburgh Society. This, the middle one in point of age, was described when he became a member as Thomas Scott, Jnr., but later dropped the use of the junior after the death of his father in 1883. The father was one of the original members of the Society. Thomas (2) was educated at Edinburgh Academy and was probably trained in his father's office. Certainly in 1899 he occupied the same office as his father had earlier used at 17 Hill Street. He also, being unmarried, had the same home address in Gayfield Square. He played golf at St Andrews and at Musselburgh. He was a member of the Council of the Society in 1884-1887. In 1882 another Thomas Scott was admitted to membership of the Society. This third Thomas, described in 1899 as Junior, had then an address in San Jose, Costa Rica. It seems possible that he was a grandson of the original, and used the "junior" to distinguish himself from his C.A. uncle.

H. K. SHIELLS

b. 1856 E 1879 d. 4-viii-1917

H. K. Shiells was one of the founders of the well-known Edinburgh firm Scott Moncreiff, Thomson & Shiells. His father, John Lyall Shiells, was an Edinburgh merchant.

During his training Shiells won the Society's bursary for success in the third year examination in 1875.

He became a member of the Council of the Society in 1899 and from 1906 he was one of the Society's representatives on the General Examining Board.

JAMES AUGUSTUS SINCLAIR (Earl of Caithness)

b. 31-v-1827 A 1867 d. 1891

James A. Sinclair, son of Colonel J. S. Sinclair, R.A., was one of the twelve original members of the Aberdeen Society and was, according to the standpoint taken, the first chartered accountant to be a peer or the first peer to be a chartered accountant. Sinclair was accountant first and peer later.

He was in practice in Aberdeen from 1850 till 1890. In the latter year he was adjudged heir to the earldom of Caithness which had fallen into abeyance on the death of the 15th earl in 1889. He did not live long to enjoy his new status as he died in London in 1891, to be succeeded as the 17th earl by his son, John, whose mother was Janet Macleod, daughter of Roderick Macleod, M.D., of London.

Sinclair had trained as an accountant with Archibald Borthwick whose family were also concerned in a succession claim to an old Scottish peerage. While in practice in Aberdeen he was agent for the Bank of Scotland and seems to have regarded himself, and been regarded by the community, primarily as a banker, for he was so described in most directory references in which his name appeared. He held some important audit appointments, however, including Northern Insurance Company and, jointly, the Great North of Scotland Railway Company. He was also clerk to the J.P. Court and was a director and a trustee of Aberdeen Heritable Securities Investment Company.

Sinclair was on the Council of the Aberdeen Society in 1867, 1868, 1876 and 1877 and was President from 1873 to 1875.

ALEXANDER SLOAN

b. 1843 G 1867 d. 18-xii-1928

Alexander Sloan had a long and distinguished connection with the Glasgow Institute and with the life of the city as a whole. He was the second son of David Sloan of William Sloan & Co., shipowners, Glasgow. His maternal grandfather was the last provost of the burgh of Calton, before it was absorbed by Glasgow. His grandmother was a Tennant of Glenconner, Ochiltree, of whose father Robert Burns wrote—

"My heart warm love to guid auld 'Glen'
The ace and wale o' honest men".

The second line could well have been applied to "Glen's" great-grandson and to his son in turn.

Alexander Sloan served an apprenticeship of four years with Mitchell & Watson, C.A., remained with them for a further year and then was for two years with J. Wyllie Guild, C.A. When he applied for membership the existing 59 members were all in practice in Glasgow, but Sloan himself was still a clerk. In the circumstances, the Council took six months to consider whether to accept his application.

In the year following his admission to the Institute, Alexander Sloan became a member of the Glasgow Stock Exchange Association, and the firms of A. & C. T. Sloan and Alexander Sloan & Co., continued to carry on the combined business of accountants and stockbrokers for fully 50 years. For a time his brother Charles T. Sloan was his partner but when he resigned from the firm the name was changed from A. & C. T. Sloan to Alexander Sloan & Co.

Sloan's part in the administration of the Institute's affairs began in 1873 when he was appointed secretary. He held this position for 36 years and when he resigned from it in 1909 he was elected President and his son, D. Norman Sloan, succeeded him as secretary, holding the office until 1940 when he in turn was elected President.

When Alexander Sloan was appointed secretary in 1873 the membership of the Institute was 67; when he relinquished the office in 1909 it was 575.

When Richard Brown, his then contemporary as secretary of the Edinburgh Society, published his "History of Accounting and Accountants" to mark the jubilee of the granting of the first Royal Charters, Sloan collaborated with him in the writing of some of the chapters and in the compilation of the notes on deceased Glasgow accountants. In 1905 also he was presented with his portrait, painted by Alexander Roche, R.S.A., and subscribed for by the members. A replica was hung in the Institute's hall.

Alexander Sloan was one of the Institute's original representatives on the General Examining Board and later also on the joint committee of the chartered bodies in the United Kingdom.

He did not take part in civic affairs as

such but was interested in several charitable organisations and was secretary and treasurer of the Royal Botanic Institution of Glasgow. He was for a time a Volunteer officer, attaining the rank of major in the 4th Lanarkshire Rifle Volunteers.

He participated at various times in a number of sports. In a notice written for the *Glasgow Herald* on his death, Dr David Murray categorised his sporting achievements thus: Fisher—enthusiastic, Golfer—fair, Skater—fine, Curler—keen, Diver and Swimmer—notable. Dr Murray does not mention cricket and it could be that Sloan's interest in this sport was mainly on the administrative side. He was for a time treasurer of the West of Scotland Cricket Club.

Active till the end of his long life, Alexander Sloan died a few days after he had attended a luncheon (at which he had become unwell) to mark the taking over by the Western Infirmary, of which he was for many years auditor, of the David Elder Hospital.

CHARLES TENNANT SLOAN

b. G 1873 d.

C. T. Sloan was a brother of Alexander Sloan but had by no means such a notable career. He started his accountancy career by spending a year with Auld & Guild and then was a clerk with his brother for five years before becoming a member of the Institute. He was for some years a partner with his brother in A. & C. T. Sloan and was for five years, from 1873 to 1878, a member of the Glasgow Stock Exchange Association.

ADAM DAVIDSON SMITH

b. c 1848 E 1872 d. 20-xii-1932

Adam Davidson Smith was born in Inverness-shire. His father, Charles Smith, was the factor of Whittingehame. He was educated in Edinburgh at the High School, the Edinburgh Institution and the University. He then was an apprentice with Kenneth Mackenzie. He practised on his own until 1906 when his son became a partner and the firm name of A. & C. M. Davidson Smith was adopted.

Adam Smith was one of the first county auditors appointed under the 1889 Act. He served as an examiner for the Society and was also a member of the Council from 1888 to 1892. He was later invited to become President but declined on health grounds. Notwithstanding this doubt about his health he lived to an advanced age and he was described as a robust man physically and mentally and forthright in expression.

He was a keen curler, was secretary of the Royal Caledonian Curling Club and he figures in Martin Hardie's picture of the 1899 Carsebreck Bonspiel.

Smith was an elder in Morningside Parish Church.

ADAM GILLIES SMITH

b. 1827 E 1855 d. 8-i-1900

Adam Gillies Smith was born at Dreghorn, the son of the Rev. Robert F. Smith, who was in turn minister of Brechin and then of Old Machar Cathedral, Aberdeen. He had links with all the three cities which promoted the first chartered bodies of accountants, for he attended Aberdeen University, was trained in Edinburgh and became a member of the Society there, and was in practice for a short time in Glasgow.

He was an apprentice with Donald Lindsay. For a time he was assistant to the Accountant in Bankruptcy. He then spent part of 1860 as a partner in James McClelland & Co., in Glasgow, but returned to Edinburgh in that same year to set up on his own account.

He had as partners William Moncreiff and F. J. Moncreiff and had some substantial audit connections, which included Standard Property Investment Co. Ltd., and Scottish and New Zealand Investment

Co. Ltd. He was also employed professionally in an action by the liquidators of the Western Bank against the firm of Baird.

In 1880 he retired from practice and became manager of North British & Mercantile Insurance Co. He held that position until 1894 when he retired and went to live in North Berwick.

Smith was a man of wide literary and general culture, keenly interested in the study of political economy, to which in his retirement he devoted much of his time. He also took part in the local affairs of his retirement home, North Berwick.

He was twice a member of the Council of the Edinburgh Society and was an examinator during the years 1887 to 1891.

His only son died young soon after being called to the Bar.

JAMES SMITH

b. G 1854 d. 18-vii-1880

James Smith spent about nine years as a book-keeper and cashier with various legal firms in Edinburgh before moving to Glasgow in 1851, where he set up as an accountant. In 1857 he extended his activities to stockbroking and became a member of the Glasgow Stock Exchange Association. Things seem to have gone unfavourably for him, however, for in 1873 he gave up his Stock Exchange membership and he also ceased to be a member of the Institute, having allowed his subscription to fall into arrears.

JOHN SMITH (1)

b. c 1797 A 1867 d. 5-v-1884

John Smith, one of the twelve original members of the Aberdeen Society and its first President, was born at Woodside, Aberdeen. He was the son of John Smith who was the manager of a firm of calico printers. He completed his education at Marischal College, Aberdeen, where he graduated M.A. in 1813 at a very early age. Smith then trained in law as an apprentice with John Ewing, advocate in Aberdeen, and was then for a time with a legal firm in Edinburgh. He returned to Aberdeen and in 1819 was admitted as a member of the Society of Advocates in Aberdeen. At the time of his death he was the senior member and President of that Society, having also been President on an earlier occasion. Until 1831 he designated himself as an advocate; then, like a number of his near contemporaries, he began to designate himself "accountant".

Smith had as partners first James Blaikie and then John Blaikie. He was a director of Aberdeen Town & Country Bank, of the Scottish Provident Assurance Company and of other companies. He was also manager of the National Security Savings Bank.

After serving as President of the Society, Smith was on several occasions a member of the Council.

For some years John Smith was factor for the Milne Bequest Trustees and he wrote a "Memoir of John Milne, M.D., founder of the Milne Bequest".

He died in Paris.

JOHN SMITH, C.B. (2)

b. 9-vii-1837 E 1861 d. 25-ii-1922

John Smith, an early member of the Edinburgh Society, had a career which ranged widely both geographically and in occupation. His father was supervisor of Inland Revenue in Edinburgh, but the young John was born at Bedale, Yorkshire. Apart from that accident of birth he was an Edinburgh product, being educated at the High School and University there and apprenticed to C. M. Barstow.

Soon after he qualified as a chartered accountant, Smith was sent to America to represent a body of creditors in a liquidation and he travelled extensively through the United States on this business. His next move, in 1863, took him to the East where he joined the Bank of Bombay. The bank was forced into liquidation a few years later by the American cotton failure and Smith was appointed to act as liquidator. The liquidation was completed in 1868 and he then returned home.

For a time after his return he was in business in Hull. He was the founder and first chairman of the London & Yorkshire Bank.

Chamberlain's Bankruptcy Act of 1883 called for changes in the system of supervision of the administration of insolvent estates, and Smith was invited to take charge of the department set up for this purpose as the first Inspector General in Bankruptcy. This appointment took effect from 1st January 1884, and in 1890, following changes in the Companies Acts, he became also Inspector General in Companies Winding-up. The two offices were severed in 1904 and Smith then retired, his services having been recognised by the award of the C.B.

On his retiral he was entertained at a farewell dinner presided over by Mr Gerald Balfour, President of the Board of Trade, who paid tribute to his work in setting up what had been a new department and in contributing to the changes introduced by the Companies Acts of 1890 and 1900.

Although retired from the public service Smith remained active. He was chairman of a trust company until increasing deafness compelled him to relinquish all business.

In his retirement he lived in Croydon where he called his house "Dunedin". Smith was a keen angler. His elder son, a doctor, predeceased him. His other son was a barrister.

J. TURNBULL SMITH

b. 5-viii-1843 E 1867 d. 20-x-1929

J. Turnbull Smith's father was the schoolmaster at Kilbucho, Peeblesshire, and later at Dolphinton, Lanarkshire. He came to Edinburgh in his youth as an apprentice to Kenneth Mackenzie, C.A., and so impressed him by his ability that Mackenzie made him a partner even before he became a member of the Society. Mackenzie died in 1880 and Smith then carried on alone, He had a large general practice but nevertheless found time for other interests.

In 1883 he was elected as a director of the Life Association of Scotland, and when the manager of the Association died two years later his fellow directors asked Smith to become his successor. He thereupon gave up general practice and allocated his professional appointments to members of his staff, recommending their services to the clients. Three separate firms were founded as a result of this arrangement and two of the members of staff involved eventually became Presidents of the Society.

While still in practice, Smith had become a Fellow of the Faculty of Actuaries. He had also been secretary of Edinburgh University Club, secretary and treasurer of the Royal Maternity Hospital and was connected with other charities. He had a long interest in church affairs, was an elder in St Bernard's Parish Church, a member of the General Assembly for 30 years, and for some years was convener of the General Business Committee of the Assembly. His portrait by Fiddes Watt, R.S.A., is in the church offices. He had a particular interest in Church re-union and lived to see this effected in 1929, he having been born in the year of the Disruption.

While manager of the Life Association of Scotland Smith was also for many years a director of the Bank of Scotland. He was chairman for three years of the manager's association of the Scottish Life Offices.

Apart from the church, Smith's other great interest was education. He was for long a member of Edinburgh Merchant Company, of which he was Master in 1891-1893 and concerned himself largely with the educational work of the Company. In 1897, Edinburgh University conferred on him the degree of LL.D. in recognition of his services to education. He was also appointed a Deputy Lieutenant of the City.

In 1908 Smith retired from business and went to live in Peebles.

WILLIAM HENRY SMITH

b. E 1863 d.

Only the fact that he became a member of the Edinburgh Society in 1863 is known of W. H. Smith. He is not mentioned by Richard Brown though he probably died in the early 70's having been for some years previously in Glasgow

DAVID R. SOUTER

b. E 1854 d. 10-xi-1888

David R. Souter was in practice from about 1832 when he succeeded his uncle, J. Robertson Chaplin. He later had as a partner, from 1848, Thomas Robertson Chaplin, who was presumably also a relative. Souter was an original member of the Society and an early member of the Council. He subsequently took the name of Souter-Robertson.

JAMES T. SPENCE

b. 18-iv-1837 E 1865 d. 16-iii-1888

James T. Spence served for two years with Maclachlan & Ivory, W.S., before becoming an apprentice to Samuel Raleigh. His father appears to have died while he was a boy and an older brother was agent of the Commercial Bank of Scotland at Musselburgh. Nothing is known of his later career, except that some ten years after his admission he was in London.

NATHANIEL SPENS

b. 1850 D 1871 d. 1935

Nathaniel Spens was a son of William Spens, a prominent Glasgow citizen, and a nephew of J. A. Spens of Maclay, Murray & Spens, solicitors. In the same year that he became a member of the Glasgow Institute he also joined the Glasgow Stock Exchange Association.

He was one of the first applicants for membership of the Institute to produce, with his letter of application, a certificate showing that he had passed the prescribed examinations. He was for five years a clerk with Auld & Guild, C.A., then a partner in A. H. & J. Graham. Later, until 1890, he was a partner in Grahams, Crum & Spens.

He served on the Institute Council from 1885 to 1887. In 1890 he withdrew from Grahams, Crum & Spens, resigned from the Stock Exchange and went to London as chairman and managing director of Stock Conversion Trust Ltd. He held these offices till 1928 and was also actively involved in the direction and management of a number of finance and investment companies and with railway finance. Companies of which he was a director included Franzpoort Exploration Co. Ltd., of which he was chairman; City Property Investment Trust Corporation Ltd.; London Scottish American Trust Ltd.; Second London Scottish American Trust Ltd.; and United States Debenture Corporation. He was also a trustee of London Midland & Scottish Stock Conversion Trust.

Spens was a member of the Royal Company of Archers. His great-grandfather, Dr Nathaniel Spens, who died in 1815, had been adjutant general of the Archers and had his portrait by Raeburn hung in the Archers' Hall. An engraved print of this portrait hangs in Chartered Accountants' Hall, Edinburgh.

In 1892 Nathaniel Spens unsuccessfully contested the Govan division as a Conservative candidate. His son, W. P. Spens, K.C., was more successful and became Member of Parliament for Ashford.

ROBERT SPOTTISWOODE

b. E 1854 d. 14-xi-1876

Robert Spottiswoode, a native of Perthshire, was one of the original members of the Edinburgh Society. He was in partnership with Thomas Mansfield and T. J. Mansfield.

Spottiswoode was a member of the Council of the Society from 1869 to 1873.

WILLIAM STEELE

b. A 1867 d. 1870

William Steele, who was one of the twelve founders of the Aberdeen Society, was in practice in that city from 1852. He was secretary of Aberdeen Trade Protection Society. In the year of his death he was a member of the Society's Council.

GEORGE STEVENSON

b. 23-viii-1845 E 1871 d.

George Stevenson's father was a doctor in the East India Company's service. He was educated at Edinburgh Academy and soon after admission to membership he emigrated to New Zealand in 1872. There he spent about twelve years as accountant to two commercial concerns, but from 1884 took up farming in the Poverty Bay District.

GEORGE DUKE STIRLING

b. G 1877 d. 1913

George D. Stirling was for some years a clerk with Wilson & Rattray, C.A., then continued with John Wilson, C.A., when his partnership with Rattray was dissolved. He was assumed as a partner by Wilson in 1885, the firm at first being known as John Wilson & Stirling, but after the assumption of other partners, some years later, as Wilson, Stirling & Co. Stirling was the secretary or a director of a number of land or property companies. He was also appointed in 1889 to be auditor of the Parish of Cathcart. On Wilson's retiral in 1912 he became senior partner of the firm but died the following year.

DAVID STRATHIE

b. 1851 G 1878 d. 1925

David Strathie was born in Glasgow but was educated at Ayr Academy, his parents having settled in that area. He started his career as a clerk with D. G. Hoey with whom he spent some six years. He then went to Edinburgh where he was with Andrew Paterson, C.A., for about a year. Around 1876 he returned to Glasgow and was in the employment of Moore & Brown, C.A.

Strathie founded the firm of David Strathie & Co., which after about ninety years merged with Kerr, Macleod & Macfarlan. Before this he was for a short time a partner of John Dalgleish, an Edinburgh C.A., who had come to Glasgow. He was a director of a number of industrial companies, including United Collieries Ltd., and Glenfield & Kennedy Ltd., being chairman of the latter.

He served on the Council of the Glasgow Institute, represented the Institute on the General Examining Board on its inauguration, and was elected President of the Institute in 1918.

In 1892 he published a pamphlet on "Fixed Machinery".

From 1900 to 1912 Strathie was treasurer of the Congregational Union of Scotland.

One of his three sons, Arthur C. Strathie, was a chartered accountant and a partner in David Strathie & Co.

J. ROXBURGH STRONG

b. G 1870 d. 1-xi-1899

J. Roxburgh Strong was a son of Rev. David Strong, Dailly. A brother, W. Robertson Strong, was also a chartered accountant. Two other brothers were ministers, one in Hillhead, Glasgow, the other in Melbourne, Australia.

Strong started as an apprentice with McEwan & Auld. After four years as an apprentice he remained with them as a clerk for a further five years and then from

1866 to 1870 was managing clerk with the successor firm of Auld & Guild. In 1870 he became a partner of Moses Provan, who was then sole partner of D. & A. Cuthbertson. The firm name became D. & A. Cuthbertson, Provan & Strong and when Provan died, Strong carried on as sole partner.

J. R. Strong was several times a member of the Institute Council and in the year before his death he was appointed auditor of the Institute.

W. ROBERTSON STRONG

b. G 1878 d. 29-ix-1911

W. Robertson Strong was a younger brother of J. Roxburgh Strong, their father being minister of Dailly. Before becoming a member of the Institute, he was for seven years with Andrew Bannatyne and then for four years with Moore & Brown, C.A. For some years he was in business as an accountant in Glasgow. He then emigrated to Australia, where another brother was a minister in Melbourne. He settled first in Brisbane and then moved to Melbourne, practising as an accountant in these cities.

Some years before his death, he returned to Britain for health reasons and was living in Bedford at the time of his death. He married a daughter of William Church.

CHARLES EDWARD STUART

b. E 1876 d. 21-iv-1884

Charles E. Stuart was an apprentice with Wood & Hanna. He died young.

ROBERT MOODY STUART

b. 17-iii-1846 E 1868 d. 22-vi-1896

Moody Stuart was one of the first chartered accountants to practise in Dundee, but unlike most of the early Dundee chartered accountants he was a member of the Edinburgh Society, not of the Glasgow Institute.

He was born in Edinburgh and was a son of Rev. Alexander Moody Stuart, minister of Free St Lukes, who in 1875 was moderator of the General Assembly of the Free Church of Scotland. Robert Moody Stuart was educated at Edinburgh Academy and Edinburgh University and was apprenticed to Thomas Martin, C.A., after spending a year in the office of Henry Callender, C.A.

The year after his admission, Stuart went to Dundee to the office of J. & J. Ogilvie, Solicitors. He did not remain long with them and later in the same year set up in practice as an accountant. Among his first appointments was as auditor of Dundee Water Commission, which was founded in 1869. Another early appointment was as auditor of Liff and Bawie Parochial Board in 1873. When that parish was amalgamated with Dundee Parish, Stuart was continued as auditor of the combined board.

In 1875 Stuart invited J. C. Robertson, a member of the Glasgow Institute who had Dundee connections and had earlier worked there, to join him as a partner, so constituting the firm of Moody Stuart & Robertson.

Stuart was recognised as an authority on family trust accounts and he was the author of several articles on that subject in the *Scots Law Times*.

Moody Stuart suffered from lung trouble and following his wife's death—she predeceased him by about two years—his health was never good. His father and two brothers, one of whom was Professor of Law at Glasgow University and at whose home he died, survived him.

JOHN R. SWAN

b. G 1855 d. 1873

John R. Swan was an apprentice with John L. McKirdy. He served in the Volunteers, holding a commission as Lieutenant in No. 12 Battery of the 1st Consolidated Brigade Lanarkshire Artillery Volunteers.

He ceased to be a member of the Institute in 1869 but survived for a further four years.

ALEXANDER B. TAWSE

b. E 1855 d. 1858

A. B. Tawse was a son of Andrew Tawse, W.S. Following his admission to membership of the Society he became a partner of F. H. Carter but this partership was terminated by his early death.

JAMES TAYLOR

b. 1846 G 1877 d. 1924

James Taylor was born at Gask, Perthsire, and received his earliest training in Perth. He came to Glasgow at about the age of eighteen and for ten years was with Thomson, Johnston & Jackson, first as an apprentice and then as a clerk. In 1874 he became a partner of the firm, which later became Thomson, Jackson, Gourlay & Taylor.

Taylor took no active part in public affairs, but devoted much time to church matters. He was connected with Albert Road United Free Church. His eldest son became a partner in Thomson, Jackson, Gourlay & Taylor, as did two of his grandsons, one of whom later became a minister of the Church of Scotland.

JOHN TAYLOR

b. E 1873 d. 1917

John Taylor was for a time secretary and treasurer of Edinburgh City Club. He later emigrated to Australia where he was one of the first practising chartered accountants in Melbourne. He died there.

CHARLES W. W. THOMSON

b. 1828 E 1854 d. 12-ii-1898

Charles W. W. Thomson was one of the younger among the original members of the Edinburgh Society. He was a son of the minister of Newbattle and was a descendant of Dr Wodrow, notable as a church historian.

Trained in the office of Archibald Borthwick, he became a partner in Scott Moncreiff, Thomson & Shiells, from which he retired some time before his death. Thomson was auditor of the Edinburgh Gas Light Co.

He served for two terms on the Council of the Society.

JAMES THOMSON, JNR.

b. G 1853 d. 12-xii-1885

Before commencing to practise as an accountant in 1847, James Thomson, Jnr., had had long experience as a book-keeper in commercial concerns. He was active in promoting the formation of the Institute. From 1852 he was a partner with Alexander Ritchie in Thomson & Ritchie, having previously been a partner in James Thomson & Son (presumably as the son). That firm eventually became part of Thomson, Jackson, Gourlay & Taylor.

JOHN H. TOD

b. 5-viii-1845 E 1873 d. 2-vii-1911

A son of James Tod, W.S., John H. Tod was educated at Edinburgh Academy and in 1866 graduated M.A. before becoming an apprentice with William Wood. He was later with Scott Moncreiff & Thomson. Most of his professional life was spent as a stockbroker. He became a member of the Edinburgh Stock Exchange in 1877. He was forced by failing health to retire from business in 1906, a few years before his death.

Tod was a skilled amateur musician and

for many years was connected with the Edinburgh Amateur Orchestral Society, of which he acted as secretary.

GEORGE TODD

b. 15-xii-1813 E 1854 d. 6-vi-1873

George Todd was an original member of the Society and was in practice from 1843. He was a partner of Kenneth Mackenzie. Like many of the early members of the Society he was also an actuary and, also like many others, combined the practice of accountancy with insurance management. He was secretary of Standard Insurance Co., and manager of Scottish Equitable Insurance Co.

RUTHVEN C. TODD

b. G 1857 d. 10-viii-1887

Ruthven C. Todd was an Edinburgh man who came to Glasgow after having had experience in both a legal and an accounting office in Edinburgh. After working for a time in Glasgow as an accountant he became a stockbroker. He was first an apprentice to William Alexander, W.S., and then spent two years with William Russell, C.A., in Edinburgh. On coming to Glasgow he was employed by John C. Foulds, C.A., and after admission to membership of the Institute he became in 1859 a member of the Glasgow Stock Exchange Association. Thereafter he devoted most of his attention to stockbroking. About 1862 he allowed his subscription to the Institute to lapse but in 1880 he became Vice-Chairman of the Stock Exchange Association.

Todd served for many years in the Volunteers and attained the rank of Lieutenant-Colonel in command of the 1st Lanarkshire Rifle Volunteers.

THOMAS J. TODD

b. c 1849 E 1877 d. 2-xi-1912

Thomas J. Todd was a son of Thomas Janett Todd, customs officer in Leith. He was apprenticed to James H. Balgarnie and at the Society's final examination in 1876 was the joint winner of the fellowship then awarded to the candidate achieving first place. Most of his career was spent with Heritable Securities and Mortgage Investment Association Ltd., of which he was manager from 1890 until his death.

A man of quiet habits, his recreations were reading and gardening.

WILLIAM TOLMIE

b. G 1853 d.

William Tolmie was a partner for a number of years in Tolmie & Reid. Both he and his partner, John C. Reid, had been for some years before 1852 in the employment of James Gourlay. In that year Gourlay relinquished the greater part of his accountancy business to them; he subsequently took up a banking appointment. Tolmie's membership ceased in 1868 as he had allowed his membership dues to fall into arrear.

He had been for a time deputy treasurer of the Commercial Travellers Society of Scotland, which had been founded by Gourlay and of which he remained treasurer until his death in 1872.

PATRICK TURNBULL

b. 26-ii-1835 E 1858 d. 17-i-1887

Patrick Turnbull was born at Coldstream. His father, Phipps Turnbull, was a farmer at Crooks, Berwickshire. After attending Edinburgh Academy he became an apprentice with D. Robertson Souter. He did not, as was common at the time, begin to practise immediately on admission to membership but was for a time factor at Kinnel, Linlithgowshire, to the Duke of Hamilton. He set up in practice about 1866.

Turnbull acted as manager of National Property Investment Company Ltd. and was a director of a variety of companies—railway, tramway, coal and insurance. He joined the Volunteers in 1859 when that movement began.

JAMES TYTLER

b. A 1869 d. 1896

After being in the employment of Lachlan McKinnon, Jnr., an Aberdeen advocate, as book-keeper, James Tytler set up in business as an accountant in 1867. He also became a member of the Aberdeen Stock Exchange and later served on the committee of that body. Shortly after becoming a member of the Society he was elected as a member of its Council. He was re-elected to the Council on a number of occasions and was appointed President in 1893.

Tytler was secretary of the Royal Northern Club for a time and also of the Aberdeen Chamber of Commerce and North of Scotland Trade Protection Society. He was joint auditor with A. J. Rennie of Aberdeen District Tramways Company.

Tytler was an elder in the city's East Parish Church.

He possibly retired a few years before his death for though his name continues to appear in the local directory as a member of the Society it is not entered elsewhere in the directory under either a business or residential address in the city.

GEORGE J. WALKER

b. 15-iii-1853 E 1875 d.

G. J. Walker's father, George Walker, was a merchant in Leith. The son attended Edinburgh Academy where, in 1869, he won the Ferguson Medal. Although a member of the Edinburgh Society, Walker practised in Glasgow, where he was a partner in the firm of Walker & Marwick, and latterly continued on his own account under the same style.

JOHN WALKER

b. c 1854 E 1876 d. 3-vi-1906

John Walker was an apprentice with F. & F. W. Carter and in the Society's final examination in 1877 won the fellowship award. He was in partnership successively with Frederick Falkner (E 1883) who died young and W. A. White who had been an apprentice of Walker and who also died young. Walker himself suffered much from ill health and did not have a long life. He had a considerable practice in connection with the shipping trade, and the business of Walker & White which they built up and which Walker carried on alone after White's death was later continued by A. J. J. Brown.

PETER WALKER

b. G 1854 d. 8-iii-1886

Peter Walker was for some years on the staff of the City of Glasgow Bank. About 1848 he set up in business as an accountant and house factor. He appears to have given up his membership of the Institute around 1862.

ALEX. J. WATSON

b. 6-ii-1831 E 1855 d. 16-v-1892

A. J. Watson was another Edinburgh member who practised in Glasgow, where he was a partner of Moncreiff Mitchell. He had been an apprentice with William Low and was then with F. H. Carter. His father, John Watson, was manager of the Edinburgh Gas Light Company.

JAMES WATSON

b. 1830 E 1860 d. 10-ii-1912

James Watson was born in the parish of Newlands, Peeblesshire. He was an apprentice of Donald Lindsay, and in his indenture is described as "son of Robert Watson, coachman in Edinburgh and one of the boys of George Heriot's Hospital". He had, in fact, been dux at Heriot's in 1845 before going on to Edinburgh University. The school authorities obviously thought highly of him, and the treasurer of Heriot's Hospital, Adam Luke, is named in the indenture as cautioner along with Watson's father and as giving "his special advice and consent" to the apprenticeship.

In 1856 Donald Lindsay's partner, G. A. Esson, was appointed Accountant in Bankruptcy and when he took up his duties at Register House he took the young man Watson, not yet a member of the Society, with him as an assistant. Watson later became the head clerk in the Bankruptcy Office.

Later still, in 1871, Watson was appointed manager of Standard Property Investment Co. and held that office for 37 years till he retired in 1908 at the age of 78. For some years before this, however, his health allowed him to give only a restricted amount of time to business. Watson was an actuary as well as a chartered accountant.

When the Accountants' Company of the Rifle Volunteer Brigade was formed Watson was among the original members.

Watson was an elder in Mayfield United Free Church and was a director of the Philosophical Institution.

He had three sons, the eldest of whom succeeded him as manager of Standard Property Investment Co., while the two others were chartered accountants and partners in Chalmers & Watson.

J. GRAHAM WATSON

b. 17-vii-1850 E 1874 d. 1935

J. G. Watson was the son of James Watson, who was the manager of the Scottish Provident Institution, a position which the son later occupied also. He was educated at Edinburgh Academy. As well as being a chartered accountant Watson was a Fellow of the Faculty of Actuaries. For twelve years he served with the Forfar and Kincardine Artillery Militia, retiring as a senior captain in 1885.

JOHN E. WATSON

b. G 1855 d. 18-iv-1901

John E. Watson's father, Thomas Watson, was an auctioneer and appraiser and was a well-known man in the city. In his youth, John was in his father's office and assisted him in the administration of several important trust matters, of which the father had charge. He then set up in business on his own as an accountant and factor. He was one of the earliest members to be admitted to the Institute after examination.

Thomas Watson's household is reported to have been a rather old-fashioned one and John was first of all sent to a private school. He then passed on to Glasgow High School where among his classmates were another prominent early accountant, John Graham, and John Burns, pioneer of steamship services on the Atlantic, and later Lord Inverclyde. Watson, himself, visited America as a young man.

He served twice on the Council of the Institute and was President from 1887 to 1890. Public appointments which he held included the audit of Glasgow Savings Bank.

His extra-professional interests were varied. He was an elder in St George's Church, treasurer of West of Scotland Bible Society and a director of Glasgow Sabbath School Union and of the Western District Sabbath School Union. He was a member of the Royal Northern Yacht Club.

HENRY G. WATSON

b. 1791 E 1854 d. 2-vii-1879

H. G. Watson was a son of Captain Watson, R.N., and was one of the small number of the early members who were born in the 18th century. He had already been in practice for over a quarter of a century when he became one of the original members of the Society, having set up in business about 1825. He was a member of the original Council of the Society and on two subsequent occasions was again elected to the Council.

For a time he was a partner of T. G. Dickson, but he retired about 1870

LAWRENCE HILL WATSON

b. G 1878 d. 1893

Lawrence Watson served as an apprentice with McClelland, Son & Co., for four years and then continued with that firm and its successors as a clerk for a further five years. He was a partner of D. S. Carson in Carson & Watson, which in 1890 merged with Moore & Brown as Moores, Carson & Watson. In the same year Watson became a member of the Glasgow Stock Exchange Association.

Three years later, Watson died as a result of an accident in the hunting field.

PETER WHITE

b. 1810 G 1853 d. 5-vi-1881

Peter White was the first treasurer of the Glasgow Institute, having taken an active part in its formation. He held that office till 1864 when, on the resignation of James McClelland, the first President, he was elected to follow him as President. He subsequently served on the Council.

White had been in business as an accountant and stockbroker for many years prior to the formation of the Institute. In 1844 he had been one of the original members of the Glasgow Stock Exchange Association and after being President of the Institute he was Chairman of the Stock Exchange Association for two separate terms. He latterly devoted most of his attention to Stock Exchange business and when he died left a fortune of upwards of £200,000, a very substantial sum at that time.

For some years, in addition to his town house at 2 Woodside Place, Glasgow, White had a country residence, Newark Castle, Maybole, which had been largely rebuilt by its owner, the Marquis of Ailsa.

White was on the committee of the Glasgow Society for the Prevention of Cruelty to Animals. He was a director of Glasgow Academy, a director of the Merchants House of Glasgow and a Justice of the Peace for Lanarkshire.

THOMAS WHITSON

b. 15-i-1835 E 1872 d. 15-x-1895

Thomas Whitson, who was born at Blairgowrie, was an apprentice in Edinburgh to G. A. Jamieson and James Haldane. He afterwards became a partner in Lindsay, Jamieson & Haldane. His son was also a chartered accountant and became Lord Provost of Edinburgh. By a curious coincidence at that time the Lord Provost of Glasgow and the Lord Mayor of London were also chartered accountants.

JOHN WIGHT

b. c 1826 G 1861 d. 7-xii-1911

John Wight was a native of East Lothian and began his business career in Edinburgh, where he studied law and served a legal apprenticeship for five years. He came to Glasgow as an assistant to Andrew Thoner, then the Town Clerk of the city. Turning from law to accountancy, he was next employed by George Wink, with whom he had been for eight years when he applied for membership of the

Institute. He was later a partner with Wink.

Wight held a number of important public appointments including Town and Parish Council audits. For 33 years he was honorary treasurer of the Geological Society of Glasgow and he was also honorary secretary of Glasgow St Andrew's Society.

Although of a retiring disposition he took an active part in promoting the enactment of the Presumption of Life Limitation (Scotland) Act. He was interested in books and fond of reading.

Two of his three sons became chartered accountants and were partners in Wight, Wight & Co. He had also five daughters.

JAMES WILKIE (1)

b. c 1815 E 1854 d. 18-ix-1871

James Wilkie, who was born in Haddington, was in practice in Edinburgh from about 1841 and became a member of the Society immediately on its formation. He was also an Associate of the Institute of Actuaries. He was a member of the Society's Council from 1865 to 1869.

Among his professional appointments was that of manager of the National Guarantee & Suretyship Association.

JAMES WILKIE (2)

b. G 1853 d. 25-ii-1883

The Glasgow James Wilkie was also an original member of his local accounting society. He was already a member of the Glasgow Stock Exchange Association and had been in business as an accountant, stockbroker and insurance agent since 1845. With his brother, George G. Wilkie, he carried on these businesses as Wilkie Brothers at 135 Buchanan Street. George Wilkie did not become a member of the Institute. Both brothers lived in Cathcart.

In 1856, whether as a result of pressure of accountancy work or lack of stockbroking work, James Wilkie ceased to be a member of the Stock Exchange.

JOHN WILSON

b. 1840 G 1868 d. 1925

John Wilson was born in Kirriemuir where his father is described as being a manufacturer, but was possibly a weaver working on his own. At the age of about fifteen, he became an apprentice with G. B. Brand, Writer and Bank Agent in Kirriemuir. Four years later, his father having died, he came to Glasgow and became a clerk with McNab & Selkirk. In 1864 he set up business on his own account in a small office with one office boy. He had already made some acquaintances among the business men of the city and in the circular which he issued offering his services he named some of these as gentlemen to whom he was permitted to refer prospective clients.

John Wilson became recognised as an expert in bankruptcy matters and on that foundation his business grew. About 1869 he joined in partnership Patrick Rattray, who had set up in business as an accountant in 1867 and had joined the Institute in 1868. This partnership existed for a few years only and then again for some time Wilson practised on his own. In 1885 he assumed as a partner George D. Stirling, who had been a clerk with Wilson & Rattray and had subsequently continued with Wilson. The new partnership was at first known as John Wilson and Stirling, but later as Wilson, Stirling & Co.

After serving twice as a member of Council John Wilson was elected President in 1897. During his presidency the headquarters of the Institute moved from the original hall, in West Nile Street, to 218 St Vincent Street.

In 1912 Wilson retired from the firm and from professional activity. Outside business, John Wilson had several interests. He was a founder member of the Western Angling Club of which he was for long secretary. He was a member and for a time vice-chairman of the Franco-Scottish Society and he was a keen golfer, playing at the Douglas Park Club until he was well over 80.

RICHARD WILSON

b. 1829 E 1855 d. 15-v-1906

Richard Wilson was a son of Major Henry Wilson of Ballo, Fife. He was already in practice in Edinburgh when the Society was founded. In 1876 he was a member of the Council of the Society.

He acted for a time as manager of the Caledonian Heritable Security Co. Ltd. In younger life Wilson, who was a strong Conservative, took an active interest in politics. He was for a short time, too, a member of Edinburgh Town Council.

He was an elder in St Bernard's Church and held office in St Luke's Masonic Lodge.

Wilson retired from business a number of years before his death.

GEORGE WINK

b. G 1853 d. 17-vi-1869

George Wink was a North of Scotland man. He began his career in the office of the Town Clerk of Elgin. There he was involved with the accounting connected with landed estates and public and private trusts, a number of which were managed by the Town Clerk. He came to Glasgow and was in practice there from 1846. During that time, he was a Depute Clerk of the Sheriff Court and participated in both the civil and criminal business of the Sheriff Clerk's office. He at the same time had experience of accounting under judicial remits.

He first appears as an accountant as a partner in a firm of Manford & Wink. Then he became a partner of John Wight. A son was also a chartered accountant and was a partner with his father in a later firm of George Wink & Son.

Wink lived in 1855 in Govan, then a completely separate community.

JAMES WINK

b. G 1869 d.

James Wink was a son of George Wink, C.A. Although he did not become a member of the Institute until after his father's death, he was a partner of his father from 1864 until the latter's death in 1869. It may indeed have been his father's death which moved him to seek membership and so retain the right to the "chartered" description.

James Wink was a member of the Institute Council from 1880 to 1882.

WILLIAM WOOD

b. 1812 E 1854 d. 14-xii-1892

William Wood's father, John Philip Wood, was Auditor of Excise. He began to practise as an accountant in 1841 and was one of those who were present at the meeting at which the first moves for the formation of the Society were made. He was for a time a partner of John Maitland who became the first Accountant of Court and gave up practice. In 1868 Wood took into partnership his wife's nephew, T. C. Hanna, and this partnership continued till Wood's death.

Wood was three times elected to the Society's Council and he was also treasurer of the Society from 1879 to 1892. In the early years of the Society he acted for a time as an examinator.

Apart from his work for the Society, Wood took little part in public affairs but he devoted much of his leisure time to the financial affairs of the Free Church. An elder in Free St George's congregation, he was a frequent member of the Free Church General Assembly, though he seldom spoke there except on financial matters. A more personal link with Free Church affairs was through his marriage to a daughter of the famous Rev. Dr Thomas Chalmers.

Wood was well known in Edinburgh professional circles, and with his partner he built up an extensive practice.

ARCHIBALD WOODSIDE

b. G 1853 d. 1867

Archibald Woodside had been in business as an accountant and factor for upwards of ten years when in the year of its formation he became one of the early members of the Glasgow Institute. In the year in which he died he was for some reason excluded from membership.

WILLIAM B. WRIGHT

b. 3-v-1848 E 1877 d. 19-i-1894

William B. Wright, the son of William B. Wright, Surgeon, was educated at Edinburgh Academy and was an apprentice with Wood & Hanna, C.A. He had a relatively short life and details of his professional career are not known.

ALEXANDER WYLIE

b. G 1854 d.

Alexander Wylie was in the employment of John Fleming, one of the original Glasgow members, for five years before commencing to practise on his own account in 1849. As Fleming himself began business in 1844, Wylie must have been a very early employee, perhaps his first office boy. In 1855 Wylie was in partnership with Moncreiff Mitchell, who also joined the Institute in 1854, having then been in business for four years. They may have been partners throughout this time.

Wylie, who lived at Eastpark Cottage, Garscube Road, then on the edge of the country, ceased to be a member in 1872 because of unpaid membership subscriptions.

APPENDIX

Links with firms founded by some of the pioneer C.A.s

From the earliest days of the profession some practitioners found it convenient, and presumably also profitable, to carry on practice in partnership with one or more of their fellow accountants. To begin with, when there was very little audit or other regularly recurrent work, the element of continuity and goodwill which now attaches to the use of an established firm name was of little importance. Firm names tended to be, in effect, mere lists of the names of the partners and to change with changes in the composition of the partnership. Such changes were, as the biographical notes show, frequent.

The growth in the number of audit and other continuing appointments was, no doubt, one of the factors which encouraged the continued use of the same firm name notwithstanding changes in the make-up of the partnership; and in many cases, too, family succession justified the continued use of one or more of the patronymics included in a firm's title.

From the closing decades of the 19th century till after the middle of the present century, there was among the well-established practices a growing stability in the firm names used. The past ten or twenty years have again been a period of change in this respect. This suggested that some notes on older firm names first used by the pioneer chartered accountants and on the ways in which these names are linked with existing practices might be of interest.

The length of time which elapsed between the granting of the charters and the first publication, in 1897, of an Official Directory of Scottish Chartered Accountants, and also the absence from the early editions of that directory of any reference to firm names makes it extremely difficult to trace changes in early partnerships or to connect these with names used by firms practising in later years. No claim can be made, therefore, that the notes which follow are at all complete. They are certainly not intended even to outline the development of the firms mentioned. They do, however, provide some link with the earliest practitioners and the names of about one-third of all of these will be found in the lists of partners appended to the notes. Only those early partners who were among the pioneers of this book have been named after each firm noted. There have also been shown, where applicable, the names of any of the pioneers who served as apprentices or received their early training in the offices of such firms. The names are listed in alphabetical order within each group.

The notes have been grouped into three sections which reflect broadly the differing nature of the connections between existing firms and those founded by the pioneers. Firstly there are those firms which still practise under a style adopted by their founder(s) or very closely resembling that style. Then there are those names, often adopted following a merger or mergers, which can still be clearly linked with an earlier style. Finally there are the cases in which local practices have become linked with those of national or international firms. In some such cases the "group" name is used in parallel with the old local name; in others, especially following on the removal of the statutory restrictions on the size of partnerships, the "group" name alone is used.

SECTION I

Firm names used by early members and still in use

Barstow & Millar (Edinburgh). Business originally founded by C. M. Barstow who later had as a partner J. M. Latta when the firm was known as Barstow & Latta. Barstow was afterwards joined in partnership by Robert Cockburn Millar, and the present firm name came into use and has continued to be used since.

Partners: C. M. Barstow, J. M. Latta, R. C. Millar.

Apprentices: J. H. Balgarnie, J. M. Latta, R. C. Millar, John Smith.

Chiene & Tait (Edinburgh). This name was first used by George T. Chiene, Jr., and his partner John Tait. Chiene had earlier been in partnership with J. H. W. Rolland when the firm was known as Chiene & Rolland. For a time the firm name became Layton-Bennett, Chiene & Tait, but the older and shorter name was resumed some years ago.

Partners: John Brewis, George T. Chiene, Jr., J. H. W. Rolland.

D. & A. Cuthbertson, Provan & Strong (Glasgow). The brothers Donald and Allan Cuthbertson first practised as D. & A. Cuthbertson. Their father, William Cuthbertson, was reputed to be the originator of the accountancy profession in Glasgow but he long pre-deceased the formation of the Institute. The names of Provan and Strong were added as they in succession became partners but Strong was never in fact a partner of the Cuthbertsons.

Partners: Allan Cuthbertson, Donald Cuthbertson, Moses Provan, J. Roxburgh Strong.

Hardie & Rowan (Greenock). William Hardie, a member of the Edinburgh Society, founded two firms in the West of Scotland. His partner in the Greenock firm (R. H. Rowan) was a member of the Aberdeen Society.

Partner: William Hardie.

Hardie, Caldwell Ker & Hardie (Glasgow). This business was begun by Hardie after he had established his Greenock practice and he then became a member of the Glasgow Institute as well as of the Edinburgh Society.

Partner: William Hardie.

Mann, Judd, Gordon & Co. (Glasgow). Founded by John Mann, one of the original members of the Glasgow Institute, who succeeded to the business of Paul & Harvie. When he was joined by his son John Mann, Jr. (Sir John Mann) the firm was known as John Mann & Son and from 1910 as Mann, Judd, Gordon & Co. John Mann, Sen., died in 1910, but Judd and Gordon had then been his partners for four years.

Partner: John Mann.

Meston & Co. (Aberdeen). This firm was founded by James Meston, the man largely responsible for the creation of The Society of Accountants in Aberdeen. It is now associated with Deloitte & Co.

Partners: John K. Greig, James Meston.

Apprentice: William Richardson.

James Milne & Co. (Aberdeen). Founded by one of the original members of the Aberdeen Society.

Partner: James Milne (2).

Reid & Mair (Glasgow). A partnership formed in 1871 by Robert Reid and R. A. Mair, two of the early Glasgow members, and known by the same name ever since. Reid's son was a partner until 1960.

Partners: R. A. Mair, Robert Reid.

Apprentice: G. B. McKim.

Romanes & Aitchison (Edinburgh). Originally Murray & Romanes, the name was changed to the present style after Murray's death in 1884.

Partners: R. S. Aitchison, George Murray, James Romanes.

Apprentice: R. S. Aitchison.

Scott-Moncreiff, Thomson & Shiells (Edinburgh). A partnership of three of the Edinburgh pioneers which has continued to be known by the same name since Shiells' name was added on his assumption into the previously existing partnership of Scott-Moncrieff & Thomson. The firm can also trace links with the old Howden & Molleson partnership, as to which see Section III, Deloitte & Co.

Partners: John Scott-Moncreiff, H. K. Shiells, C. W. W. Thomson.

Apprentices: James Pollard, William Pollard.

Alexander Sloan & Co. (Glasgow). Alexander Sloan first practised on his own account, then in partnership with his brother as A. & C. T. Sloan, but since the closing years of last century the present name has been used. Another very old Glasgow practice, that of Aikman & Glen, is now merged with that of the firm.

Partners: P. H. Aikman, Ninian Glen (in Aikman & Glen), Alexander Sloan, C. T. Sloan.

SECTION II

Firms whose names which, though changed, remain clearly linked with those used by early members

McKerrell Brown & Gray (Edinburgh). James McKerrell Brown and his brother Henry, who were grandsons of the first President of the Edinburgh Society, originally used the firm name of J. & H. McKerrell Brown. Henry did not become a member of the Society until 1889. The present firm name has been in use for upwards of 50 years.

Partner: J. McKerrell Brown.

Cotton, Lawson & McNiven (Edinburgh). D. N. Cotton practised on his own account for many years. He was eventually joined by his son D. N. Cotton, Jr., when the firm name of D. N. Cotton & Son was adopted. On the admission of later partners the name was changed on several occasions, but the link with the founder's name has been maintained throughout.

Partner: D. N. Cotton.

Wyllie Guild & McIntyre (Glasgow). The practice, which was founded by James Wyllie Guild, was known during his lifetime by a number of names, including J. W. & D. R. Guild, Auld & Guild and J. Wyllie Guild & Fisher. For many years the firm name used, after Guild's death, was Wyllie Guild & Ballantine. In more recent years, after amalgamation with other practices, the name Wyllie Guild & McIntyre was adopted. This name continued to be used in parallel with that of Binder, Hamlyn, Singleton & Fabian, with whom the firm is now associated.

Partners: William Auld, D. R. Guild, James Wyllie Guild, Walter Mackenzie.

Apprentices: Andrew Bannatyne, Hugh B. Barclay, T. A. Craig, Arthur Hart, Walter Mackenzie.

Grahams, Rintoul & Co. (Glasgow). The firm was founded by the brothers John and William Graham, who began to practise about 1867, as J. & W. Graham. At a fairly early date the name became J. & W. Graham & McCall. Later, following an amalgamation, the firm name for a long period was Grahams, Rintoul, Hay, Bell & Co. This long title was in comparatively recent years, and following a general trend, contracted to the present style. The firm is now associated with Tansley, Witt & Co.

Partners: John Graham, William Graham, John C. McCall.

Apprentice: John C. McCall.

Turner, Hutton & Lawson (Glasgow). The first partnership to include the name Hutton in its firm title was McFarlane & Hutton, a partnership between George McFarlane, previously senior partner of McFarlane & Houston, and James Hutton. Later the firm was known for many years as McFarlane, Hutton & Patrick, but on amalgamation with two other firms the first and last names were dropped and the present style adopted.

Partners: John Houston, James Hutton, George McFarlane.

Apprentices: P. H. Aikman, Ninian Glen.

Watson & Galbraith (Glasgow). John E. Watson began to practise on his own account in the 1850s. His son became a member of the Institute in 1887 and, on his joining his father as a partner, the firm name of John E. Watson & Son was used. Later names were John E. Watson & McHarg and John E. Watson & Co. Following amalgamation with the long-established Glasgow firm of Walter & W. B. Galbraith, the present name was adopted. The firm is now associated with Spicer & Pegler and with firms in Dundee and Aberdeen.

Partner: John E. Watson.

SECTION III

National or International firms of which Scottish firms founded before 1879 now form part

(1) **Coopers & Lybrand.** Several of the early Scottish firms of Chartered Accountants are now incorporated in or associated with firms described as "founder firms" of The Institute of Chartered Accountants in England and Wales. The first of these to be noted is Rattray Brothers, Alexander & France which, in 1957, became associated with Cooper Brothers & Co., now Coopers & Lybrand.

For a few years after he became a member of the Glasgow Institute in 1868 Patrick Rattray was in partnership with John Wilson. This partnership was dissolved, and Rattray formed a new partnership with his brother David (G 1881). They later merged their practice with that set up by H. F. Alexander (G 1900) and W. G. France (G 1901), the combined firm being known as Rattray Brothers, Alexander & France.

Partner: Patrick Rattray.

(2) **Deloitte & Co.** No fewer than five old Scottish firms whose founders figure in the preceding biographical notes can be linked with Deloitte & Co., another of the English Institute's founder firms. Two were Edinburgh firms—Howden & Molleson and Romanes & Munro; two were Glasgow firms—Kerr, MacLeod & Macfarlan and David Strathie & Co.; the fifth was the Aberdeen firm, James Meston & Co.

The links with the Edinburgh firms are rather less direct than those with the others. Howden & Molleson grew from the successive partnerships established by Archibald Borthwick, but ceased to have a separate existence in 1964. The first of Borthwick's partnerships was with Samuel Raleigh, to whom James Howden succeeded, to be joined later by James A. Molleson. Through these changes the firm name changed with the partners, but eventually Borthwick's name was dropped and the practice continued as Howden & Molleson until 1964. When in that year the partnership was dissolved, some of the then partners joined Scott-Moncreiff, Thomson & Shiells, a firm already noted in Section I of this Appendix, and the others joined the firm of Graham, Smart & Annan and through that firm came into the Deloitte group.

Romanes & Munro was formed in 1884 when Charles S. Romanes (E 1877), who had been practising on his own, assumed as a partner C. J. Munro, then newly admitted to membership of the Society. The name is still in use, but in 1970 the firm became associated with Harmood-Banner & Co., which four years later merged with Deloittes.

The two Glasgow firms had amalgamated in 1971 before joining Deloitte & Co. The older, Kerr MacLeod & MacFarlan, originated in 1805 when Henry Kerr's father commenced to practise on his own account. Henry Kerr formed a partnership with William Anderson in 1842, and the firm name, at first Kerr & Anderson, underwent many changes, reflecting changes in the constitution of the partnership—Kerr, Anderson & Brodie; Kerr Anderson & Muir; Kerr, Anderson, Muir & Main, and finally and most lastingly Kerr, MacLeod & MacFarlan, the Kerr name being the permanent element. In contrast the Strathie firm during its existence of some ninety years used only two names—Strathie & Dalgleish (relatively briefly) and David Strathie & Co.

Meston & Co. was established by James Meston, who subsequently played a leading part in the formation of the Aberdeen Society. The name is still used for certain purposes, but the firm became associated with Deloitte & Co. in 1973.

Partners: *In Howden & Molleson and its predecessor firms:* Archibald Borthwick, James Howden, James A. Molleson, Samuel Raleigh.

In Romanes & Munro: C. S. Romanes.

In Kerr, MacLeod & MacFarlan's predecessor firms: H. K. Anderson, James Anderson, Wm. Anderson, W. J. Anderson, John A. Brodie, Henry Kerr, John T. Main, James Muir, J. C. Robertson.

In David Strathie & Co.: John Dalgleish, David Strathie.

In James Meston & Co.: John K. Greig, James Meston.

Apprentices: *With Howden & Molleson and its predecessors:* John Brewis, Alex Dunlop, Jr., Thomas Dymock, James Ellis, T. C. Hanna, Wm. Hardie, J. Wilkie Logan, David Marshall, James R. Molleson, Samuel Raleigh, Peter Ronaldson, J. A. Sinclair (Earl of Caithness), J. T. Spence, C. W. W. Thomson.

With Kerr, MacLeod & MacFarlan's predecessors: H. K. Anderson, James Anderson, W. J. Anderson, D. S. Carson, Henry Leck, Alex McIndoe.

With James Meston: William Richardson.

(3) **Thomson McLintock & Co.** The firm next to be noted is now, like the others in this section, international in its spread, but is of more distinctively Scottish origin. The founder, Thomson McLintock, set up in practice in 1877 and became a member of The Institute of Chartered Accountants in England and Wales in 1880, but did not become a member of the Glasgow Institute until 1892. He does not, therefore, as an individual, figure among the pioneers of this book. The firm which he founded, however, now incorporates practices founded by a number of these. These include the successor firms of A. & J. Robertson and of Wm. Home Cook & Coy., two of the earliest Edinburgh firms of chartered accountants; Moody Stuart & Robertson, the first firm of chartered accountants in Dundee; and Frame, Kennedy & Forrest, the successors of Robert F. Cameron, who was the first chartered accountant to practise in Inverness, where he was latterly in partnership with George Forrest (E 1900).

A. & J. Robertson was founded by the first secretary of the Edinburgh Society, Alexander Weir Robertson. He commenced to practise about 1842, and about 1870 was joined by his son J. A. Robertson (later Robertson-Durham). After a number of amalgamations this firm, at the time of the merger with McLintocks in 1975, was known as Robertson & Maxtone Graham. Another part of that firm went back to Bringloe & Penney, who were two early Edinburgh members.

Robert Moody Stuart, an Edinburgh member, commenced to practise in Dundee in 1869. In 1875 he invited J. C. Robertson, a Dundee man but not yet a member of any of the chartered bodies, although he had been for a couple of years a partner in a Glasgow firm, to join him as a partner. Robertson became a member of the Glasgow Institute in 1878. The firm name of Moody Stuart & Robertson, adopted when he returned to join Moody Stuart in Dundee, remained unchanged till 1975.

Partners: *In A. & J. Robertson; Bringloe & Penney:* Francis A. Bringloe, J. Campbell Penney, A. Weir Robertson, J. A. Robertson(-Durham).

In Mylne & Cook; Wm. Home Cook & Coy.: William Home Cook, W. R. Mylne.

In Moody Stuart & Robertson: John C. Robertson, Robert Moody Stuart.

In R. F. Cameron & Forrest: R. F. Cameron.

Apprentices: *With A. & J. Robertson:* W. P. Wilson Brodie, Robert McNair, J. A. Robertson(-Durham).

(4) **Thornton Baker & Co.** Two old Glasgow firms, each of which had practised from the 1840s under a succession of names, merged in 1968 to form Kidston, Jackson & Co. That firm is now part of

Thornton, Baker & Co. After the 1968 merger only the Jackson name remained to perpetuate the firm's connection with early Glasgow members, but until that time the name Thomson, Jackson, Gourlay & Taylor had on one side been in use unchanged since 1877, while Thomson had been part of the firm name since its foundation as James Thomson & Son in 1847. The other firm involved in that merger had developed from a practice founded in 1844 by Robert McCowan. Through numerous changes McCowan's name continued to be used in conjunction with others until 1892 when McCowan, Findlay & Kidston, as the firm had been called from 1885, became Findlay, Kidston & Goff.

Partners: *In Thomson, Jackson, Gourlay & Taylor:* Robert Craig, John Gourlay, Thomas Jackson, Alexander Ritchie, James Taylor, James Thomson.

In McCowan firms: W. Brown, W. T. Duncan, A. M. Houston, Robert McCowan.

Apprentice: *With Thomson, Jackson, Gourlay & Taylor:* Robert Carswell

(5) **Touche, Ross & Co.** Another instance of old-established Edinburgh and Glasgow firms becoming connected through a common link with an international group is provided by the association of A. T. Niven & Co. and Wilson, Stirling & Co. with Touche, Ross & Co. In the case of the former firm there is also an element of family reunion involved.

A. T. Niven carried on business in Edinburgh from the early 1850s, at first as a sole practitioner, then as Niven & Cowan and latterly as A. T. Niven & Co. His apprentices included George A. Touche, who later founded accounting firms on both sides of the Atlantic. A partner in Touche's New York firm of Touche, Niven & Co. was A. T. Niven's son John B. Niven. Touche, Niven & Co., Touche, Ross, Bailey & Smart and George A. Touche & Co. are all names which have now gone out of use, and the whole of the present group, which also includes one of the founder firms of the English Institute—Kemp, Chatteris & Co.—is known as Touche, Ross & Co.

John Wilson set up in practice in Glasgow in 1864, before he became a member of the Institute. Some years later he had for a time as a partner Patrick Rattray who after leaving this partnership founded the business which became Rattray Brothers, Alexander & Frame, a firm which is now, as noted above, part of Coopers & Lybrand.

Partners: *In A. T. Niven & Co.:* R. C. Cowan, John F. Moffatt, Patrick Morrison, A. T. Niven.

In Wilson, Stirling & Co.: Patrick Rattray, George D. Stirling, John Wilson.

Apprentice: *With A. T. Niven:* John F. Moffatt.

(6) **Turquand, Youngs, Barton, Mayhew.** This group also brings together an English founder firm, Turquand, Youngs & Co., and a very early Edinburgh firm, A. & C. M. Davidson Smith, latterly Davidson Smith, Wighton & Crawford. In each case there had first been a more strictly national merger. Adam Davidson Smith practised on his own account from the 1870s till 1906, when his son became his partner under the firm name of A. & C. M. Davidson Smith.

Partner: Adam Davidson Smith.

(7) **Whinney, Murray & Co.** Here again is a case of a founder firm of The Institute of Chartered Accountants in England and Wales uniting with a Scottish firm which had already established itself in England, and further afield. In fact two of the earliest Glasgow firms were involved, because in the 1940s the old-established firms of Brown, Fleming & Murray and Aitken, Mackenzie & Clapperton had amalgamated under the former name. The latter firm had been founded as Aitken & Mackenzie by two of the original members of the Glasgow Institute, but the name had undergone a number of changes over the years, reflecting successive changes in the partnership.

William S. Brown (G 1877) assumed J. Gibson Fleming (G 1880) as a partner early in the 1880s and they practised as Brown & Fleming. The name continued in use, after Brown's early death, until R. A. Murray became a partner and his name was added to the firm title.

Partners: *In Aitken, Mackenzie firm:* Robert Aitken, R. Easton Aitken, Hugh B. Barclay, Walter Mackenzie.

In Brown, Fleming firm: W. S. Brown.

Apprentices: *With Aitken, Mackenzie firm:* R. Easton Aitken, Theo E. Keyden, George Millar, George Moffatt, John Moffatt.

(8) **Arthur Young, McClelland, Moores & Co.** This is the only one of the international firms which still includes in the firm name the names of any of the Scottish pioneers. The group includes Glasgow and Edinburgh firms originally founded by some of the very earliest chartered accountants, though only the Glasgow firms are recalled in the present professional style. These firms were McClelland, Ker & Co. and Moores, Carson & Watson, which amalgamated in 1958 as McClelland, Moores & Co.

James McClelland, the first President of the Glasgow Institute, his sons and other partners practised under a number of names from 1824, but until after the end of the century no one name was in use for more than twenty years, when, between 1872 and 1892, the firm was known as McClelland, Mackinnon & Blyth. The name McClelland, Ker & Co., adopted in 1901, proved more enduring and lasted until the merger with Moores, Carson & Watson in 1958. That name had been used from 1890, when the firms of Moore & Brown, founded by Alexander Moore in 1856, and Carson & Watson, set up by D. S. Carson and Lawrence Hill Watson in 1878, had amalgamated.

Two of the oldest Edinburgh firms, Lindsay, Jamieson & Haldane and Richard Brown & Co., merged in 1967 as Haldane, Brown & Co. and a few years later joined Arthur Young, McClelland, Moores & Co. The first of these Edinburgh firms numbered among its early partners three of the original members of the Edinburgh Society—G. A. Esson, Donald Lindsay (the firm name was at first Lindsay & Esson) and G. Auldjo Jamieson. When Jamieson became a partner the firm name was extended to Lindsay, Esson & Jamieson; changed after Esson's death and the admission of James Haldane, to Lindsay, Jamieson & Haldane, which continued without further change until the merger with Richard Brown & Co. That firm was founded by Richard Brown about 1885, and the name Richard Brown & Co. adopted when he assumed his first partners some eight years later.

Partners: *In McClelland, Ker & Co.:* Robert Blyth, A. S. McClelland, James McClelland, James McClelland, Jr., Walter Mackenzie, Wm. Mackinnon.

In Moores, Carson & Watson: Wm. Brown, D. S. Carson, Robert McCowan, Alex Moore, Alex Moore, Jr., Laurence Hill Watson.

In Lindsay, Jamieson & Haldane: Findlay B. Anderson, G. A. Esson, James Haldane, G. Auldjo Jamieson, Donald Lindsay, Francis More, Thomas Whitson.

In Richard Brown & Co.: Richard Brown.

Apprentices: *With McClelland, Ker & Co.:* James Affleck, Robert Blyth, Charles Gairdner, A. S. McClelland, James McClelland, Jr., Andrew McEwan, Walter Mackenzie, W. W. Naismith, Arthur O'Kell, Laurence Robertson, Laurence H. Watson.

With Moores, Carson & Watson: Adam E. Black, W. R. M. Church, Alex Moore, Jr., Robert Paterson, Patrick Rattray.

With Lindsay, Jamieson & Haldane: Findlay B. Anderson, Francis Anderson, F. A. Bringloe, R. S. Cameron, G. T. Chiene, Jr., R. C. Cowan, T. G. Dickson, Hon. F. J. Moncreiff, R. L. Oliphant, J. Campbell Penney, A. Weir Robertson, J. H. W. Rolland, James Romanes, Adam Gillies Smith, Thos. Whitson.

Chronological Index of Chartered Accountants 1854-79

Pre-1879 Chartered Accountants arranged by dates of admission

Within each year the pioneer members' names are arranged alphabetically, and appended to each name is the initial letter of the city of whose local body he was a member.
A = Aberdeen. E = Edinburgh. G = Glasgow.

Members admitted in 1853 or 1854 before the granting of charters

Robert Aitken	G
William Anderson	G
William Auld	G
John M. Baillie	E
Robert Balfour	E
John Barrow	E
C. M. Barstow	E
Alexander Black	G
Arch'd Borthwick	E
John A. Brodie	G
James Brown (1)	E
James Adam Brown	E
T. G. Buchanan	G
Charles Cairns	G
Henry Callander	E
F. H. Carter	E
Thos. R. Chaplin	E
Robert Christie, Jr.	E
David Cormack	E
William Cowan	G
Charles Cunningham	G
Alan Cuthbertson	G
Donald Cuthbertson	G
James J. Dickson	E
Thomas G. Dickson	E
Christopher Douglas	E
David Dreghorn	G
George Dundas	E
G. A. Esson	E
John Fleming	G
Robert Forrester	G
John C. Foulds	G
J. C. Fraser	E
Charles Gairdner	G
Archibald Gibson	E
Richard Gordon	E
James Gourlay	G
John Graham	G
Thomas Grant	E
J. Wyllie Guild	G
Dundas Hamilton	G
William Hendrie	G
Arch'd Horne	E
James Howden	E
John Hunter, W.S.	E
Alex Jamieson	E
G. Auldjo Jamieson	E
William Jamieson	G
Henry Kerr	G
Henry Leck	G
Joseph M. Liddell	E
Donald Lindsay	E
William Low	E
J. M. Macandrew	E
James McClelland	G
Robert McCowan	G
David McCubbin	G
Andrew MacEwan	G
George Macfarlane	G
Kenneth Mackenzie	E
Walter Mackenzie	G
J. L. McKirdy	G
David Maclagan	E
William McLean	G
William McNaughton	G
Arch'd McNicoll	G
John Maitland	E
John Mann	G
Thomas Mansfield	E

David Marshall	E
Thomas Martin	E
George Meldrum	E
John Miller	G
George T. Mitchell	E
Moncreiff Mitchell	G
John Scott Moncreiff	E
Wm. Moncreiff	E
Patrick Morrison	E
David Murray	E
George Murray	E
William Myrtle	E
A. T. Niven	E
James J. Ogilvy	E
John S. Ogilvy	E
David E. Outram	G
Andrew M. Paterson	E
Charles Pearson	E
Donald S. Peddie	E
Samuel Raleigh	E
George Ramsay	E
John C. Reid	G
Alexander Ritchie	G
A. Weir Robertson	E
George Robson	G
William Russell	E
Robert Scobie	G
R. E. Scott	E
Thomas Scott	E
James Smith	G
D. R. Souter	E
Robert Spottiswoode	E
C. W. W. Thomson	E
James Thomson, Jr.	G
George Todd	E
William Tolmie	G
Peter Walker	G
Henry G. Watson	E
Peter White	G
James Wilkie (1)	E
James Wilkie (2)	G
George Wink	G
William Wood	E
Arch'd Woodside	G
Alex. Wylie	G

Admitted in 1855

James H. Balgarnie	E
George T. Chiene	E
James Coventry	E
Alex. Craig	E
Thomas Dall	E
R. H. Douglas	E
D. R. Guild	G
Alex Henderson	E
John Houston	G
D. C. Kerr	E
James Latta	E
James McClelland, Jr.	G
Robert Murray	E
John Ogilvy	E
Andrew Paterson	E
Charles Robertson	E
Laurence Robertson	G
David Scott	E
Thomas Scott, Jr.	E
Adam Gillies Smith	E
John R. Swan	G
Alex. B. Tawse	E
Alex J. Watson	E
John E. Watson	G
Richard Wilson	E

Admitted in 1856

James Anderson	G
James Haldane	E
Moses Provan	G
William Reid	G

Admitted in 1857

William Brown	G
James R. Carphin	E
W. J. Carswell	G
William Church	G
Robert Craig	G
Alex Moore	G
Wm. Mudie	G
Ruthven C. Todd	G

Admitted in 1858

Patrick Turnbull	E

Admitted in 1859

J. T. Bowie	E

Admitted in 1860

Alex Dunlop	E
Wm. McBean	E

W. C. Maughan	E
J. A. Molleson	E
Robert Rainie	E
James Watson	E

Admitted in 1861

E. Erskine Scott	E
John Smith	E
John Wight	G

Admitted in 1862

Andrew Bannatyne	G
William Drew	G
Robert Forman	E
Robert Lumsden	G
David Pearson	E
R. Hope Robertson	G

Admitted in 1863

Henry Budge	E
George L. Craik	G
Henry A. Finlay	E
Wm. H. Smith	E

Admitted in 1864

Robert C. Cowan	E
T. C. Hanna	E
J. Wilkie Logan	E
Colin McCuaig	E
R. L. Oliphant	E
James Romanes	E

Admitted in 1865

Alexander Downie	E
John F. Moffatt	E
James T. Spence	E

Admitted in 1866

James Grahame	G
Arch'd Lumsdaine	E

Admitted in 1867

Alexander Brand	A
John Crombie	A
Robert Easton	G
Robert Fletcher	A
William Gardiner	E
James Hutton	G
John G. Leslie	A
William Lunan	A
William MacKinnon	G
George Marquis	A
James Meston	A
William Milne	A
George Moffatt	G
John Moffatt	G
James A. Murray	A
J. A. Sinclair	A
Alex Sloan	G
John Smith	A
J. Turnbull Smith	E
Wm. Steele	A

Admitted in 1868

Fred W. Carter	E
Hugh Miller	E
Charles Prentice	E
Patrick Rattray	G
R. Moody Stuart	E
John Wilson	G

Admitted in 1869

Hugh Blair	E
James Blair	G
George T. Chiene, Jr.	E
James Galt	G
William Graham	G
Andrew M. Houston	G
C. H. Hughes	E
Wm. McLean, Jr.	G
James Martin	E
George Miller	G
Wm. R. Mylne	E
Wm. Ross	E
James Tytler	A
James Wink	G

Admitted in 1870

R. Easton Aitken	G
Hugh B. Barclay	G
John Gourlay	G
D. G. Hoey	G
Theo. E. Keyden	G
A. S. McClelland	G
David Maclean	G
James Muir	G

James Pringle	E
J. A. Robertson(-Durham)	E
Peter Ronaldson	E
J. Roxburgh Strong	G

Admitted in 1871

Francis A. Bringloe	E
W. H. Glynn	E
Harvey Hall	A
R. A. Mair	G
Thomas J. Mansfield	E
A. W. Miller	E
Eric M. Noble	E
J. H. W. Rolland	E
Wm. Saunders	E
Nathaniel Spens	G
George Stevenson	E

Admitted in 1872

Finlay B. Anderson	E
Robert Blyth	G
Robert Carswell	G
David Cowan	G
James Drummond	E
T. B. Drysdale	E
W. T. Duncan	G
J. Forbes Moncreiff	E
Adam Davidson Smith	E
Thomas Whitson	E

Admitted in 1873

John Dalgleish	E
Francis Dickson	E
James Ellis	E
Henry Forrester	G
Thomas W. Galloway	E
Arthur Hart	G
Henry Keith	G
James Milne (1)	A
David F. Park	E
James Pollard	E
C. T. Sloan	G
John Taylor	E
John H. Tod	E

Admitted in 1874

B. R. Bruce	A
John E. Dovey	E
John Lamb	E
Alex. Machray	A
J. Graham Watson	E

Admitted in 1875

John W. Brodie	E
D. S. Carson	G
John C. McCall	G
Hon. F. J. Moncreiff	E
Francis More	E
Douglas Murrie	E
William Pollard	E
Robert Reid	G
George J. Walker	E

Admitted in 1876

H. K. Anderson	G
W. J. Anderson	G
R. F. Cameron	E
Thomas Dymock	E
John K. Greig	A
A. F. Hamilton	G
John T. Mair	G
A. J. Rennie	A
Wm. Richardson	A
Charles E. Stuart	E
John Walker	E

Admitted in 1877

James Affleck	G
P. H. Aikman	G
David Bird	G
Adam E. Black	G
W. P. Wilson Brodie	E
William S. Brown	G
W. R. M. Church	G
T. A. Craig	G
Ninian Glen	G
Thomas Jackson	G
David Macritchie	E
R. C. Millar	E
James Milne (2)	A
Alex Moore, Jr.	G
R. Leef Murray	E
Arthur O'Kell	G
Robert Paterson	G
J. Campbell Penney	E
T. C. Robertson	G
C. S. Romanes	E

George D. Stirling	G
James Taylor	G
Thomas J. Todd	E
Wm. B. Wright	E

Admitted in 1878

Robert S. Aitchison	E
Francis Anderson	E
James Brown (2)	E
T. Bennet Clark	E
W. Home Cook	E
D. N. Cotton	E
Alex. Fleming	G
T. P. Fleming	E
John Gray	A
F. D. V. Hagart	E
Wm. Hardie	E
James McOmish	G
Alex. Murray	G
J. C. Robertson	G
T. Eaton Robinson	G
David Strathie	G
W. Robertson Strong	G
Laurence Hill Watson	G

Admitted in 1879

John Brewis	E
Richard Brown	E
Archibald Grierson	G
Robert C. King	G
Alex McIndoe	G
George B. McKim	G
Thomas McKim	G
Robert McNair	G
W. W. Naismith	G
H. K. Shiells	E

Endpaper map:—

Map of the City of Glasgow and Suburbs, from the Glasgow Directory, published by W. McFeat (1825)

Scale: 5 inches = 1 mile

The major part of the map is shown. Garden Square (now Blythswood Square) was at the western limit of the built-up area of the city. There was little change between 1825 and 1854.

Nile Street (not yet styled West), where the first Chartered Accountants' Hall was located, in 1874, runs north and south, nearer to George Square.

Cut of Junction
Dobbies Loan
Dobbies Street
Lunatic Asylum
Magdalene Asylum
Cowcaddens
Garden Square
Regent St
George
St Vincent
Terrace
Waterloo St
Cadogan St
Union Place
Queen Street
Argyle
Jamaica St
Robertson St
York
Broomielaw
Quay
Clyde St
Centre
Dale
King St
Nelson St
Bridge
Carlton
Wallace
Hyde Park

Glasgow 1825
Dunchattan
Quarry
Bridewell
Duke Street
College
London Street
Court House
and
Prison
Nelsons
Monument
GREEN
CLYDE
Adelphi St
Wellington Pl
Cattle
Market
Glasgow
Water Work

For Product Safety Concerns and Information please contact our EU
representative GPSR@taylorandfrancis.com
Taylor & Francis Verlag GmbH, Kaufingerstraße 24, 80331 München, Germany

www.ingramcontent.com/pod-product-compliance
Ingram Content Group UK Ltd.
Pitfield, Milton Keynes, MK11 3LW, UK
UKHW020203200926
475702UK00004B/585
* 9 7 8 0 3 6 7 5 3 2 5 5 0 *